U.S.
INTELLIGENCE
AT THE
CROSSROADS

OTHER TITLES IN THE BRASSEY'S INTELLIGENCE AND NATIONAL SECURITY LIBRARY

Roy Godson • *Dirty Tricks and Trump Cards: U.S. Covert Action and Counterintelligence*

Hussein Sumaida with Carole Jerome • *Circle of Fear: My Life as an Israeli and Iraqi Spy*

Abram N. Shulsky • *Silent Warfare: Understanding the World of Intelligence* (Revised Second Edition)

William Hood • *Mole: The True Story of the First Russian Spy to Become an American Counterspy*

Adda B. Bozeman • *Strategic Intelligence and Statecraft: Selected Essays*

U.S. INTELLIGENCE AT THE CROSSROADS

AGENDAS FOR REFORM

EDITED BY

ROY GODSON, ERNEST R. MAY, AND GARY SCHMITT

BRASSEY'S
Washington London

Library of Congress Cataloging-in-Publication Data

U.S. intelligence at the crossroads: agendas for reform/edited by
    Roy Godson, Ernest R. May, and Gary Schmitt.
        p.   cm.
    ISBN 1–57488–036–5
    1. Intelligence service—United States.   I. Godson, Roy, 1942– .
    II. May, Ernest R.   III. Schmitt, Gary James, 1952– .
JK468.I6U18   1995
327.1273—dc20   95-3477
                                                              CIP

10 9 8 7 6 5 4 3 2 1

Printed in the United States of America

CONTENTS

INTRODUCTION

Roy Godson, Ernest R. May, and Gary Schmitt

T he essays in this volume were originally presented at meetings of the
Working Group on Intelligence Reform or were authored by members of the Working Group. The Working Group, established in early
1992 by the Consortium for the Study of Intelligence,[1] is cochaired by
Roy Godson of Georgetown University and Ernest May of Harvard
University, with the assistance of Gary Schmitt, former executive director of the President's Foreign Intelligence Advisory Board. Still active,
the Working Group draws its participants from both inside and outside
of government. Its principal function is to provide an unclassified
forum for specialists in the area of intelligence and national security
affairs to discuss proposals for reforming U.S. intelligence and to
exchange ideas on how to improve its effectiveness. In addition, the
Working Group has provided a vehicle for senior officials from within
the Intelligence Community to explain the changes they are making to
improve performance and/or address new security concerns.

What led to the Working Group's establishment in 1992 was the
sense that the reform debate—especially as exhibited by the debate
taking place in Congress—was itself in need of reform. Although there
was substantial rhetoric on the need to reform U.S. intelligence in light
of the end of the Cold War, initial efforts had a relatively narrow focus.
With some exceptions,[2] the principal goal was to redesign a community
that could do as much or more in the future (in meeting the government's intelligence requirements) with less (funding) than in the past.
Even bills proposed in 1992 by the leadership of the Senate and House
intelligence committees—although ambitious—were keyed to the
somewhat limited concerns of "reorganization," "reducing duplication," and "increasing the DCI's management authority over the [Intel-
ligence] Community."[3] Those were important issues. However, for
many observers of U.S. intelligence, this effort did not address a number of key intelligence topics or, equally important, prescribed measures that missed the mark substantively.

Shortcomings in the intelligence reform debate in the early 1990s are apparent when that debate is set alongside the deliberations about military reform in the late 1970s and early 1980s. In the case of the military reform movement, there was a relatively extensive debate on the lessons to be learned from past military successes and failures, and the advantages and disadvantages of how other nations organized their defense efforts. Although that debate was far from perfect and not free of departmental and bureaucratic parochialism, overall, the military reform movement generated an impressive brief in support of the changes that were eventually made, largely through the Goldwater-Nichols Defense Reorganization Act of 1986.

The intelligence reform debate has not so far been comparably far-reaching or consequential, though, in fairness, it should be noted that the intelligence reform debate has begun more recently and has been conducted under far more stringent constraints. The military reform debate had a long history prior even to passage of the National Security Act of 1947, while the public debate over intelligence reform has little history prior to the 1970s. In addition, any discussion of intelligence reform is handicapped because so much of what intelligence agencies do is necessarily done in secret.

The intelligence reform effort of the early 1990s failed to generate much support, either substantively or politically. Also, the turnover in leadership of the two intelligence committees and changes made to the Intelligence Community by the then–Director of Central Intelligence (DCI) Robert Gates curtailed interest in reform and reduced the impetus to overhaul U.S. intelligence.[4] Absent the sudden rise of a new and pressing security threat or the revelation of some striking intelligence failure, the organizational changes made by the community itself seemed sufficient to most policymakers, intelligence professionals, and members of Congress.

The arrest of Aldrich Ames in 1994, a KGB mole in the heart of the Central Intelligence Agency's (CIA) operations directorate, of course, was precisely the kind of failure that gave new life to the reform debate. But this time the debate was far more pointed. In the early 1990s, the central question had been how best to organize the Intelligence Community in the face of a new security environment and the expected reductions in personnel and resources. After Ames, the questions were more fundamental, asking whether the CIA and the rest of the U.S. intelligence establishment were still effective organizations or even necessary ones. If the debate in the 1970s was something of a "mid-life crisis" for the Intelligence Community and the post–World

War II democracy it served, then the reform debate in the mid-1990s became a dispute over whether U.S. intelligence had reached a kind of bureaucratic "old age," was no longer up to its job, and was perhaps incapable of changing its ways.

Asking such questions presumes that one knows what the Intelligence Community should do and that there exists some agreed-upon standard for judging its effectiveness. In the changed security environment of the post–Cold War era, these and related questions are not easily settled. It is not surprising to find that both critics and supporters of U.S. intelligence have pushed for a fundamental examination of the Intelligence Community's basic roles, missions, and methods of operation. As with the Pentagon before it, the U.S. Intelligence Community now faces its own "Bottom Up Review."[5]

The eighteen essays in this volume cover a wide range of intelligence issues and are intended to complement that review. They are not by any means the final word, but each is a thoughtful review of a piece of the intelligence puzzle.

The volume is divided into three sections. The first set of essays (chapters 1–5) addresses intelligence topics from a broad perspective, beginning with the question: "What is intelligence?" (The answer: two essays, two very different views.) The essays that follow review recent efforts at intelligence reform, challenge some of those efforts' key premises, and, in turn, offer suggestions for what might be done to enhance intelligence performance in the United States.

The second set of essays (chapters 6–12) focuses on the core activities of U.S. intelligence—analysis, collection, counterintelligence, and covert action—and the current security environment. The one essay in this section that at the time it was written might have been thought the least relevant, "Angleton's World," is at the heart of current concerns. Specifically, in analyzing how Aldrich Ames could operate as a mole as long as he did within the CIA's Directorate of Operations (DO), former DCI James Woolsey argued that the DO's culture was decisively formed by its reaction against the excesses of James Angleton, former head of the CIA's counterintelligence staff.

> In the years that Ames was spying, the fact is that counterintelligence was not coordinated well with personnel security. We should not excuse what happened. But we must understand the roots of the environment within which Ames was able to operate so that we do not change it in a way that re-creates the problems of a still-earlier era. We all at the CIA want to continue to serve in today's Virginia, not in 17th century Salem.[6]

Yet, as William Hood's essay on Angleton and the comments by former Federal Bureau of Investigation (FBI) and CIA officials James Nolan and Samuel Halpern suggest, Woolsey's view of Angleton's legacy, though widely accepted, is not undisputed.

The final set of essays (chapters 13–18) addresses intelligence's relationship to specific policy concerns and policymakers in general. Although not every topic is covered, the essays discuss an array of subjects that either are of particular concern in the post–Cold War era or propose new ways of thinking about how intelligence can better address the needs of national security officials.

In general, the essays in this volume are designed to raise questions and, where necessary, to challenge the prevailing conventional wisdom with respect to intelligence issues. But one view that is apparent in all the essays is that intelligence still matters. This has not always been the case. Clausewitz, writing at the dawn of the modern military era, maintained that intelligence was generally irrelevant to the conduct of war and grand strategy. Today, with the lessons of two world wars, the reconstruction of Europe, the Cuban Missile Crisis, the war in the Persian Gulf, and other key events, it would be difficult to sustain that view. Although intelligence may never be as critical as it was during World War II, states cannot assume that intelligence will or will not play a significant role in the military and foreign affairs of the future.

The real question, thus, is not whether intelligence will be a factor in the future but whether the large intelligence bureaucracies spawned by World War II and the Cold War continue to suit U.S. national security needs. U.S. intelligence is at a crossroads. We hope that this volume will help scholars, officials, intelligence professionals, members of Congress, the news media, and the public at large to see a little more clearly where alternative paths may take us.

PART I:

DEFINING THE DEBATE

1

WHAT IS INTELLIGENCE? INFORMATION FOR DECISION MAKERS

Jennifer Sims

For those who follow the ins and outs of Washington politics, it appears the Intelligence Community is being whipsawed. Some want it to address a multitude of new and complex threats such as economic competition, weapons proliferation, and multilateral disarmament. Others demand that the community contract, releasing its "fair share" of the defense budget in the process. Further stirring these currents have been recent press reports that have focused attention on national intelligence "failures" ranging from the failure to predict the collapse of the Soviet Union to losing track of North Korean ships on the high seas.

Leaving aside the damage that can be caused by such contradictory forces, the prospect of massive budget cuts and large-scale reorganization does concentrate the mind, driving one swiftly and usefully back to first principles. What, after all, is intelligence and how do we know when it has failed? Such questions raise provocative theoretical issues. Moreover, the answers are useful because they provide a way to probe practical problems through a back door. Theory affords an escape from the "turf fights" and "bureaucratic" debates over the value of what currently exists, and allows one to think about such issues on a plane where money and politics may be temporarily ignored.

Of course, in Washington, money and politics cannot be ignored for long. Hence, this paper, which begins with theory, will end with a discussion of the practical implications of such a theory in a period of budget reductions and community-wide reorganization.

This paper was first presented on April 29, 1992.

The Theory

There is no shortage of definitions of *intelligence*. Webster's dictionary defines it as "the gathering of secret information, as for military purposes." Jeffrey T. Richelson defined it as "the product resulting from the collection, evaluation, analysis, integration and interpretation of all available information which concerns one or more aspects of foreign nations or of areas of operation which is [*sic*] immediately or potentially significant for planning."[1] In turn, Robert Bowie defined it simply and elegantly as "information designed for action."[2]

While Richelson's and Webster's definitions are too narrow, Bowie's may be too broad. Intelligence need not involve secret information exclusively. Nor does it, as Richelson's definition suggests, refer only to products as opposed to raw data. And although Bowie's definition underscores an essential aspect of intelligence—purposefulness—it does not distinguish intelligence from advertisement, propaganda, or advocacy, all forms of information "designed for action."

DEFINITION

Intelligence is best defined as information collected, organized, or analyzed on behalf of actors or decision makers. Such information may include technical data, trends, rumors, pictures, or hardware.

Intelligence may be collected from open (newspapers, books, radio, television), clandestine (national technical means, human agents), and "gray" sources. Gray sources include private citizens or companies willing to divulge information during private conversation. A schoolchild who overhears two teachers discussing an upcoming test over lunch has acquired "gray" information. A schoolchild who sneaks into the classroom after hours and takes a copy of the test from the teacher's desk has acquired the information clandestinely. If the teacher provides a pretest to all the students the day before the exam, she has provided open-source information. All this collected information can be regarded as intelligence.

Limitations do apply: information, to be intelligence, must be collected, organized, or analyzed "on behalf of" the consumers of that information. The "or" in this sentence is critical. If the information is not collected for the decision maker, then it must be organized or analyzed for him. A pile of newspapers on a decision maker's desk does not constitute intelligence. Even a set of clippings of those newspapers, organized by subject matter, is not intelligence. A subset of clips, selected expressly for the needs of the decision maker, is intelligence. This is true, one should note, even though the original collector of the information was a reporter. It is the particular organization of the material for the decision maker that may turn publicly available news into intelligence.

Similarly, information collected on behalf of a decision maker but not organized or analyzed for him is also intelligence. For example, the National Security Agency (NSA) may retain raw data that have not been organized or analyzed for the consumer but that fit the expressed needs of the consumer and are accessible on request. This, too, is intelligence.

Intelligence *analysis* digests information and refines it for the purpose of assisting the policymaker. Analysis implies not just the organization of information but its examination as well. Analysis becomes estimative when it renders judgments about the implications of the findings. For example, intelligence analysis may point out that X has always been seen with Y, whereas an estimate might, given evidence of X, predict the likely existence of Y.

Intelligence analysis and estimation must be performed on behalf of the consumer, not the analyst, and should be as objective and relevant as possible. This threefold requirement is difficult to satisfy, but is key to the integrity of the product. Relevance, measured by the consumer's ability to assimilate and use the product, requires constant interaction between the analyst and the consumer. Objectivity, on the other hand, demands a certain distance and a willingness to consider all variables—not just the ones the analyst or his consumer has deemed most important in the past.

In the real world, however, human nature intervenes to distort intelligence in several ways, two of which will be discussed here: politicization and privatization. *Privatization* refers to the use of the intelligence process for personal or bureaucratic advantage; it is probably an outgrowth of any intelligence process in which personal recognition is limited. As analysts become experts in their areas and in their consumers' needs, they tend to become selective in their information gathering. They naturally acquire a professional stake in their record and reputation and are inclined to defend it vigorously. Judgments, premises, and assumptions derived from past work tend increasingly to shape current work. While such maturation is desirable to a point, if it leads to intellectual rigidity it may also contribute to intelligence failures.

Institutions can also privatize intelligence. For example, if a military service's intelligence arm notes and fails to report an adversary's termination of a key weapons system for fear it might lead to cancellation of one of its own, this is a misuse of intelligence for particularistic ends. To reduce the likelihood of this happening, the Intelligence Community has adopted several institutional reforms. Differing estimates of Soviet missile capabilities by each of the military services during the 1950s led to the establishment of the Defense Intelligence Agency (DIA), which was responsible for integrated defense intelligence. More recently, concern that the military services' Science and Technology Centers might not be totally objective in appraisals of foreign technologies led Congress to put several of these centers under DIA budgetary and operational management.

Privatization is the use of intelligence for personal or private institutional ends; *politicization* is the skewing of intelligence to influence policy outcomes or vindicate policy choices. Whereas privatization is found at all levels of the intelligence service, politicization may be most evident at the higher levels, where the ability to influence policy decisions is greatest.

Although politicization and privatization are difficult to identify in practice, charges of one are usually accompanied by countercharges of the other. Thus, during the nomination hearings of Robert Gates for the position of director of Central Intelligence before the Senate in the fall of 1991, several former intelligence officers charged that the nominee had altered their analyses in the past for political purposes, while, in turn, defending themselves against accusations that their own analytical rigidity and ideological agendas had skewed their products. Where some observers saw martyrs, others saw careerists with bruised egos and frustrated personal ambitions.

Given the broad definition of intelligence, the actors or decision makers whom intelligence serves can be anyone from a soldier or government official to a shopkeeper or kindergartner. *National intelligence* involves the collection, organization, or analysis of information solely on behalf of national actors or decision makers.

A *national intelligence service*, in its most efficient form, handles only that portion of the intelligence process that requires the security and secrecy such a service affords. Secrecy is necessary if the sources (e.g., national technical means, spies) or the policy areas (e.g., trade negotiations, defense policies) are sensitive. In the latter case, intelligence may include open-source material. Unfortunately, to the extent that policymakers' information requirements are not met by their own departments, they will tend to look to the Intelligence Community to meet them—whether or not the information could have been acquired elsewhere.

THE INTELLIGENCE PROCESS

The intelligence process involves everything from the establishment of collection requirements to the dissemination and assessment of collected information. An intelligence service is created to manage and appraise the process but not to assess it for policy purposes. Assessment is the responsibility of the consumer/decision maker. A functioning intelligence process thus depends on both the intelligence officer and the consumer.

Because information must be tailored to consumer needs, the process is correctly thought of as more two-way than unidirectional. The intelligence analyst should understand the needs, perspectives, and working constraints of the consumer, including the types of contingencies he faces. The analyst also plays the critical role of apprising intelligence collectors of changing needs, including types of collection assets that might usefully be developed, while at the same time relaying information on collection capabilities, constraints, and policy options to the decision maker. The decision maker, in turn, must understand the limits of knowledge on which the intelligence is based, and factor them into a realistic assessment of the intelligence received.

While intelligence officers may, because of their contacts with collectors, foreign colleagues, and operators, be able to offer policy options, it is the decision maker who must assess its significance for policy options or contemplated actions. The distinction here is not just of theoretical interest. Careful delineation of responsibilities for intelligence estimating and assessment is a practical safeguard; it increases the chances that a good decision will be made even if the policymaker has not shared all of the information with the Intelligence Community. Unfortunately, consumers often fail to appreciate that the intelligence service manages an information bank where the withdrawals of each depend on the deposits of all.

A breakdown in the intelligence process occurs whenever either the intended consumer does not get the information collected, organized, or analyzed on his or her behalf, or if the policy community fails to provide the proper feedback or to alert the service about changing requirements or priorities.

SECURITY AND COVERT ACTION

The foregoing discussion suggests that process is integral to the meaning of intelligence. It is not surprising, then, that a substantial portion of national intelligence expenditures are devoted to protecting the process as well as intelligence itself from foreign penetrations, public disclosures, and external influences.

Public disclosure or foreign penetration might lead not just to the release of secrets, but also to the disclosure of the national intelligence process itself and thus how it might be influenced or its efforts foiled. As a result, intelligence derived from open sources may still need to be classified if it is organized or analyzed in a way that reveals sensitive sources or the inclinations of a policymaker engaged in sensitive negotiations.

Finally, the definition of intelligence used here does not embrace covert action, which is properly understood as policy execution, not intelligence. Such activities nevertheless tend to fall under intelligence management simply because they must remain secret to be effective. Although classification systems are generally instituted by intelligence services, countries without such services can still conduct covert actions as part, for example, of their military or diplomatic operations.

Quality National Intelligence

This discourse on the concept of intelligence is useful for exposing one's premises and for suggesting a rich set of measures for evaluating its quality. An effective intelligence process affords timely, relevant, and objective information to decision makers. A superior national intelligence service protects and fine-tunes this process in order to increase a decision maker's knowledge. The relevance, timeliness, and accuracy of intelligence products are indicators of a well-functioning service. However, the theoretical discussion above suggests a number of additional, less well understood criteria for evaluating a national intelligence process. Six of these may be most important:

• Degree to which consumers are well identified and adequately trained

• Degree of institutional and resource flexibility

• Number of sources and collection methods used

• Competitiveness of the analytical environment

• Adequacy of the balance struck between the requirements of security and the nurturing of community-wide debate

• Strength of central, community-wide management

WELL-IDENTIFIED AND WELL-TRAINED CONSUMERS

All government decision makers are consumers of intelligence in that they depend on organized information handling. However, only some need support from a national intelligence service—namely, those whose effectiveness requires either secret decision making or access to publicly unavailable information. In democracies secret decision making is typically restricted, usually to the national security establishment, although intelligence can serve others as well. If clandestinely placed sensors would assist the Drug Enforcement Agency, the Commerce Department, or the Environmental Protection Agency, or even an international organization, officials in these organizations may be identified as consumers who need the intelligence service's support. In the U.S. government, the identification of officials who require support from the Intelligence Community (along with some judgment of their respective priority as consumers) is the responsibility of the president on the advice of the DCI.

All consumers of intelligence interact with those who provide them with information, and a superior intelligence service, recognizing the importance of consumer feedback, will educate the consumer about the intelligence process in order to increase its effectiveness. Policymakers must understand their role in evaluating the utility of the intelligence product; in providing personally acquired information back into the intelligence archive; in explaining changing intelligence requirements; and in describing, when possible, desirable collection capabilities for development. Such knowledge is specialized. Consumers cannot be expected to intuitively understand the importance of information sharing or of their role in determining what new technical collection capability might best be developed.

INSTITUTIONAL FLEXIBILITY

A high-quality intelligence service will also be highly flexible. It must be able to shift resources and information flows swiftly between consumers without overloading communication or distorting intelligence in other areas. Whereas in peacetime a Washington-based assistant secretary of state might receive priority support for arms control negotiations, in wartime the mission of an F-15 pilot in a theater far removed from the United States may become the immediate priority. An intelligence service must be evaluated on the basis of its ability to make such adjustments, building and disassembling support infrastructures as required.

Keys to institutional flexibility are community-wide structures that develop networks across institutional lines, an ethic of teamwork, rigorous training programs in cross-marketable skills such as languages, communications technologies, and HUMINT (human intelligence) collection techniques, and maneuverable collection assets.

The Iraqi invasion of Kuwait tested the flexibility of U.S. national intelligence. On one hand, there was a flood of intelligence products as analysts, skilled in relevant functional areas such as mobile missile hunting, applied their knowledge to the Iraqi theater. New tasking and dissemination arrangements were quickly established, including mechanisms for providing support to an array of newly allied governments. The community's capacity to build, to disassemble, and to build again was laudatory and sustained. In the aftermath of the war, the Intelligence Community not only shifted quickly to a peacetime mode, but also reorganized rapidly to support the United Nations' (UN) disarmament operations that followed. The institutional flexibility exhibited by the community during this crisis was remarkable and perhaps unprecedented.

On the other hand, there were problems in the intelligence support for operations against Iraq. Some national intelligence organizations had difficulty making their products useful to new or demanding consumers who, in turn, were unfamiliar with what they could expect from some parts of the Intelligence Community. During the war, the CIA and even the DIA were occasionally criticized for the lack of relevance, such as when General Schwarzkopf bemoaned the tendency to pronounce a bridge partially destroyed when what he needed to know was whether it still functioned as a bridge. Similarly, transmittal of imagery in the theater was obstructed or delayed by "hardware" incompatibilities.

Such problems are often—though not always—rooted in institutional rigidities. As suggested earlier, the worst rigidity stems from the institutional privatization of intelligence in which organizations withhold intelligence for fear of being wrong or in order to gain bureaucratic leverage. While privatization does not seem to have been a significant problem during the Persian Gulf War, it does appear to have infected some of the initial efforts to provide support to the UN Special Commission.

MULTIPLE SOURCES AND COLLECTION METHODS

The more sources of information available to an intelligence service, the fuller the archive of information available to the decision maker and the greater the likelihood that unreliable sources will be exposed. To a certain extent, redundancy also protects the intelligence process from loss or compromise of one of its collectors. It also enhances the community's flexibility and adaptability.

Redundancy can, however, be expensive and can even lead to overloaded communications in certain circumstances. It is the responsibility of intelligence managers to ascertain the proper collection mix, but they cannot make such evaluations in a vacuum. They must rely heavily on intelligence officers "in the trenches" to identify what is needed to sustain and develop sufficient sources. This is especially true in the technical collection area. Yet managers can and should ensure that the laboratory infrastructure that supports collectors is sufficiently integrated with the rest of the intelligence process so that consumers, as well as analysts, are aware of current and anticipated capabilities.

COMPETITIVE ANALYSIS

Intelligence must live with an irony: the relevance and timeliness of intelligence are enhanced if intelligence analysts work side by side with those they serve, while such proximity may be the greatest single source of temptations to privatize and politicize intelligence. One solution to this dilemma is the institutionalization of competitive analysis.

Quasi-redundant analytical shops ensure that a marketplace of ideas exists even within the highly regimented intelligence hierarchy. Although analysts distributed among executive agencies, departments, and military services will not necessarily generate alternative views, they are more likely to do so than if they responded to a single consumer hierarchy.

The president, as the ultimate decision maker, rightfully expects an integrated product. Therefore, a superior intelligence service will also have a small, centralized analytical shop to drive analytical debate forward and to ensure that competing analysts are not talking past one another because of fundamentally divergent frameworks or assumptions. Moreover, a central, "back-stopping" analytical shop can usefully identify distortions and seek to counter them before damage is done.

In no case, however, should a central analytical shop seek to interpose itself between policymakers and the officers who directly support them. The president is the most important consumer of the integrated product, although access to it should be available to all.

BALANCING SECURITY, INSTITUTIONAL FLEXIBILITY, AND INTERNAL DEBATE

A superior intelligence service will have a well-developed security system to ensure that intelligence is protected from unauthorized influence or disclosure. Compromised intelligence is not only no longer useful to the policymaker; it can also reveal a great deal about the policymaker to potential adversaries, putting the policymaker in a worse situation than if no intelligence had ever been available initially.

The need for strict information security can lead, however, to over-classification and too much compartmentation. If security is perceived as an unqualified "good," then institutions and officials may be tempted to use it to exclude others from knowing what they know and thus to exercise undue control over the intelligence process. In severe cases this can result in policymakers acting on intelligence products without key information.

The more those in the Intelligence Community know about the work of their colleagues, the better their products and general support to the policymakers will be. Ideally, analysts should be well aware of the capabilities of technical collection systems as well as what capabilities are being developed for the future. A superior intelligence service will therefore couple stringent security clearance procedures with stringent but simple, standardized classification requirements and minimal compartmentation.

STRONG, CENTRALIZED, COMMUNITY-WIDE MANAGEMENT

The need for strong central management of intelligence is a recurring theme throughout this analysis. Without such management, competitive analysis can quickly lead to trench warfare, resources cannot be shifted efficiently, new consumers cannot be identified in a timely fashion, and an effective balance between security and free debate cannot be achieved. Perhaps most important, the president cannot be ensured access to integrated intelligence products when the national security is at stake.

That the need for centralized management must be coupled with sensitivity to departmental interests is also a recurring theme and need not dilute one's commitment to a strong managerial hand. It simply suggests that in providing for strong, centralized management, the debates generated on a community-wide basis should be nurtured, occasionally disciplined, but certainly not shut down as excessively disruptive.

Implications for U.S. Intelligence

Using the indicators of quality suggested above, the U.S. intelligence system would appear quite healthy, incorporating multiple sources and collection methods, highly competitive analysis, and considerable institutional flexibility. The system has also enjoyed relatively strong central management, which, in recent years, has encouraged community-wide coordination of collection and production. Still, few would say the system is perfect.

While definitions should never drive policy, the insights provided by such basics can help clarify the policy debate. The previous discussion suggested a number of points, of which two will be explored here: the importance of the changing consumer mix and the urgent need to improve the handling of open-source information. They inspire three recommendations:

Think creatively about who the priority intelligence consumers will be in the future and how they will be trained and served.

There are several dimensions to the "new consumer" issue. First, the end of the Cold War may increase the need to share intelligence with nontraditional allies or nongovernmental institutions such as the UN Security Council or the International Atomic Energy Agency (IAEA). Procedures for evaluating finished products for this purpose on a time-urgent basis could improve institutional performance during future crises. Internationalizing certain national technical collection assets may also be useful and would help ease intelligence costs. Landsat serves as a model of how this internationalized collection capability could be achieved, although declassifying a clandestine collector for more general use is also feasible and worth considering, if only to defray costs.

Second, there is no reason to assume that the U.S. Intelligence Community must serve only the national security establishment as traditionally defined. The Treasury Department, the Commerce Department, the Environmental Protection Agency, the Drug Enforcement Agency, and the Centers for Disease Control may all become increasingly important recipients of intelligence information. Nevertheless, nonnational consumers, such as U.S. industry, should not become involved in the government's intelligence functions. Industry's orientation toward profit making and competitive advantage, and the close working relationships that are desirable between intelligence analysts and consumers, would turn portions of the Intelligence Community into a hothouse for the growth of privatized and politicized intelligence.

Third, considerable attention should be paid to Congress as a legitimate consumer of intelligence. Although security clearances are liberally distributed among staff and automatically provided to elected officials, the Intelligence Community and members of Congress tend to consider the latter's role to be more that of a watchdog than of a consumer. Given the information revolution and increasing congressional influence on broad matters of policy (including the intelligence budget), it may be best to consider congressional leaders and their staffs as decision makers intent on engaging in intelligence assessments, fully informed or not.

Once their role as consumers is recognized, individuals should be trained to understand their role in the intelligence process. At stressful times, decision makers may lean on the Intelligence Community to make difficult choices for them. Before the war with Iraq, for example, numerous senators and representatives pressed intelligence officers for a "bottom line": Would sanctions work, or not? Intelligence officers, struggling to assess the intelligence themselves without engaging in policy debate, were quickly labeled either evasive, mushy, or politicized, depending on their willingness to reach a conclusion. Yet it was elected officials who needed to do the assessment, and to do this required knowing the right questions to ask the right people.

Ignorance of how to use the intelligence service is not confined to Capitol Hill; it is widespread within the civilian policy-making community. (The military services are far better at establishing appropriate relationships between analysts and decision makers because intelligence is a key aspect of strategy, tactics, and, therefore, military training.) Policymakers tend to think of intelligence as a service, not as a process that requires their active participation.

Although the establishment of community-wide centers on functional issues represents a step forward, consumer ignorance is partly the fault of the Intelligence Community. It has not done a good job of empowering the front and back ends of the intelligence process (i.e., decision makers and intelligence collectors) by making each aware of and knowledgeable about the other. As an example of this problem, six months after the creation of the Nonproliferation Center—which serves as the intelligence focal point and liaison with the policy community on the issue of Iraqi disarmament—elements involved in the training and support of inspectors had never heard of the center, nor had they been visited by any of its officials.

Tackle the issue of open-source collection aggressively by recognizing that (1) consumers may find these sources the most useful and (2) properly organizing them in data banks will free the Intelligence Community to focus its more expensive and higher risk collection techniques on information not publicly available.

Fear of national involvement in industrial espionage should not obscure the need for U.S. intelligence to provide better economic intelligence. Relevant open sources are currently poorly processed and disseminated because of unwarranted classification methods within the Intelligence Community and archaic notions of information management in some U.S. agencies. The result is often duplication of work within the government, a lack of tasking from policymakers, and growing public resentment over lack of timely access to government information.

The Intelligence Community should consider coordinating open-source information management with certain agencies and departments to create a national commercial information archive. Such a data bank, accessible to the public as well as to the Intelligence Community, could be a depository of unclassified information, for instance, from commercial attachés as well as information gleaned from the texts of foreign technical journals translated by the Intelligence Community. As such, it could serve as an immediate dumping ground for open-source intelligence that needs to be "laundered" as well as an information bank by which to determine what information clandestine activities may be uniquely able to acquire.

Encourage intelligence analysts to publish and to brief their own work.

Increased visibility may reduce the frustrations that can lead to privatization of intelligence. Personal briefings would also ensure that the coordinated intelligence studies produced by an iterative process are balanced by more individualistic work. Authors would gain greater exposure to policymakers' requirements while helping the latter to develop contacts in the Intelligence Community.

Conclusion

This discussion of "what is intelligence?" will not satisfy everyone. However, it does expose the assumptions and analytical strengths and weaknesses behind some current arguments for intelligence reorganization and reform. A number of the reforms suggested above are already being implemented by the Intelligence Community or are under consideration by Congress. Unfortunately, in some circles, simple budget cutting, not cost-effectiveness, may be receiving more attention. If one believes that intelligence, in addition to keeping tabs on existing strategic threats, also monitors emerging ones, then accompanying defense cuts with intelligence cuts for the sake of "fairness" makes little sense.

2

WHAT IS INTELLIGENCE?
SECRETS AND COMPETITION AMONG STATES

Abram Shulsky

A number of important points were raised by Dr. Sims in chapter 1. Rather than treat them individually, however, I intend to go directly to the heart of the matter: our fundamentally different views of what intelligence is. For Dr. Sims, intelligence is the information necessary for decision makers. By implication, this seems to mean *all* the information that is necessary for the decision makers. That strikes me as an overly broad definition. Moreover, what makes me suspicious about such a definition is that it nowhere mentions secrecy. And it is secrecy, I believe, that provides an essential key for understanding what intelligence is, and what it is not.

At one level, this dispute over the meaning of intelligence may seem academic. Obviously, there must be some mechanism by which decision makers get the information they need. For example, if there is a coup in Fredonia, they must be made aware of it. It might seem, at first, that it does not make much difference whether it is called current intelligence or news reporting. However, upon reflection, it does have important effects on how the government organizes the gathering and processing functions with respect to policy-relevant information.

This requires that the problem be viewed from a broader perspective. Much of the information that government officials need to do their jobs, they get via informal, unstructured mechanisms—the general news media, diplomatic and other official conversations, travel, contacts with academic specialists, business executives, and so on. It is clear, however, that such mechanisms are not sufficient. A government official needs organized, structured mechanisms for providing at least some kinds of information. The question is: What are these structured mechanisms, and are they the same as intelligence?

This paper was first presented on April 29, 1992.

Genesis of an Idea

I will approach this question by looking at the history of intelligence in the United States because it provides the reason we tend to take the view—which I think is a particularly American view—that intelligence is all the information that is necessary for policymakers.

First, there was the experience of the Office of Strategic Services (OSS) during World War II, in particular, the famed Research and Analysis Branch, which was able to derive a great deal of valuable information for the war effort from open sources. These open sources provided information about German industry, transportation facilities, and so on, which was very useful targeting information for the strategic bombing campaign.

That the U.S. government had to scramble around in 1943 to find this information in the stacks of the Library of Congress reflected the fact that the United States did not have a very big and active military establishment before the war. This was information that the Army Air Corps would have been collecting if it had viewed Germany as a potential enemy in the 1930s and if it had the resources and structure necessary to plan for the war. That is the kind of information that under other circumstances would have been contained in the encyclopedic studies assembled by the German General Staff, but the United States did not have an equivalent to the German General Staff. The United States did have, however, one of the most impressive groups of social scientists, historians, and other academics ever gathered under the auspices and in the pay of the U.S. government. Such intellectually high-powered staffs did not exist elsewhere in the foreign policy arena before that time.

At the onset of World War II, when everyone was patriotic, when everyone wanted to contribute to the war effort, it was possible, according to a recent book, to move the faculty of Yale University to Washington, D.C., practically en masse. The result was a tremendous wealth of human talent that could be applied to research questions relevant to the war effort, many of which could be answered from open sources. It was part of an intelligence agency (OSS) because "Wild Bill" Donovan understood that these academics could make important contributions.

Second, after the war, a different kind of intelligence problem was posed by the Soviet Union, for which there was in the early postwar years very little open-source information. Information that other countries published as a matter of course (e.g., the defense budget or maps) was regarded as secret in the Soviet Union, and either was not published or was published only in a distorted fashion. Therefore, specialized methods and structures were necessary to learn almost anything of national security interest about the Soviet Union.

In addition, traditional human intelligence methods did not work well. The solution was that the United States developed a tremendous array of technical collection assets to acquire basic information about the Soviet Union. This represented a new kind of intelligence. Various sorts of technical collection existed previously, but this new type of intelligence had the important characteristic that it did not totally depend on the other side not knowing that you were engaged in it. In some cases, the other side can know a fair amount about what you are doing and you can still collect useful intelligence; in this sense, it was very different from human intelligence collection.

The result was that the Intelligence Community had a quasi-monopoly on national security information about the Soviet Union. It was not a complete monopoly because there were other sources such as the "Kremlinology" that academics developed in the 1950s to "tease out" bits of information from Soviet open sources. Much of the information, including information that the academic community used in its work, had to come originally from the Intelligence Community. This changed later on as the Soviet Union eased its restrictions on travel and contacts between its people and the outside world, but the Iron Curtain that Churchill talked about was a barrier that made it very hard to know what was going on on the other side.

The point of recounting this history is to show why the notion that intelligence is all policy-relevant information took root. Although the historical circumstances were different, they both supported the idea that an intelligence agency should deal in all information, either because it was the only government agency equipped to deal systematically with the available open sources, or because useful open sources hardly existed.

This idea was given theoretical expression in Sherman Kent's *Strategic Intelligence for American World Policy* (1949). According to Kent, intelligence includes all information necessary for conducting foreign policy. This idea reflects, in part, the historical experience discussed above. It might also reflect the practical response to the rapid turnover in policymakers in the U.S. government and the resulting loss of experience and knowledge available for making decisions. Intelligence analysts tend to remain in their positions much longer and, hence, are likely to become more expert in their subject matter than the policymakers they are advising. But I think Kent reflects something else that is perhaps less noted in this type of discussion. I think he reflects the tremendous optimism of the social sciences of the 1940s and 1950s.

Kent's book discusses research with admiration; he describes it as the sole method that Western civilization has found that can serve as the source of reliable information, and so forth. This reflects a belief that was common in the social sciences in the 1940s and 1950s, a belief that the new methodology of social science would begin to bear fruit and result in a much more scientific understanding of human behavior. The belief was that social science would develop on the model of the physical sciences and, as in those fields, greatly expand the ability to explain and predict events—in this case, human events.

Former DCI William Colby, in an article published in 1980 in *Information Sciences*, takes Kent's optimism about intelligence to an extreme by treating intelligence as a universal social science able to bring all its methodologies to bear in order to produce solid scientific results. From the point of view of academic social science, this has a familiar ring. In the 1960s it was still very much the case that the profession tended to believe that if social science's Newton had not yet arrived, he or she would come in the near future. On the other hand, if one attends an American Political Science Association meeting in the 1990s, it is apparent that there is an awareness that "scientific" social science is much more problematic and that the model of the physical sciences is not applicable. This undercuts Kent's belief in intelligence as a universal social science and forces us back to the main issue of how the information needs of a government should be met, what types of structures are useful in that regard, and what distinguishes intelligence from other types of information potentially available to the policymaker.

The Future

The future intelligence agenda is clearly different from that of the past as a result of important changes that have occurred in the world. These changes affect what information is available to policymakers and is needed by them. Most obvious is the collapse of the Soviet Union. Russia and the other states on the territory of the former Soviet Union and in Eastern Europe are still important intelligence targets, but it is much easier to find out what is going on there. There are all sorts of information available—open sources, diplomatic and other personal contacts, and so forth. At the same time, the future shape of the international system also deals with the policies of countries that are relatively open and where political debate goes on much as it does in the United States. It is important to know about the future policies of countries such as Germany and Japan, which have the potential to become major actors in the international system. However, the clandestine means that were needed to obtain information about the Soviet Union are not necessary in these cases.

With respect to proliferation issues, which have come to the fore as intelligence questions, the situation is more complicated. On the one hand, technical intelligence is still needed and, as indicated by the experience with Iraq in the 1990s, can be difficult to obtain. On the other hand, there are many other available sources of information useful for keeping abreast of the proliferation problem. Some type of mechanism is required to collect and use this information to best advantage.

Consider Iraq's nuclear weapons program, for example. Iraq was not a closed society in the Soviet sense. It was a difficult human intelligence target because Iraq had a good counterintelligence capability. On the other hand, Iraq did not manufacture everything or even most of what it needed for its nuclear program. Instead, it bought most items from Western countries. So, in a sense, the Western countries had, or could have had, access to an important part of Iraq's nuclear program. In addition, many of Iraq's scientists and technicians were trained in Western countries.

In principle, this should have made the job much easier. But it turns out that it was not easy to obtain a list of all Iraqi students who were trained in nuclear physics in the United States, let alone in Western Europe. The same is true of the provision of relevant materials or equipment, where the issue is further complicated by the trade competition among Western countries.

In this case, then, nontraditional information of this sort can be as important as the ordinary sorts of intelligence information. It may even be that items like export license requests can provide earlier indications of a nuclear program than can technical intelligence assets, especially if the country involved has undertaken sophisticated concealment and deception measures. Thus, there must be a structured and sophisticated mechanism for processing all of these sorts of relevant information, and the process must be as sophisticated as the one now used for the more traditional types of intelligence information.

Should all of this information be considered intelligence? To answer that question, several items must be considered. It is not merely a matter of definition, although if one wishes to define intelligence as equal to all necessary information, that certainly can be done. But things have changed dramatically since World War II, and institutional arrangements that came into existence during and immediately following the war should not be automatically or uncritically accepted.

Since World War II, there has been an increase in the number of organizations that are involved in the collection and analysis of policy-relevant information but that are by no means intelligence organizations. There are national security think tanks such as the Rand Corporation and many others; in-house think tanks of the military and other departments of the government (e.g., the Institute of National Strategic Studies at the National Defense University); national laboratories of the Department of Energy (e.g., Livermore, Los Alamos, and Sandia); the Federal Research Division of the Library of Congress; and so forth.

Within the government are many specialized staffs of various sorts—policy planning staffs, specialized analysis units in law enforcement agencies, the Office of Net Assessment in the Department of Defense, and so forth. These organizations deal with classified information if necessary, but they are not ordinarily regarded as intelligence organizations. In addition, there are numerous research centers on policy-relevant questions that have no, or minimal, ties to the government. Included in this category are various academic organizations that study questions of interest, as well as business-oriented risk assessment outfits and other types of research centers.

The basic point is that the U.S. Intelligence Community must be able to more fully tap the knowledge that exists within the society as a whole; it cannot exist in just one place. When Chairman of the Senate Intelligence Committee David Boren introduced his bill in 1992 to reorganize the Intelligence Community, he talked of creating a world-class think tank at Langley. In one sense that would be a good idea, but in another sense, it is impossible; there is simply too much information necessary and available for one to be able to centralize it and organize it in one place.

When viewed in this manner, the real problem is how to reach out and tap the information that exists throughout the whole society. An interesting subpoint is that the OSS did precisely that; it drew people from throughout society. Circumstances were different then, however; it was not necessary to tap the information that existed throughout the whole society because the whole society could be and was being restructured to win the war. The OSS did not have to contact Wall

Street businessmen to find out what they knew about European business conditions because they had already moved to Washington to work for the OSS.

The situation is quite different now, but the government still must have some way to make use of all the relevant information that is available in other parts of the society.

The clearest case of this is economic intelligence. It makes little sense to use the current model of an intelligence organization (i.e., to assign a government agency to collect and analyze intelligence to produce the economic information that the government needs) because that information already exists in various segments of society. The government cannot, and should not try, to duplicate all the information that exists throughout society, and it certainly cannot match the salaries and rewards provided by private companies to individuals for gathering and understanding that information. For example, if the government wanted to hire someone to analyze the Japanese auto industry, it would be competing with Morgan Stanley for the same talent; and the government would not be able to pay the analyst close to the amount Morgan Stanley would pay.

On the other hand, the government is not trying to use the information to trade on the stock market; its interests do not conflict with those of Morgan Stanley. Thus, the government should be able to purchase the information from Morgan Stanley (which is paying $350,000 or more per year to produce that information) at a much reduced price.

In this area of economics, furthermore, one cannot realistically distinguish between foreign and domestic information: understanding the Japanese auto industry requires understanding the American auto industry as well. Certainly any government policy that deals with the former does so primarily because it wishes to help the latter. In contrast, Sherman Kent emphasized that intelligence was foreign information, not domestic information. Similarly, in a speech before the Economic Club of Detroit in April 1992, then-DCI Robert Gates discussed economic intelligence, saying that his intelligence analysts would work on both the international economy and on the domestic economic performance of countries around the world. That leaves an important gap: the domestic economic performance of the United States. That is not an inconsequential part of the puzzle and yet the CIA is not going to be working on it. But if one wants to set economic policy, it cannot be ignored. Of what use would an analysis of international economic trends be without information about U.S. domestic performance?

Law enforcement data present similar problems. To deal with narcotics intelligence requires understanding the links between foreign suppliers of narcotics and domestic consumers. Most such data will be developed by law enforcement agencies in the performance of their duties, and much of it will deal with domestic activities and with Americans. As such, the full analysis of the narcotics problem cannot be an intelligence issue, although some specialized intelligence information may be useful.

Finally, there is the delicate question of the stigma that is still attached to intelligence. There is and will probably continue to be an unwillingness in certain elements of society—primarily in academia but in other sectors as well perhaps—to cooperate with anything that is labeled intelligence. And yet there is a need to use the expertise of these groups of people. There is nothing "cloak and dagger" about most of what would be involved, but as a public relations matter it is much easier to stop calling it intelligence than it is to convince a professor who has just returned from a conference in Kiev that it is "politically correct" to discuss matters with the CIA.

A government-sponsored Center for Ukrainian Studies could perform most of the analytic work that one would want done about Ukraine. For the most part, it is not a question of access to secrets. One could look through every government file in Kiev and still not find a document that clearly lays out what the Ukraine's long-term military policy is—because it does not have one. That must be determined by other analytic means based on available data, data that will consist primarily of open-source materials and information gained in conversations at conferences, in business dealings, in government-to-government communications, and so on.

My conclusion is that the goal should not be to centralize all the necessary information inside the government, let alone inside one part of the government. In many cases, we cannot distinguish clearly between foreign and domestic information. Similarly, there is a problem in making use of both intelligence and law enforcement information. The law—to say nothing of traditional U.S. views—implies a dichotomy between these two types of institutions; this alone would seem to force us to create new types of institutions when we want to deal with an issue such as international narcotics trafficking, which involves both intelligence and law enforcement aspects.

Finally, and perhaps even more important as a practical matter, we cannot distinguish as clearly as Kent implies between intelligence and policy. My impression is that Kent was thinking about the fact-value distinction familiar in the social sciences; that is, intelligence, like social science, will provide the "facts" but someone else—the policy official in this case—must provide the "values." Unfortunately, in most foreign policy issues, values are not of primary concern. The real problem is determining what measures are likely to work and what measures are not.

For example, the major debate on U.S. policy toward the Persian Gulf in late 1990 concerned a question of "fact": Would sanctions induce Saddam Hussein to withdraw from Kuwait or not? If intelligence could have provided a solid answer to that question, then the debate would have ended immediately; but, of course, it could not provide such an answer.

There is an important risk in combining what one might call "hard" and "soft" intelligence (i.e., real nuggets of information that the Intelligence Community knows and that policymakers do not know until the community tells them, as opposed to judgments that the Intelligence Community may be able to make in a somewhat—but only somewhat—more informed fashion than the policymaker). The risk that one runs is the politicization of intelligence. The danger is that the "hard" information that the Intelligence Community really knows will be devalued in the minds of the policymakers if one habitually presents it in a sort of mélange of hard fact and analysis that directly tries to answer the policymakers' questions about what is going to happen in the future. Such a prediction is almost always going to be complex, because the hard nuggets of fact available will not be a sufficient basis for it; a large amount of speculation will typically also be required.

The adverbial qualifiers *really* and *almost always* in the preceding sentences are not simply rhetorical; there are some cases (e.g., the Battle of Midway) when intelligence really is in a position to predict the future. The point is that, when such a situation occurs, one wants the policymaker or commander to believe the intelligence, and not reject it because of previous experiences in which intelligence "predictions" turned out to have an evidentiary base similar to that of scholarly articles or other sources of informed speculation.

In conclusion, if the pundits are correct in telling us that we are in the information age, handling information must be viewed as a major function of government. Although this has always been true, to a greater and greater extent, government is going to have to be organized and structured in order to become better at obtaining and using information. This parallels developments in the business world, where the tendency has been to decentralize the gathering and exploitation of information and diffuse it throughout the corporation.

Intelligence Properly Understood

In this age of information, it becomes important to try to focus on what intelligence is, specifically, on what is unique about intelligence. Given that the processing of information will become more widespread throughout the government, and that the government will have to rely more and more on information that is gathered and analyzed elsewhere in society, what part of that process should be considered "intelligence" and treated in a special manner? This is where the link between secrecy and intelligence, noted at the outset, becomes apparent.

For example, one category of information that requires protection is information that would reveal sources and methods. This is fairly obvious and does not require much discussion, but it will become a more and more complicated issue as the overhead imagery capabilities available in the civilian, commercial sector (such as Landsat or the French SPOT [*Satellite Pour l'Observation de la Terre*] system) improve. While specific characteristics of technical intelligence systems require protection (and hence intelligence products that would reveal the existence of those capabilities must be likewise protected), attempts to extend that protection too far may be counterproductive and lead to pressures to disclose too much. In addition, intelligence analysts must be fully aware of the extent to which technical collection capabilities are understood by their targets; a picture that the intelligence target knows is being taken may be useful, but its usefulness cannot be as great as that of a picture that the target is unaware of.

This raises another important issue in deciding what should be, or should not be, considered intelligence. Concern about, and protection against, being deceived is a specific intelligence sensitivity and responsibility that the rest of the government's and society's information-processing apparatus is not likely to have. If one loses the sense that the gathering, analysis, and exploitation of intelligence is at least potentially a contest with someone who does not want one to gain an advantage by means of having that information, then one runs a great risk of being deceived and misled. Many of the nontraditional subjects proposed for intelligence concern (e.g., environmental issues) do not have this aspect to them. Trying to centralize consideration of them in an intelligence apparatus is, from this point of view, not necessary. Conversely, requiring the intelligence apparatus to deal with many such topics may dull its sensitivity to the possibility of deception in those areas where it is very important.

Finally, there is the "aura" of intelligence—within the policy world, intelligence remains a trump card to be played in the course of policy debate or recrimination, especially when it is at the point of leaking out into the media. The implication is that to make a policy decision "against" intelligence is simply a form of irrationality. As discussed above, this is not really true most of the time, because the "intelligence" that is most relevant to the specific policy question is the analyst's speculation, which may or may not be more trustworthy than that of other experts.

But because of the implication that the analyst's speculation is based on secret information unavailable to others (there may well be such information, but the question is how crucial it is to the conclusion), what should be a relatively wide-open debate about what policy to follow risks becoming a hidden struggle to shape the intelligence judgment. Why fight it out on policy grounds if one can win by manipulating the intelligence product and arrogating its aura for one's position? Yet this is the temptation one creates when one extends the sphere of intelligence to include virtually all policy-relevant information and its analysis.

The alternative would be to try to focus the term *intelligence* and all of its aura and prestige on the hard and reliable information that it is able to obtain and that it would be irresponsible to ignore. As for the rest of the information processing that must go on and that is in fact a government-wide and indeed society-wide operation, we must recognize that its structure should depend on the particular type of information involved, on who has the greatest chance and incentive to collect it, on what the legal ramifications of centralizing or dispersing it would be, and so forth. And as for the suggestion that a single center for information gathering and analysis, a center on which the government would place primary reliance in determining the entire range of its national security policies (including international economic, environmental, and health issues, to say nothing of international terrorism and drug trafficking), we should recognize that for the utopia which it is.

3

THINKING ABOUT REORGANIZATION

James Q. Wilson

R eorganization is a favorite Washington activity, not because it is a proven method for achieving certain policy goals, but because it is a strategy that can accommodate so many different motives that almost everyone can join in, whatever their goals. Reorganizations are undertaken to reward constituencies, achieve efficiencies, reduce duplication, enhance White House power, acquire prestige, display symbols, undercut opponents, simplify oversight, and "do something" without actually spending money.

Some History

I say this not in a spirit of detached cynicism, unaware of the efforts of the many serious people who have tried hard to improve how the government works. On the contrary, I briefly served as a government reorganizer in the early 1970s when involved in the creation of the Drug Enforcement Administration. That experience left me keenly aware of how difficult it is to achieve a given outcome by changing an organizational chart. As someone once said, reorganizing an agency is like pushing a wet string.

There have been only a few serious academic studies of reorganization, most written in the aftermath of the major reorganization efforts of the 1950s and 1960s.[1] Drawing on these, and mindful of my ignorance of the newest research, as well as of the limitations of the older studies, I offer the following tentative generalization: The least successful reorganizations have been those that sought to change the behavior of frontline agency personnel or otherwise alter the programmatic outputs of the agency.

The reorganization that created the Drug Enforcement Agency (DEA) out of the old Bureau of Narcotics and Dangerous Drugs

This paper was first presented on June 10, 1992.

(BNDD) and parts of the Customs Service was intended to improve the way cases were made against drug dealers and to eliminate interagency competition in these investigations. BNDD had been under fire for relying too much on undercover "buy and bust" tactics that led to the arrest of many low-level drug dealers and few high-level drug bosses, and BNDD and Customs both had been under fire for their intense rivalry, which led on occasion to members of one agency placing under surveillance those from the other. The new DEA generally continued the operations of the old BNDD, and absorbed many Customs agents.

Three main difficulties afflicted this reorganization plan. First, there was no real effort by the advocates of the plan to understand the daily work and operating culture of the BNDD and Customs investigators and to think through the relationship between these routines and incentives on the one hand and specify policy objectives on the other. Second, the advocates of reorganization were under heavy pressure from their political superiors to do something dramatic about a highly visible issue, and to do it quickly. Third, to overcome resistance within Congress and among agency personnel the advocates promised more than could be accomplished by reorganization alone. The second and third difficulties accentuated the first; the desire for quick, decisive, comprehensive, and low-budget action minimized the likelihood of thoughtful analysis of what changes should be made, although I suspect that the analysis probably would have been inadequate even without those pressures.

The reason for my suspicion is that reorganization plans tend to be developed by staff people who are brought in from outside the government to serve political appointees or legislators and who, as a consequence, know relatively little about the agencies they propose to change and who quickly discover, when they consult members of those agencies, that most employees can think of numerous reasons why a reorganization is either not needed or will not work. These staffers must therefore develop a change strategy with the aid of only their own instincts supplemented by the complaints of dissident agency members (or former members). The reorganization plan tends, as a result, to reflect general proverbs of good administration (End wasteful duplication! Clarify lines of authority!) reinforced by negative stories from people unhappy with their lives in government.

The previous probably overstates the matter, but if so, only to dramatize a point made by Rufus Miles, a man with vast and lengthy experience in public affairs. He wrote in 1977: "Repetitive reorganization without proper initial diagnosis is like repetitive surgery without proper diagnosis; obviously an unsound and unhealthy approach to the cure of the malady."

Even when reorganization plans are prepared by committees of insiders, they are often quick and dirty exercises written under heavy time pressures by people who are told to look kindly on reorganization or who are recruited from among those who already think that way.

By 1981 the DEA again faced a top-down demand for reorganization, which led this time to a most unusual outcome: it became a wholly owned but quasi-independent subsidiary of the Federal Bureau of Investigation (FBI). Many people believe that this reorganization really improved matters, but if that is true, I am sure that it was the result of a happy accident and not the "proper diagnosis" of which Miles wrote.

Making a proper diagnosis will differ depending on the kind of agency being studied. There are generally two kinds of agencies: those that produce an outcome that can be specified in advance (Type One) and those that do not (Type Two). The Internal Revenue Service (IRS), the Social Security Administration, and the Bureau of Public Roads are, in general, examples of the first type: we can say in advance what we want the agencies to achieve and we can be fairly confident of our ability to tell whether or not they have achieved it. We want complete and honest tax collections subject to a budget constraint; we want retirement checks sent out promptly and in the correct amounts; and we want certain cities linked by highways built to certain specifications. The State Department, the FBI, the DEA, and the CIA are agencies of the second type: we cannot say in advance or with much precision what we want these agencies to produce and we will not find it easy to agree on whether they have produced it. (We may think we can evaluate their products, but that is only because it is so easy after the fact to criticize their apparent failures. For example, if Gorbachev is the object of a coup that not even Gorbachev saw coming, should the CIA be blamed for not predicting it? If drug dealing increases, is it the fault of the DEA? If Yugoslavia collapses because of irresistible internal pressures, should the State Department be held responsible for not keeping it in one piece?)

The central task facing anyone proposing to reorganize a Type Two agency is to think through exactly what operating culture we wish to produce among rank-and-file employees and then to design an organizational structure that will increase the chances of that culture being created and sustained. Defining that culture requires us to understand the key processes that we wish to see under way despite not knowing for certain what outcome those processes will lead to. A culture is important because we must trust rank-and-file personnel to define ambiguous situations, take "appropriate" action, and motivate one another through peer pressure to work hard at difficult and dangerous tasks.

A corporate executive managing a research and development laboratory or attempting to meet the demands of a fickle public responding in unpredictable ways to rapidly changing market and technological conditions understands the need for empowering and motivating lower-level personnel. But business management techniques cannot be easily assimilated to governmental realities; the political problem is much more difficult. There is no "customer" whose preferences, registered in a market, can unambiguously signal success or failure back to the executive. Government serves many customers with conflicting preferences that are ambiguously expressed. That is, agencies must serve a variety of partially inconsistent goals. Therefore, we must create a set of independent, somewhat inconsistent organizational cultures and then find ways to create linkage mechanisms that make it possible for people with very different cultures to work together on overlapping or common tasks.

Thinking this way about reorganization, it is clear that, at least for Type Two agencies, there is no "one best way" to organize; the conflict among and within agencies is not only inevitable but (up to a point) desirable, and a great deal of time and effort must be devoted to understanding existing organizational cultures and thinking through how they can be adapted to serve the kinds of functions that we suspect may be important. A rational reorganization effort would be characterized by prolonged inquiry, internal self-examination, and external monitoring, with heavy attention paid to understanding those historical cases in which the agency did well and those cases in which it did poorly. In all likelihood, it would recommend not a grand plan, but a series of piecemeal changes aimed at remedying certain specific problems.

Intelligence: A Few Questions

I have had a variety of experiences over the last several decades with government agencies, culminating in a five-year stint on the President's Foreign Intelligence Advisory Board (PFIAB). Despite this experience, I do not think I know how to organize what is called "The Community" nor have I met anybody who has a good enough grasp of all of the parts of the community to qualify as a certified expert. I do not wish to give the impression that I am an academic whose stock in trade is sneering at the good faith efforts of practical people, but thinking as I do about bureaucracies, I have some reactions to the reorganization proposals put forward in 1992 by the then-chairmen of the House and Senate intelligence committees.

My first reaction was puzzlement. After receiving the House and Senate plans, I requested copies of the studies that had been done that described the existing system, highlighted its defects, and explained why certain changes might lead to certain desirable outcomes. I was told there were no such studies. I inquired further, and got the same answer, modified by the suggestion that some staff people who compiled the plans might have kept notes.

This was almost exactly the state of affairs that existed when I was involved in creating the DEA. I recall being asked by a member of Congress for some written examples of the need for a reorganization. I called back to the White House to get the study. There was nothing that could be called a study. There was only The Plan. After some scurrying about, I was furnished, orally, with some horror stories and reminded that my job was to tell people that this administration was going to put an end to "wasteful duplication." (A digression: Why is duplication always wasteful? When we shop for a new car, we do not point to the existence of ten auto dealers as evidence of wasteful duplication. When the astronauts go up in the space shuttle, they do not point to the existence of three redundant computers as evidence of wasteful duplication. Of course, some kinds of duplication are wasteful; the task is to specify what and why.)

Perhaps a study was carried out. If so, I hope it raised questions of the following sort and asked what answering them implies about organizational structure and incentive systems. First, after several decades of attempting to gather human intelligence in Castro's Cuba, Castro pointed out publicly that virtually all of the CIA's assets in Cuba were in fact Cuban double agents. What is there about our system of acquiring assets abroad that makes it relatively easy for a hostile power to supply us with doubles? What is there about this system that can lead us to reproduce this mistake for decades, without detection, and to reward with promotions those responsible for such "recruitments"?

Second, CIA officers are stationed in U.S. embassies and operate under official cover. While offering certain advantages, this creates at least two problems. First, the host nation knows that U.S. intelligence officers are in the embassy (and usually knows exactly who they are); this simplifies their job of keeping secrets from us and planting false "secrets" on us. Second, the important dynamics of a regime are often found in the economic ventures, ethnic pressures, and military bases located on the periphery and not in the capital of the host nation. Why do we resist placing intelligence officers at the periphery under nonofficial cover?

Third, counterintelligence (CI) has long been a suspect part of the Intelligence Community. Intelligence officers are rewarded for acquiring assets; CI is charged with evaluating these assets skeptically. As a consequence, CI is viewed, at best, as a party pooper. The resultant career rewards are about what one would expect; the route to the top of the CIA traditionally has been via covert collection and operations; occasionally, an analyst will make it, but CI specialists rarely get near the top. Some CIA executives justify this situation by declaring that we must never again risk letting a James Jesus Angleton use CI to exercise a chilling effect on collections. But even those no longer possessed by the Angleton specter view CI as a suspect stepchild. How can the CIA best enable CI to play an effective role in evaluating assets and make a career in CI personally rewarding?

Fourth, intelligence analysis is important. But what do we mean by *analysis* and what, exactly, are analysts supposed to do? If the task of analysis is to synthesize everything that is known about another country or an international issue and present a crisp summary, together with dissenting opinions and an account of what is not known, then it is not clear why analysis is an intelligence activity at all. Universities, consulting firms, and the National Academy of Sciences do exactly this all the time; what can intelligence analysis add to that, especially since most of the sources for any summary are publicly available? The answer seems to be that an analytical unit adds information from secret sources to that from open sources. But that answer is only valid if the information gleaned from secret sources is materially different from or better than information gleaned from public sources. It is not clear how often that is the case.

Thinking through this issue is important, because to the extent that analysis is a government function, especially a classified one, there will be enormous pressures to produce consensus estimates or to tell policymakers what they want to hear. It usually takes something akin to a coup d'état to produce competitive estimates internally. (Recall the bitter legacy of the Team A/Team B exercise.) But it is business as usual to produce competitive estimates externally. Should we try to have the best of both worlds by relying on competitive external sources for most of the analytical work, using an internal unit only for the specialized task of adding to these estimates information too secret to be shared outside a small number of people?

And finally, the military, especially theater commanders, have intelligence needs that are different from those of the White House or the State Department. It is as implausible to think that a separate, essentially civilian agency can supply timely and valuable war-fighting intelligence as it is to think that the military can supply timely and valuable diplomatic intelligence. There is no easy answer to this question. But I am deeply skeptical of the view that when two agencies have overlapping missions the inevitable conflict and slippage can be overcome by creating czars or by interagency coordination.

Neither coordination nor a drug czar has reconciled the roles of DEA and Customs. Intelligence is an even vaguer, more general activity than drug enforcement, and it is quite unlikely that either an intelligence czar, interagency committee, or shared executive personnel will reconcile the many discrete missions and tasks that make up intelligence. The Joint Chiefs of Staff, at least until the installation of the Goldwater-Nichols reforms, did not produce much coordination of the armed services. It has taken decades of effort to coordinate effectively army infantry and air force tactical strikes. Most important, there has not been, at the working level, a high degree of coordination between the FBI and the CIA or between the State Department and the CIA.

The burden of proof must be on the individual who suggests that interagency coordination will solve the problem of war-fighting intelligence. Is there a case for coordination so plausible, so well-grounded in past experience, that it is superior to giving the military its own intelligence service? It is no answer to say that a separate military service will produce "wasteful duplication." Duplication, as mentioned previously, is not inherently wasteful; duplication is a means, one of many, by which to attain stated objectives.

Conclusion

I am not confident that I have the answer to the above questions, but I am reasonably confident that no one has produced a government document that even addresses, much less answers, the questions. The document need not be the result of a five-year research effort. It is only necessary to think through, as best one can, how to organize and motivate people so that they will want to find real secrets and not just countable "assets"; so that prospective assets are honestly evaluated; so that working outside the embassy and outside the capital is viewed as exciting and rewarding even though it means acquiring greater language skills and cultural knowledge than is now possessed by most of those who get embassy postings; so that analysts will know what they do and how it is different from what professors or consultants do; and so that military personnel will be able to serve their commanders with information from technical and human resources that are focused on an enemy's (or would-be enemy's) intentions and capabilities. Until that happens, I think there is no case, or at best a very weak case for reorganizing the Intelligence Community.

4

INTELLIGENCE: BACKING INTO THE FUTURE

Ernest R. May

Congress considered legislation in 1992 to reorganize the U.S. Intelligence Community. As drafted, the bills would have solved problems of the past, not problems of the future. The National Security Act of 1947 created the Central Intelligence Agency (CIA). That act and later executive orders govern what is called the Intelligence Community, which extends far beyond the CIA. Early in 1992 the chairmen of the Senate and House intelligence committees, David Boren and David McCurdy (both Democrats from Oklahoma), introduced nearly identical bills designed to replace those mandates and reshape the structure of intelligence.

The Boren and McCurdy bills called for replacing the current director of Central Intelligence (DCI) with a director of National Intelligence (DNI), who would preside over four separate agencies, one agency for each major category of collection—human intelligence, signal intelligence, and imagery—and a fourth agency to produce analyses of the intelligence received. The DNI would have also controlled most of the government's spending for all kinds of intelligence.

Both Boren and McCurdy hoped for debate. Neither proposed that his bill be enacted exactly as drafted. This was a sensible approach; the 1947 charter did duty for forty-five years, and any new charter should also be designed to last.

Looking Forward

The main premises and objectives of the two bills were correct: the world has changed; and yet there is still a need for secret intelligence. We also need to ask, as did both bills, whether in this changed world

A version of this article was published in *Foreign Affairs* 71:3 (Summer 1992), and was originally adapted from testimony before the Senate and House intelligence committees.

the Intelligence Community will serve "the needs of the government as a whole in an effective and timely manner."

First, *change*. Both bills said that a new era is opening. The Senate version allowed only that the threat from the former Soviet Union had "considerably diminished." The House bill acknowledged the "end of the Cold War and the collapse of the Soviet Union."

In actuality, three changes occurred, all potentially revolutionary. The virtual disappearance of the Soviet threat was one. A second change was the near disappearance of any comparable threat. Before the Cold War, there were the Axis powers and fascism and, earlier still, monarchism. Americans now face no menace from any foreign military power or any hostile ideology.

The third change was in warfare. Strategic intelligence has become tactical intelligence and vice versa. In the Persian Gulf War satellites that had originally been designed to track Soviet intercontinental ballistic missiles provided target data to tank commanders and pilots. Field operatives' reports on morale among Saddam Hussein's Republican Guard meanwhile influenced presidential decisions in Washington on suspending hostilities. The odds are that in future conflicts front-line commanders will be demanding satellite imagery while White House staffers plead for intelligence information cables.

Second, *continuing need*. Absurd as are leaked Pentagon fantasies about future wars, Americans would be foolish to forget how little can be foreseen. When the USS *Lexington* was launched in 1927, almost no one imagined that it would be needed fifteen years later in the Coral Sea to check Japanese conquest of the mid-Pacific. Given the revolution in warfare Americans would be doubly foolish not to ensure that, if peace fails, U.S. battlefield commanders have eyes and ears keener than any enemy's.

The premises of an impending new era, however, imply other secret information needs. These include intelligence on sub-rosa flows of narcotics, weapons, and associated money, perhaps cross-checks on other data about trade, the environment, migration, or disease. Serving "the needs of the government as a whole" implies generating information and analysis about new subjects and for new consumers.

Looking Back

Certain features of the Boren and McCurdy bills, however, were at odds with these premises. Those features included provisions regarding the National Security Council (NSC), budgets, a revamped CIA, and the proposed new analysis agency. These provisions of the bills looked backward rather than forward.

Provisions of the bills referring to the NSC assumed the Intelligence Community would serve the same consumers as it had in the Cold War. The community would not only remain under the NSC, but would also look to an NSC subcommittee for "overall policy direction" and determination of "overall resource needs." These provisions supposed that the NSC would remain the paramount policy forum for the president. That may prove untrue.

The NSC is in some respects an anachronism. It was established in 1947 to satisfy a demand of the military services for a voice in diplomacy. Arguing that the State Department ignored the costs of diplomatic commitments, the armed services had begged since 1919 for a consultative committee equivalent to the British Committee of Imperial Defense. In the 1950s, when arms competition dominated the Cold War, roles reversed. The State Department sought a voice in defense policy. The NSC provided a forum. Presidents meanwhile found the NSC increasingly convenient for guiding both Defense and State. Under Henry Kissinger and Zbigniew Brzezinski, the NSC became a superdepartment, but for more than a decade since, however, the organization has not been what it then was. If the national agenda changes, the NSC may cease even to be primus inter pares among White House staffs.

The NSC has not dealt well in the past with nontraditional issues. In the early 1980s debt default by foreign governments was one of the greatest threats to U.S. national security. Outstanding loans, chiefly to Mexico and Brazil, equalled over 200 percent of the capital of America's nine largest banks. Insiders at the Treasury and the Federal Reserve Board feared a financial collapse worse than what occurred in 1929.

The NSC's senior director of economic affairs tried to get a warning to the president, and CIA analysts helped him build a case. But it took more than two years to place the matter on the NSC agenda. By that time, luckily, the danger had lessened. Neither the Treasury nor the Federal Reserve had seen the NSC as a natural venue for a problem in their domains, and neither agency had or has a comfortable relationship with the Intelligence Community. They succeeded in keeping their worries to themselves.

The NSC has since shown no sign of becoming better able to seize economic issues. President Bush's January 1992 trip to Japan is evidence. Staff work even approaching that on Cold War political-military issues would surely have forestalled the president's appearing as a tour guide for corporate campaign contributors. Nor does the NSC show any ability to plan a "war on drugs" or prepare for international negotiations about the environment.

In the future the NSC may handle traditional political-military issues. Other staff groups parallel in stature may handle other matters. The Clinton administration has a National Economic Council parallel to the NSC that sometimes takes the policy coordination lead. If defined by statute as "intelligence adviser to the National Security Council," the head of the Intelligence Community would not have automatic access to other staff agencies. He would be even worse off if beholden to an NSC subcommittee for guidance on policy and resource allocation. It would be better if new legislation separated the Intelligence Community from the NSC. The most that is needed is statutory provision for a "principal intelligence officer for the president."

Again, Looking Back

The second backward-looking element in the proposed bills concerned the intelligence budget. The DCI was originally expected to coordinate spending, but no DCI has ever done so. Signals intelligence remained with the Department of Defense in what became the National Security Agency. As satellites and other high-cost collection systems came on line, the Defense Department managed them as well. One-time DCI Richard Helms once estimated that the secretary of defense controlled 85 percent of all intelligence spending.

The Boren and McCurdy bills would have put the entire intelligence budget under the new DNI. The secretary of defense would have become "responsible for ensuring that the policies and resource decisions of the director of national intelligence are implemented by elements of the Department of Defense."

At the beginning of the missile and satellite era such a policy might have been wise. In a period of spending cutbacks the contrary may be true. Collection systems would fare less well as big items in a small intelligence budget than as small items in a big defense budget.

An intelligence czar could find himself in the situation of the old Atomic Energy Commission (AEC). Congress gave that agency all responsibility for nuclear weapons and nuclear propulsion; the armed services could thus make demands on it without counting the costs. The AEC became little more than a caterer. An intelligence czar could likewise end up spending money mostly to satisfy requests from the

Pentagon. Either way, the nation could lose. There could be too few systems to satisfy battlefield commanders, or there could be plenty of systems but little capacity to make sense of what they collect.

Experience in the Persian Gulf War suggests that the military establishment should retain collection systems with tactical military uses. If intelligence analysts deal increasingly with nonmilitary issues, they may have less use for signal intercepts or imagery. The president's principal intelligence officer may need only the power to ask Defense for the information his analysts wish to hear or see.

Operators and Analysts

The third backward-looking element in the bills concerned the CIA. The agency would have evolved into what is now its dubious image: an organization for spies and "dirty tricks." The large components of the CIA that do analysis would have moved elsewhere. All that would have remained would have been the clandestine service and a small staff to coordinate other human intelligence resources (e.g., as embassy attachés).

At the height of the Cold War this change, too, might have made sense. When Congress studied the CIA in the mid-1970s it saw an agency dominated by operators. Allen Dulles, director through most of the 1950s, had been called "the Great White Case Officer." The career men who later headed the CIA, Helms and William Colby, came from the clandestine service. While analysis was not distorted, it was sometimes muffled or mischanneled. In 1961 the CIA's analysts knew that Fidel Castro was popular in Cuba, but they had no chance to report this until after the Bay of Pigs fiasco. During the Vietnam War analysts poured out reports on potential military targets. Few studied the politics that might affect decisions in North Vietnam. In those years independence for the CIA's analytic directorates might have given them greater status and voice.

But the 1990s are different. The Iran-Contra affair was probably the last heave of a slain dragon. Within the CIA, by all accounts, the directorate of intelligence more than pulled abreast of the directorate of operations. Centers that focused on terrorism and counternarcotics made analysts and operators into colleagues. As director, William Webster put analysts in key managerial posts, and his successor, Robert Gates, came from the analytical side of the agency.

Today the relevant question is different. What becomes of the operators if they are cut adrift from analysts? Absent the preoccupying task of combating communists, how does one choose collection targets? In the CIA prefigured in the Senate and House bills the clandestine service would get nearly all guidance from the very top. That is not enough. Knowledge of the analytical issues that decision makers face must influence human intelligence collection at every level, from the stations on up.

This does not mean that the CIA should be left as it is. Both its operators and analysts come from cultures conditioned by the Cold War. The former think of penetrating police states and coping with conspiracies; the latter think of piecing together rare facts, like archaeologists. Neither group may successfully adapt to a world that is more like that of a Washington news reporter, that is, challenged not to find information, but to avoid being inundated by it.

In business corporations, attempts to change cultures usually fail. They may fail in the CIA. It may prove better to create a new clandestine service and a new corps of analysts, bringing in veterans only as and if they meet newly defined needs. The Cold War CIA took shape in that fashion, for Harry Truman had shut down its predecessor, the World War II Office of Strategic Services (OSS). Though new managers took in some OSS hands, they picked and chose. Even in radical reculturing, however, operators and analysts should be kept together.

Analysis and Estimates

The fourth feature of the bills that was at odds with their own premises is the grouping of most analysts now in the CIA, NSA, and elsewhere into a new autonomous Directorate for Estimates and Analysis. While this proposal looked more forward than backward, it focused on too short a distance in the future.

The general goal of the Boren and McCurdy bills was to organize intelligence for a new era. The goals served by bunching analysts in one agency are symmetry and economy. A box for analysis on the same plane as boxes for human and signal intelligence and imagery will make for a neater organization chart. Consolidation could save a few dollars; the CIA and other elements of the community have overlapping analytic offices.

Here, however, a backward look ought to warn against such a change. For any example of wasteful duplication, a counterexample shows the value of competition. The CIA deflated military intelligence estimates of a "bomber gap" in the 1950s. In 1973 NSA analysts noticed signs of an approaching Middle East war that analysts in other

agencies ignored. The Team B exercise of the mid-1970s found estimates of Soviet missile programs by the Defense Intelligence Agency
to be better than any others.

An example nearer the new agenda is the misgauging of the Soviet
economy. From the 1950s onward CIA economists described the Soviet
economy as comparatively robust. They had all the available data, and
they worked from a complex input-output model. Their periodic
reports, published with the imprimatur of Congress's Joint Economic
Committee, acquired the status of scripture.

Emigrés' tales did not jibe with these reports. They said, for example, that economists overestimated Soviet production of television sets.
While the numbers might be accurate, they left out large numbers of
sets that blew up and caused fires. Emigrés also said that the CIA had
misjudged Soviet agricultural output. Economists counted potatoes
harvested but not the quantities that ended up as rotting landfill.
Because economists could not fit such anecdotal data into their models, they mentioned them in fine-print footnotes on "externalities."

Late in the Gorbachev era outside analysts challenged CIA estimates. Then the Soviet Union collapsed. The whole world saw its hol-
lowness. Competition among analysts—including competition from
noneconomists—might have made the revelation less astonishing.

While competition does cost money, it does not cost much. As CIA
veteran George Carver said at a House Intelligence Committee hearing, the entire community-wide budget for analysis could be covered by
mere rounding off in the defense budget. Analysts can help collectors
get the most out of their expensive hardware. Electronic eavesdroppers
and overhead picture-takers need guidance just as much as do case
officers. If a key aim is closer integration of intelligence and policy, the
case is also strong for scattering analysts of intelligence in among the
users.

To argue that all analysts should not be segregated is not to oppose
the bills' proposals for a quasi-independent National Intelligence
Council. That could be a useful body. Boren and McCurdy proposed
pulling analysts out of the CIA partly because they think that many of
America's best and brightest may be averse to working in an organization that also handles spies and covert operations. Most of that concern comes from memories of bygone times; in the 1990s CIA
recruiters generally find themselves welcome on college campuses. The
concern is not entirely baseless, however, and a wholly separate
National Intelligence Council might indeed attract analysts whose
image of the CIA is still influenced by the films *Missing* or *Three Days*

of the Condor. Such a council could also be an easier home for analysts on leave from universities or laboratories, especially if it required no polygraph tests.

To be most useful, a small new National Intelligence Council should have three characteristics distinguishing it from the pre-1992 National Intelligence Council and that council's predecessor, the Board of National Estimates. In practice, the council is already evolving in these directions.

First, the analysis needs a wide range of talent. The earlier council was organized to emphasize political-military analysis. Its prize product was its annual estimate of Soviet strategic forces. Such expertise is still in demand, but less so. For analysis and estimates the council needs men and women familiar with matters such as banking, immigration, disease, climate, and police procedure.

Second, the council needs to scan more widely. For new issues much of the information is in open sources. Much analysis is done outside the government. Future intelligence officers will more often have to specify the increment in understanding that secret intelligence provides. Decision makers will want to be told tersely and exactly what is *not* in the *New York Times* or on Cable News Network.

Third, and most important, the council needs continuous communication with intelligence users. That may entail including among its staff the analysts who head liaison offices such as those in Treasury, Commerce, and the Office of the Special Trade Representative. That would be only a partial step; some liaison offices are little more than mailboxes. Few have even occasional access to the policy process of the State Department's Bureau of Intelligence and Research. Nonetheless, those intelligence officers who regularly see top decision makers should get some sense of what is on their minds or, at least, on their calendars.

A complementary step would place intelligence officers on decision makers' staffs. The new national agenda calls for imaginative policy planning, such as that of the 1940–1941 Rainbow planners or George Kennan and Paul Nitze in the early Cold War State Department. This time intelligence should help. There need not be repetition of mistakes, such as first underestimating the Japanese, then overestimating the Russians.

Yet another link could run through think tanks. A model is the Rand Corporation of the 1950s. While analysts in its strategic studies wing did classified research, few had access to intelligence data. Those who did tactfully steered their colleagues so that Rand reports implicitly took account of, for example, U-2 photography of the Soviet Union and intercepts from tapped telephones in East Berlin. Those specially cleared analysts also carried questions back to the Intelligence Community. That could happen in the future in, for example, panels of the National Bureau of Economic Research or committees of the National Institutes of Health.

The head of the Intelligence Community must also identify needs that decision makers do not see. He or she has to do the equivalent of launching the *Lexington*. But that official must have many lines reaching into operating elements of the executive branch and Congress if, in either the short or long run, the Intelligence Community is to meet "the needs of the government as a whole in an effective and timely manner."

Conclusion

New legislation for the Intelligence Community should equip it for the future. It should provide for a principal intelligence officer not necessarily linked to the NSC. While it might create a National Imagery Agency as a counterpart of NSA, it need not move either agency out of the Defense Department. In no circumstances should Congress strip the collecting agencies of their analysts. In fact analytical staffs should probably increase. The more attention paid to the reasons for collection, the more the nation is apt to get its money's worth from high-cost hardware. A new analytical agency, if any, should serve the mission of making intelligence maximally useful for policy.

In addition, there are subjects that were not touched on by either the Boren or the McCurdy bill. The boundary between foreign and domestic intelligence is one example. Because of the march of technology, threats to privacy constantly increase. Limitations that worked when the major threat came from communists in Moscow may not work, however, when the enemies are moving drugs or migrant workers or hot money or are themselves viruses or ultraviolet rays.

Other equally difficult subjects include classification, clearance, and dissemination. In the past secrecy has limited the usefulness of intelligence. Flag and general officers routinely complain of not even knowing what they *could* have been told. If the operational uses of intelligence expand, the problem will change in kind, not just degree. If the ultimate actors are local law enforcement officials or bankers or businessmen or doctors or scientists or others who are not even employed by the government (perhaps not even U.S. nationals), effective dissemination is going to require new rules, and that may mean new statutes.

Most of what is needed, however, does not call for legislation. The president and others in the executive branch must establish processes to cope with the new challenges. Congressionally mandated organizational changes could make this harder, not easier. The intelligence oversight committees can give most help by prodding the executive to prepare for the future instead of just conserving what was built up in the past. To do that the committees themselves need to keep their eyes on the horizons.

5

INTELLIGENCE REFORM: BEYOND THE AMES CASE

Abram Shulsky and Gary Schmitt

Ames and "a CI Mentality"

Within hours of the arrest of Central Intelligence Agency (CIA) officer Aldrich Ames for espionage, unnamed CIA officials were telling reporters that Ames was a drunk and a mediocre case officer. In the weeks that followed, former superiors and fellow officers described him as inept, dull, unsophisticated, and lackadaisical. Such comments were not surprising. Agency employees wanted to distance themselves from the alleged traitor, and so were quick to point out that Ames was neither well regarded nor typical of the caliber of personnel within the CIA component that handled clandestine human intelligence activity, the Directorate of Operations (DO).

What was surprising to many, however, was the nonchalance with which an officer of Ames's low caliber was allowed to proceed from job to job in the DO, without anyone in a managerial position focusing on the fact that the organization had a problem on its hands. As the agency's inspector general subsequently noted, Ames was "not going anywhere and no one cared."[1]

Nevertheless, CIA comments at the time of Ames's arrest are revealing. After all, the officer whom the anonymous agency sources were trashing (and who was judged by the CIA at one point to be the third-worst officer among two hundred at his rank) had been only a few years before entrusted with one of the most sensitive posts within the Intelligence Community: chief of the counterintelligence branch of the Soviet–East European (SE) division of the DO. The damage he could and did do to U.S. and allied intelligence operations in the Soviet

---

A version of this article was published in *The National Interest* (Winter 1994/95).

Union was immense.² That the agency was willing to give Ames this position says as much about how important the CIA considers counterintelligence (CI) as any stack of pronouncements to the contrary from a succession of directors of Central Intelligence (DCIs.)

Of course, this is not news. For twenty years, since the forced retirement in 1974 of James Angleton, long-time chief of the agency's counterintelligence staff, CI has been a subordinate discipline at Langley, occasionally called upon but generally reviled and ignored. A Capitol Hill staffer had an occasion to learn about this view firsthand some years ago, in the course of explaining to a DO officer a bit of Machiavellian maneuvering going on in Congress. With a big smile on his face, and a professional comic's sense of timing, the officer replied: "You know, you have a CI mentality . . . and where I come from, that is not a compliment."

The record indicates that this attitude is not exceptional. For example, we now know that virtually all East German and Cuban spies recruited by the agency for more than a decade were in fact double agents, controlled by those states' intelligence services. In the absence of an effective, in-house counterintelligence capability to review and challenge these recruitments, the CIA was manipulated by the Cuban and East German services, which fed the agency inconsequential, or perhaps even deliberately deceptive, reports.

Paradoxically, against this background (but only against this background), the handling of the Ames case reflects a bit more credit on the agency than has been recognized. After a succession of its agents had been "rolled up" by the KGB in the mid-1980s, the leadership within the DO knew it had a serious problem and began to investigate. The question facing the CIA was: How, precisely, were its operations being compromised? Was it connected to the treachery and subsequent defection of ex-CIA officer Edward Lee Howard; the lapse of embassy security associated with the Marine Guard scandal in Moscow; a compromise of a communication channel used by U.S. intelligence; or, perhaps, a combination? Or, was it any clandestine service's worst nightmare, a mole?

Investigating the possible causes and eliminating those that do not pan out is the heart of the CI effort in such instances. A major complicating factor in investigating the possibility of a mole was the fact that initially nearly two hundred individuals were thought to have had access to the information associated with the failed operations.³ In addition, the failures were not continuous. Although the pattern suggests a mole whose access varied over time—as Ames's did⁴—its significance can only be grasped in retrospect.

The agency's effort to find the cause of its losses was nevertheless, according to the inspector general's (IG's) review, marked by "almost complete indifference" on the part of the CIA's leadership. This indifference, combined with the lack of resources given to the investigation and the fact that it was bureaucratically splintered between the CI Center, the CIA's Office of Security, and SE, meant that the molehunt would inevitably become a tragic comedy of errors. Ames, by any measure of the clandestine art, was a buffoon; yet, for nearly a decade, he escaped arrest.

This judgment is not intended to make light of the difficulty of combining aggressive collection efforts with the skeptical eye of counterintelligence. A too strong CI hand can have a "chilling effect" on operations. However, if the opposite is true, the collectors are apt to play down signs they are being deceived and to ignore indications—such as Ames's lifestyle and behavior—that one of their own has betrayed them and their country.[5] Although admittedly hard to do, it appears that the agency has for some time stopped trying to establish the proper balance between CI and "positive" intelligence collection.[6]

What's the Point?

With the Intelligence Community already under pressure to reform and downsize, the Ames case has further fueled post–Cold War skepticism about intelligence in general and espionage in particular. The case seemed to prove the essential irrelevance of human intelligence: an intelligence service perfectly places a mole inside the enemy's service, but its side loses anyway. As a *New York Times* editorial (May 8, 1994) put it: "Spy wars are a sideshow of passionate interest to the actors, but of marginal significance for national policy."

Nor are this and related sentiments espoused only by liberals. Angelo Codevilla, former Republican staff member of the Senate Intelligence Committee and conservative critic of U.S. intelligence performance, has pointed out that it is better for a country not to have a clandestine service at all than to have one that has been penetrated. While it is certainly true that a penetrated operation is positively harmful, and hence worse than not having that operation at all, one cannot conclude that, because one of its operations is compromised, all of a clandestine service's activities are worthless.

Similarly, Edward Jay Epstein, an author generally supportive of Angleton's theories about intelligence and CI, argued in a recent article[7] that the danger of being misled by moles and double agents is not worth the benefits sought through espionage, especially during times of peace. "In peacetime, the products of espionage tend to be things like reports about policy discussions, which are rarely verifiable. . . . In a protracted peace . . . espionage data become not only less urgent but also increasingly subject to manipulation."

It is far better, according to Epstein, to gather information by "spy satellites" and "other licit" means, such as news stories, diplomatic reports, and the like. Although such collection mechanisms will probably not provide the kind of intelligence on the secret intentions of other nations that policymakers would normally want, this shortfall can be adjusted to by having those officials routinely base their national security decisions and policies "on a worst-case analysis, leavened by common sense." Epstein's argument is that the United States is not very good at the business of espionage and should, rather than run the risk of being misled, just get out of it.

The record, however, is more mixed than the agency's critics are willing to admit. Although the KGB, GRU, and their Warsaw Pact allies had successes, the U.S. intelligence effort was not a total disaster. Oleg Penkovskiy, Dmitri Polyakov, Adolf Tolkachev, and Ryszard Kuklinski are just a few of the more important spies run by U.S. intelligence during the Cold War. The intelligence they provided on Soviet missiles, intelligence operations, military reseach and development (R&D), and battle plans for Europe was extremely valuable. At the end of the day, the human intelligence (HUMINT) scorecard may favor Soviet intelligence, but the United States was far from shut out.

In any case, as the U.S. failure with respect to the pre–Persian Gulf War Iraqi nuclear program shows, "open" sources and high-technology means of collection are not sufficient or can themselves be misleading. Despite its massive size, Iraq's program to develop nuclear weapons went largely undetected by U.S. reconnaissance satellites. By using carefully planned denial and deception measures, Saddam Hussein was able to keep the United States thoroughly in the dark about the program until after the war, when an Iraqi defector began to provide key data on Iraq's effort to build a bomb. The general capabilities of U.S. reconnaissance satellites, remarkable as they are, are becoming more and more known to the world; against a clever opponent, they can no longer be expected to make up for a lack of human reporting as they once did for countries behind the Iron Curtain.

Further, with the end of the Soviet empire, the number of "hard targets"—countries whose internal security services and security practices are so extensive that they make human operations especially difficult—

has dropped dramatically. While Stalinist regimes such as North Korea still exist, espionage is likely to be more, rather than less, useful in the post–Cold War period, as U.S. intelligence operates more in weak or failed regimes short on counterespionage capabilities and where a moderate amount of hard currency safely tucked away in a Swiss bank account can go a long, long way.

Human intelligence is not only easier to collect; in many cases it is more important. Technical collection allowed us to keep track with some precision of the Soviets' military capabilities, which were the core concern. But most countries cannot threaten the United States in the same fashion. In Haiti, Serbia, or other similar states, what U.S. policy-makers care about are the intentions of a small number of leaders, information that generally can be obtained only through clandestine human collection. Even where our concern is about capabilities—such as in the area of proliferation—human intelligence may be the only effective means to overcome the target's ability to hide the precise scope of its operations from overhead reconnaissance (e.g., through extensive tunneling, a North Korean specialty) and international inspections.

Epstein's alternative in such instances is to forgo HUMINT and base U.S. national security decisions on worst-case analysis. Leaving aside the fact that it is not necessarily clear what this means for policy in places like Haiti or Somalia, how can one expect the public and Congress to support defense and foreign policies that constantly say the "sky is falling" or that the "wolf is at the door"? Although it would be foolish to believe that one's espionage operations will never be penetrated by the other side, it is just as impractical to believe that the United States could actually conduct its national security affairs from such a perspective. In a time of declining defense expenditures and general uncertainty in key areas of the world, intelligence is no less important than it was in the past, and clandestine human collection probably more so. As the margin of U.S. safety and preeminence slips in the years ahead, there will be an even greater need for the foresight provided by high-quality intelligence, not less.

To Centralize or Not

The more extreme views aside, the main issue is how best to organize and/or reform U.S. intelligence to maximize the quality of what it produces. The most recent, significant effort to address this issue was incorporated in bills introduced by the chairmen of the House and Senate intelligence committees in 1992. Although neither bill was enacted, then-DCI Robert Gates put watered-down versions of some of their ideas into force administratively.

Although in 1992 these reforms were put forward as a response to the end of the Cold War,[8] the proposals actually predate 1989. In fact, they reflect tendencies that have been operative in the national security establishment since the beginning of the Cold War, when, in 1947, the Central Intelligence Agency was created, the armed services were subordinated to a unified Department of Defense, and the National Security Council (to which the CIA was to report) was created as a centralized national security policy organization. The main theme of this reform agenda is increased centralization of the Intelligence Community in the name of efficiency and objectivity. In this regard, the agenda mirrors the major changes in the Defense Department, from its beginning through the Goldwater-Nichols Act of 1986—the continued effort to strengthen the "central" bureaucracies such as the Office of the Secretary of Defense, the chairman of the Joint Chiefs of Staff, and the commanders in chief of the "unified" commands and Joint Staff at the expense of the services.[9]

While centralization might promote efficiency in public administration textbooks (and probably only in a rather old textbook, at that), it is less obvious that it does so in actual practice. Certain types of duplication of effort may indeed be wasteful; with respect to major issues, however, a certain amount of what is called "competitive analysis" is probably a good idea. Bringing to bear the differing perspectives of, say, the State and Defense departments, is a prudent step to take given that the cost of becoming captive to a particular strain of "conventional wisdom" can be so high.

Similarly, centralizing intelligence collection may seem like a good idea if it can avoid inefficient overlap and duplication of effort. On the other hand, different parts of the government have differing intelligence requirements, and the various formal processes for compiling these requirements are often too simplistic to capture all the nuances. Thus, having some collection capability under the control of policymakers with specific needs, such as the military, is likely to make the resulting intelligence more relevant, even at the risk of making the process by which it is collected less efficient.

In general, centralization moves the locus of the intelligence effort further and further away from the policymakers who need to make use of the intelligence product. To be useful, the intelligence output must be produced with the policymakers' needs in mind; often, the most useful interchange occurs, not by means of the written report, but in the course of briefings and meetings in which the policymakers can ask questions, distinguish between what is known and what is only surmised, probe analytic assumptions, begin to understand what types of information can be collected and what types are unlikely to be, and gain an appreciation of the timing and credibility of the likely warning that can be expected prior to a major change in the situation. This type of responsiveness is more reasonably expected from an intelligence agency bureaucratically close to its customers than from a distant one.

From this perspective, Senator Boren's ambition of creating a "world-class think tank" at Langley is misplaced. Indeed, as suggested above, the thinking behind this drive for centralization is rather old-fashioned, as if one wished to model an automobile company on Henry Ford's model of mass production rather than on Toyota's lean production. The current business literature emphasizes that a successful corporate "intelligence" office must be located close to the senior policymakers, rather than isolated from them.

In addition to the argument from an efficiency standpoint, however, is another motive for centralization: a "central" intelligence agency would be free of the biases of an intelligence agency that was part of a government department (such as State or Defense) and possibly led to modify its results to support its parent organization's policy or budgetary preferences. Historically, much of this debate concerning the objectivity of intelligence derived from the difficult question (especially in the presatellite 1950s) of estimating Soviet military capabilities. Major debates involving the issue of Soviet military capabilities—the "bomber gap" and "missile gap" issues—had important consequences for the defense budget; the CIA saw itself as an important "corrective" to military intelligence organizations, which, it could be argued, had an ulterior motive for overestimating the Soviet threat.

While objectivity is an important goal of any intelligence organization, it is unfortunately much more difficult to attain than the traditional argument for a central intelligence agency suggests. First, the absence of policy or budgetary preferences on the part of an organization does not guarantee the absence of ulterior motives. As the above example suggests, the CIA acquired a bureaucratic interest in portraying military estimates of Soviet military capabilities as excessive; if defense estimates were not excessive, then no "corrective" to them was needed, and the CIA's role in this area could be constrained. Similarly, strategic arms control, with its major requirement for verification of detailed treaty provisions, enhanced the CIA's role in this area.

Second, and more generally, any bureaucracy can acquire, over time, a set of beliefs about important issues—"conventional wisdom"—that it then has a bureaucratic interest in preserving and defending. This might be especially true in the case, such as the one discussed above, in which those beliefs distinguish it from some other bureaucracy. Thus, for many years in the 1960s and early 1970s, the CIA held to the view that the Soviet Union had accepted many of the U.S. assumptions about strategic nuclear weapons that underlay the doctrine of mutual assured destruction.

Third, the absence of a tie to departmental policymakers does not, and cannot, mean "independence": intelligence always works for, and is subordinate to, some policymaker. With respect to the recent debate over the Intelligence Community's negative assessment of Haitian President Jean-Bertrand Aristide's personality, one angry Democratic lawmaker said that the CIA should remember who won the 1992 election. Insofar as this legislator was saying that the CIA works for the president, he was right. But he was wrong not to realize that the CIA serves the president best when it "tells it like it is," not like the president wants it to be. The safeguard for objectivity cannot be sought in "independence"—backbone vis-à-vis policymakers' wishes will always be necessary.

Finally, the entire issue of objectivity is often confused because it is not realized just how speculative are most of the analytic products about which the claims of "cooking the books" tend to swirl. Debate arises around those conclusions of intelligence analysis that are, rightfully, most subject to debate.

Intelligence analysts will claim that any refusal to accept their conclusions results from the policymaker's stubborn or politically motivated attachment to his own policies or views, and, in some cases, they may be right. In other cases, however, the policymaker may be reasonably relying on his own knowledge of the area and his own contacts with foreign diplomats, leaders, and other experts. A diplomat who has had extensive dealings with Aristide, for example, may feel that his own judgments have as much validity as those of an intelligence analyst who has never met the man. He may not be right, but he is not being unreasonable if he rejects the observations of others (even if they are labeled "sources") in favor of his own.[10]

Thus, the question of objectivity and bias is much more complicated than it might appear at first glance. A truly open mind is difficult to retain under any circumstances, and mere bureaucratic arrangements cannot guarantee it. Nor can they guarantee backbone against undue pressure from political or organizational superiors, which is equally important and equally difficult to possess. Bureaucratic arrangements, at best, can help to identify the most common or characteristic failings of an organization and take institutional measures to correct or ameliorate them.

In the case of the national security bureaucracy, the most characteristic failing seems to be the bowing to the power of "conventional wisdom," a problem, at least to some extent, found in bureaucracies worldwide. Achieving consensus in a bureaucracy—inducing all the relevant parties to "sign off" on an assessment or judgment—is such a laborious task that it is not surprising that, once such a consensus has been achieved, there is a strong incentive not to revisit an issue unless changed circumstances make it absolutely necessary.

In the United States, however, there is an additional incentive: government service, below the very top levels, is not particularly prestigious. Those engaged in it who have any intellectual pretensions do not wish to be seen as "Neanderthal" or "out of it" by those in the much more prestigious realms of academia or the mainstream, national-level media. This tends to reinforce a tendency toward the "conventional wisdom"; it is distressing how often highly classified assessments of political issues closely resemble op-ed pieces.

For this reason, "competitive analysis" (i.e., the existence of competing centers of intelligence analysis) is a necessary corrective, regardless of how inefficient it might seem in terms of public administration theory. Similarly, closeness to policymakers, despite the threat to "objectivity" that entails, makes sense if it grounds the analysts in concern for concrete policy issues that must be addressed in instrumentally useful ways.

"New Age" Intelligence

Another part of the reform agenda that was taken up in the 1992 bills was an emphasis on "open source" collection (i.e., the exploitation of newspaper and magazine articles, radio and television broadcasts, and other publicly available sources of information) as opposed to more traditional "human intelligence collection" (i.e., espionage).[11] Again, this was presented as a reaction to the end of the Cold War, although the same theme was prominent in various "reform" attempts during the Cold War as well.

In fact, some of the impetus behind this idea came from the difficulty of conducting espionage in the Soviet Union, given the closed nature of its society, and its suspicious and all-pervasive counterintelligence culture. Thus, topics such as intra-elite politics, which, in other regimes, could be learned about by means of espionage, had to be approached indirectly: one of the means of doing this was dubbed "Kremlinology," the discipline of deducing the ins and outs of Kremlin politics from the minor hints that surfaced in the open press. Thus, when secret police chief Lavrenti Beria was omitted from an otherwise complete list of politburo members attending the opera, it was not because he did not like opera—something much more important was being communicated: his removal from the leadership. Although the clever use of open sources remains an important and cost-effective way of obtaining otherwise hidden information, it is arguably of less importance in the post–Cold War world, in which many intelligence targets, as noted earlier, are much more vulnerable to traditional espionage than was the former Soviet Union.

Finally, the reform agenda, especially the call for a "world-class think tank," derives in part from the view that, in the post–Cold War world, there will be numerous new topics for the Intelligence Community to concern itself with: environmental concerns, economic competitiveness, demographic issues such as refugee flows and epidemics, and so forth. Thus, there will be a need for experts on a whole range of new topics, aside from the traditional ones such as military, political, and diplomatic affairs.

No one who has worked in the executive branch of the U.S. government is likely to oppose the notion that it could use better (and more convenient) sources of information on a wide variety of topics. But, the question remains: Why should this plea for a more effective government information system be addressed to the Intelligence Community, rather than any other organization or organizations? (For that matter, why not consider the creation of a new organization, an executive branch counterpart to the Congressional Research Service [CRS] of the Library of Congress?) In most nations, the notion that the intelligence service should provide information on the climatic and other effects of ozone depletion would seem strange.

Part of the reason such a notion does not seem so strange in the United States lies in the fact that during World War II the Office of Strategic Services (OSS, the CIA's predecessor and prototype) became the intellectually most sophisticated part of government. In what must have seemed, to paraphrase the New Testament, a scandal to the armed forces and foolishness to the State Department, "Wild Bill" Donovan, head of the OSS, recruited large numbers of historians, social scientists, and other professors and intellectuals to work in the OSS Research and Analysis Branch (RAB). These researchers discovered that the answers to a lot of important questions could be found in the Library of Congress; for example, an old travel book might contain a picture of a North African beach that planners of an amphibious assault might find useful.

Similarly, systematic analysis of German domestic propaganda provided clues to the thinking of the leadership, their assessment of the situation, and, on occasion, their plans for the future. Studies of the prewar German economy provided not only detailed technical information on its railroad system, but also provided hints for those trying to determine the most lucrative targets for the strategic bombing campaign. The RAB demonstrated that, subjected to careful and sophisticated analysis, open-source information could provide clues to information that, during wartime, at least, was considered secret and withheld from publication.

The Soviet Union, the main post–World War II intelligence target, operated, with respect to the publication of data, as if it were at war. Information that other states routinely published (such as accurate maps, or the size and breakdown of the defense budget) was withheld or distorted. Thus, many of the same techniques developed by RAB during World War II were applied to the study of the Soviet Union; additional techniques, such as Kremlinology, were invented specifically for the purpose.

Consequently, the CIA became responsible for determining a whole range of information about the Soviet Union, information that under more ordinary circumstances would not have required the use of an intelligence agency. For example, one of the biggest and nastiest intra–Intelligence Community debates of the 1970s focused on the actual size of the Soviet defense budget and the percentage of Soviet gross national product (GNP) that it represented. The comparable numbers for the United States were routinely published.

Thus, the Intelligence Community in the United States was viewed as the government's general information service rather than as that part of the government that deals specifically with secrets—protecting U.S. secrets and discovering those of others. The current "new age" agenda being proposed for the Intelligence Community merely builds on that perception, but there are good reasons that the Intelligence Community is not the best locus for much of this work.

Because so much of the Intelligence Community's work will have to remain secret, the "reform" agenda effectively imposes many of the

burdens of secrecy—security clearances for personnel, special communications and information-handling facilities, physical security of office
space, and so forth—on work and workers that have no real requirement for it. It also hampers the ability of analysts to reach out to those
elements of the society—academia, nonprofit organizations, business,
and the media—that have expertise on a given topic. Aside from security considerations, it remains a reality—unreasonable as it may be—
that intelligence still carries something of a stigma, especially in many
of these circles. A professor who would expect to be praised for landing
a contract with an outside research center (thereby bringing new
resources to the campus) may well feel that getting involved with the
CIA could have untoward consequences that it would be imprudent to
risk.

Furthermore, the differing nature of government involvement in
these issues and the different types of expertise required suggest that
the proper structure of an organization for studying them should be
determined on a case-by-case basis. If, for example, the U.S. government decides more work should be done on tracking epidemics on a
global basis, it would make sense to assign that task to the Centers for
Disease Control and Prevention in Atlanta; trying to duplicate that
medical expertise in Langley would be wasteful. To take another example, the appropriate group for analyzing an issue of international economic competitiveness might be a planning group in the Department
of Commerce or the Treasury, which could be close enough to the policymakers to understand what kind of information and analysis would
be useful to support the specific policy tools at their disposal; a group
of economists operating independently might come up with a brilliant
analysis that is irrelevant to the (rather limited) ways in which policymakers can deal with this particular issue.

Less Is More

This broadening of the focus of intelligence work would also dilute the
key competitive advantage (as opposed to other sources of information) of the Intelligence Community, which is in dealing with secrets.
Given the small role likely to be played by secret information, there is,
for example, no reason to expect a midlevel intelligence analyst to out-
perform a Wall Street analyst when analyzing the economics of the
world automobile industry. On the contrary, given that a Wall Street
firm is likely to pay an analyst five to ten times the salary the CIA can
offer, it should be able—in general—to obtain higher quality results.

What is needed is some way for the government (which, after all, is not in competition with the brokerage firm) to obtain and exploit the results of the analysis undertaken for other purposes. These results can probably be obtained more easily if the government representative does not represent the Intelligence Community. In any case, the government's point of contact for this work should be as close to the relevant policymakers as possible (i.e., the officials in the Commerce Department who deal with issues concerning the auto industry, rather than analysts in a "world-class think tank" who have to go through multiple levels of bureaucracy in order to transmit a memorandum to those who are able to use it).

Perhaps most important, this focus on a broadening range of issues tends to blur the very characteristic that makes intelligence work distinctive from other kinds of intellectual activity—the fact that, at its core, it is the attempt to obtain certain kinds of information—secrets—access to which an adversary is deliberately trying to deny. An intelligence analyst must be alert to the possibility that the raw data he is relying on may not only be false (that can happen to any researcher) but also may be deliberately distorted in order to mislead him. By ignoring the "spy versus spy" aspect of intelligence work—the fact that the intelligence analyst, as well as the spy, is working against a human adversary who is trying to mislead or thwart him—one paves the way for counterintelligence disasters.

Thus, instead of pursuing the Cold War reform agenda of broadening the Intelligence Community into a universal information service for the government, we should attempt to restore a more narrowly focused intelligence agency with a revived human intelligence capability. Such an agency could help significantly in the post–Cold War world, where a few well-placed agents in the Somali militias or the Haitian military and business worlds could help avoid embarrassing and potentially costly disasters. The opportunities for useful human intelligence collection have not been greater in a half century.

One way to use these opportunities would be to expand the ways in which U.S. clandestine human intelligence operates. During the Cold War, it made sense to disguise most case officers as diplomatic personnel in U.S. embassies abroad, where they could easily come into contact with Soviet counterparts, who were their main targets. In the 1990s, however, it may sometimes be more important, for example, to understand the internal dynamics of a developing nation's military establishment. Because military attachés, military advisers, and security assistance officers are most likely to come into contact with another country's military officers, it is sensible to expand (and professionalize) military human intelligence collection capabilities.

One of Parkinson's laws is that, by the time a bureaucratic organization gets a fancy new headquarters building, it is well past its prime. By that standard, the CIA's salad days were when it was still located in ugly World War II–era temporary structures in downtown Washington. The move to its 1950s-modern Langley headquarters was an ominous sign. That, however, was nothing compared to the recent additions to the headquarters complex, complete with a glass-covered atrium that any suburban hotel or shopping mall would be proud of.

Senator Daniel Patrick Moynihan has suggested the abolition of the Central Intelligence Agency and the distribution to other organizations of its component parts. A diminished human intelligence capability, which he believed perhaps might not be necessary at all, would be transferred to the Department of State. Although unlikely to happen, the underlying instinct might be sound.

A separate human intelligence organization could be the best way to proceed. Because its founding would be in part a reaction to the Ames case, it might be bereft of the anticounterintelligence bias that exists in the CIA. (Never underestimate the power of an organization's "founding myth"—even now, reference is often made to Pearl Harbor to justify the need for "central" intelligence.) Such an organization could exploit the opportunities of the post–Cold War world and provide assistance in dealing with the myriad of crises in which, even in the absence of a global rival, the United States is still entangled.

PART II:

THE ELEMENTS AND REFORM

6

THE TRADECRAFT OF ANALYSIS

Douglas J. MacEachin

Tying the need for change in the Central Intelligence Agency's (CIA's) Directorate of Intelligence (DI) to the end of the Cold War has caused the focus for change to be on size and subject matter. There is the belief—inside the agency as well as outside—that the organization that emerges from the change process will be smaller and that the reductions will be achieved mainly by cutting resources committed to the threats formerly posed by the Soviet Union. The need for change goes beyond size and subject matter, however; dramatic changes in national priorities and the resulting funding reductions require a reexamination of the fundamental purposes and process of intelligence analysis. Basic questions must be addressed: What does the DI do and what is the best way to do it?

This chapter will describe corporate efforts under way in the DI to deal with these questions. It is not intended as a critique of past practices or of the quality of analysis carried out in the directorate. There has been much that has been good, but there is also much that needs changing.

Charting a course for the future requires facing existing problems. Designing change requires an analysis of what problems the change must correct and how the changes will make it better. Change in any large organization comes at substantial cost, and therefore it must be demonstrated—to both the work force and outside critics—that the gains outweigh the costs.

Following are descriptions of changes that have been made or are under way in the DI in fundamental areas.

• *What does the DI do?* Making the needs of the user—the policy-maker—the driving factor in intelligence production; defining the contribution to those needs as the measure of performance; and

---

This paper was first presented on February 7, 1994.

eliminating practices that encourage production aimed at fulfilling internally established conventions for achievement and recognition.

•*How does the DI do it?* Redefining the analytic tradecraft to emphasize "facts" and the "findings" derived from them. This does not mean that opinions are no longer valued, but it does require that their credibility be established through intelligence practices that clearly identify what is known, how it is known, and with what level of reliability; what is not known that could have important consequences; the "drivers" or "linchpins" that are likely to govern the outcome of dynamic situations; the analytic calculus underlying all conclusions and forecasts; and the uncertainties in any of the components of the analysis and the implications of those uncertainties for alternative outcomes. Adherence to these principles of analytic tradecraft are to be the standard of professional excellence—the "professional ethic"—of the directorate.

These changes are not directly tied to the changes generated by the end of the Cold War. There is, in fact, consensus among the corporate leadership of the DI that these changes have been needed for some time. They represent major cultural change, however, which entails sizable cost and pain, and it has taken the events generated by the end of the Cold War to make clear that not making these changes would ultimately entail even higher costs.

•In sum, the need for change has existed for some time, but the end of the Cold War generated force for change and provided the occasion and conditions for implementing change.

This is not an argument against proposals to reduce the amount of resources devoted to intelligence or to realign the substantive focus of those resources for the post–Cold War world. A major effort is under way to create a smaller DI with a more streamlined supervisory structure and greater organizational flexibility to respond to more diverse and rapidly changing requirements.

Without systemic changes such as those described below, however, change would merely mean doing the same things in different boxes, and that is not sustainable in a post–Cold War world. Therefore, while examining issues of resource allocation and ways to improve efficiency at lower levels, DI management has given first priority to fundamental changes in how the DI defines its mission and carries out its work.

The Mission: Focusing on the User

Crafting mission statements is a difficult and at times a metaphysical task. For this review, a short descriptive mission statement is useful:

Provide U.S. policymakers with information and analysis *they* need to carry out *their* mission of formulating and implementing U.S. national security policy.

This statement leaves open such questions as what constitutes "national security policy," and therefore which substantive areas are addressed and which policymakers are the intelligence users. It is also broad enough to encompass what is often referred to, in intelligence jargon, as short-term "tactical intelligence" and longer term "strategic estimates," and is also neutral with regard to "clandestine" versus "open-source" debates. Such discussions have bearing on issues such as breadth of coverage, and ultimately on resource levels, but they do not affect the basic principle of the statement—that all considerations of the intelligence mission start with the user, who is the U.S. policymaker.

Some will argue that this is not new, that this has always been the mission. Indeed, a decade ago the answer probably would have been much the same. However, back then the statement did not always drive what the DI did in practice nor how it did it. Although great strides were made in the 1980s toward exposing DI officers to the policy world and gaining greater understanding of its operation and needs, the business practice for a time evolved in ways that allowed the DI's internal goals and measures of quality to have a greater influence on the product than did the question: Who is my user and what does my user need? In recent years more emphasis has been placed on direct customer service, and that trend is accelerating.

The Publish or Perish Factor

A simple description of the dynamic that previously existed supports my analysis.

• Success in the DI meant showing a "production record" that included published papers. To get their products published, analysts had to get them through a review process that contained at least four and sometimes more layers, from the immediate supervisor to the head of the directorate. Not every written product had to go through this process, but those that did not counted for less in the rewards and advancement system.

• Once a paper cleared this process, it was disseminated according to a list of "user profiles" maintained in the office that did the formal printing. Publication was, de facto, a decision made separately from a detailed identification of the audience.[1]

The published products that counted most for demonstrating analyst achievement—and which, therefore, counted most for analyst advancement—followed the general rule that long was better than short because it demonstrated full scholarly effort. The "Intelligence Assessment" (IA), which was both long (incorporating extensive research and description) and "analytic," carried the most prestige within the DI culture. It was considered more reward worthy than the "Research Paper," which, while as long or longer, was more informational and descriptive than judgmental. Both, however, outranked—for purposes of rewards and promotions—the shorter memoranda, despite the fact that the DI's most important consumers consistently found the latter the most useful.

Production criteria for advancement also included production of a certain amount for the daily current intelligence publications. In some substantive areas, a high volume of current intelligence production could carry an analyst up the promotion scale, but sooner or later analysts had to prove their fundamental mettle by publishing one of the "big" papers.

• Analysts knew that to advance their careers, they had to get papers published, and they knew what kinds of papers counted most for this purpose; managers knew they had to demonstrate component production records.

Most of this production-based promotion process was instituted for what were viewed as sound, constructive reasons. For example, the IA was the most challenging product of the DI in terms of demands placed on the individual producer. But the IA reflected a system of evaluating products on "degree of difficulty" rather than on utility to the consumer. Similarly, the complex system of reviewing products was an appropriate tool used by management to impose accountability and greater rigor on the products. Yet, the way these factors combined caused the DI to drift away from customer focus toward internal criteria, one of the most common problems of large organizations, including those in the private sector.

Changing the System

In the mid- to late 1980s, many efforts were made to address these problems and there was particular progress made in diversifying the product line. This trend was further accelerated by the Production Task Force, one of many task forces set up by Director Gates in 1992. Another important step was taken by John Helgerson at the beginning of 1993 when he eliminated the mandatory seventh floor review of finished products. Since then, the individual offices have taken responsibility for the review, and they have instituted further flexibility on the level and amount of review required. The principle of management accountability still demands review of most products at some level, but the effort is to have it done as low in the supervisory line as possible, commensurate with the need for timeliness and the sensitivity of the issue addressed.[2]

• Today, the DI front office engages in predissemination review only on request—if, for example, a production component desires another view on a particularly sensitive or venturesome product—or in the event the product is one that was directly assigned by the deputy director for intelligence (DDI) or his assistant, the assistant deputy director for intelligence (ADDI).

• During 1993, these factors led to DI review of no more than about one dozen products.

The practice of drawing up DI publication target lists for each fiscal year has been discontinued. Any publication lists that are prepared are prepared at the production office level, and they are used only for office-level planning and for coordinating resource use with other intelligence producers such as the Defense Intelligence Agency (DIA). No percentage tallies are kept; the focus is on quality and impact, not numbers or quotas.

The annual directorate-level planning exercise, which formerly produced the publication targets, now focuses on strategic lines of analysis as a basis for resource allocation decisions and, in turn, collection and research planning. Research strategies developed in this effort are designed as capital investment in the DI intelligence production capabilities, not as a publication rationale.

Some in the DI have expressed concern that the changes mean that less value is placed on research. That is incorrect. What is being done is to establish a difference between "research" and "publication." Research is critical to the DI's effectiveness, and constitutes capital investment. What we are is what we know, and how well we analyze what we know. But the standard we want to apply to assessing the value attached to any given research effort is the knowledge gained and its contribution to the mission as a whole, not whether it fulfills a publication target.

• The results of individual research efforts probably will, as a rule, be compiled in some written form to exploit the learning and knowledge-sharing benefits, but dissemination in hardcover form will be a separate decision based on demonstrated need by the policymakers.

• The results of a single research project can be disseminated in several forms: a relatively long written compilation of the information for other members of the Intelligence Community and selected components of the policy community that engage in in-depth studies; a short Intelligence Memorandum, a few pages in length, describing for senior policymakers the principal findings and implications of the larger body of research; and a one-page version for the cabinet principals.

• Other research efforts might result in one or none of these products, and instead become part of a database.

The DI will continue to devote resources to some products that are disseminated to a broad and diverse audience, including the National Intelligence Daily (NID) and various specialized periodic journals that have high value to the users. The DI will also produce long-term strategic assessments when there is a clear need. The key to all of these, however, is a demonstrated need by the user, not continuation of a routine activity on the part of the DI.

The most important strategic change has been directed at institutionalizing the principle that DI analyses are for people, not publications. The measure of achievement is not the publication of a paper, but the delivery of intelligence information and analysis to a user that is critical to the user's needs. Written products are a means and not the only means of communication; face-to-face briefings are in many cases more useful to the consumer.[3]

This means customizing products according to issue and user. A paper or briefing designed to be useful to 100 to 200 people is not likely to be of significant value to the small group of people (from a handful to perhaps 30) who are most deeply engaged on a given policy issue.

These officials are almost always going to be up-to-date on events that affect their most pressing policy concerns. They have staffs that are dedicated to keeping them informed, and they have ready access to reporting through diplomatic and defense channels, open sources, and even raw intelligence. They also routinely talk to foreign counterparts, journalists, academicians, contractors, and lobbyists.

Intelligence products for such consumers must be governed by the principle of "value added." Accumulation of information and views is not sufficient by itself to warrant a publication. Unlike the publish or perish system, more is not a criterion for better. The threshold for production is defined by the needs of a specific set of users, and the contribution of information and analysis to those needs—not whether the product qualifies for the publication scoreboard.

Moreover, the written product on a given issue need not, and often should not, be the same for each user. For example, an intelligence report or memorandum prepared for the deputy secretaries of the various departments and members of a senior interagency working group would properly be paralleled by a one-page highlight version for cabinet principals.

Facts and Findings: The Professional Ethic of Analytic "Tradecraft"

For a long time it has been an article of faith in much of the DI that the primary value added from a DI product—written or oral—are DI judgments. Consumers present and past, however, have been virtually unanimous in emphasizing that the first element of critical importance to them is facts. First and foremost, they want the answers to the questions: What do we know? How do we know it? Is it from a spy, an intercepted telephone message, a picture, or an embassy report? What important factors don't we know? The products also must make clear the critical difference between what is known to be a fact versus what a source reports or national technical means indicate or diplomatic observers calculate.

Some DI analysts believe that this means their opinions are being devalued. On the contrary, opinions are indeed highly valued, but to be so they must be anchored in sound and clear argumentation that lays out what is known and with what degree of reliability, what is not known that could have significant consequences, and the analytic logic that forms the basis for the findings.

Findings are critically dependent on the analysts' ability to bring their expertise and knowledge base to the evidence. The patterns, relationships, and trends that analysts detect in the evidence are combined with the knowledge they bring to bear from both their training and education and from their daily scrutiny of the endless flow of classified and open-source material. And this process of synthesis must be explained to the recipient of the findings so that answers to the following kinds of questions are clearly seen as based on thoroughgoing analysis, not mere opinion.

• How do things usually work in country "X" regarding weapons acquisition or economic corruption or manipulation of elections?

• What is increasing, decreasing, new and different regarding terrorist incidents, diversion of resources to military objectives, money laundering?

• What is the relationship between meetings, speeches, and action on the part of leader "Y"?

Some have suggested that including descriptions and sources of the evidence and laying out the analytic calculus are contrary to the need to make the products short and sharply focused, but the DI's experience in implementing these principles has shown that this is not so. A quick review of the evidence followed by a delineation of the analytic logic for any conclusions makes for a short, to-the-point paper. What has tended to make papers long has been the practice in the past of writing them for general audiences, thus requiring long background and explanatory sections that the informed, engaged policymaker does not need on the issue. (These background and educational contents were also needed for the several layers of review that had to be cleared.)

Some DI analysts also have expressed concern that laying all of this out in their products will lead the consumers to do their own analyses. Most consumers, particularly those directly engaged on a policy issue, are already doing that with or without the intelligence product. They have their own channels of information, often they have much of the same raw intelligence possessed by the analyst, and they often know the main foreign players from direct interaction.

Consumers, present and past, have consistently stated that for them, the value added—and the credibility—of the intelligence product is directly dependent on the information conveyed, its reliability, and their understanding of the analytic logic that supports the conclusions. If these are not made explicit and clear, the intelligence product becomes simply an opinion that may be agreed with or swept aside.

Forecasting Versus Fortune-Telling: Identifying the "Linchpins"

Most consumers understand the difficulties of dealing with the unknowable. The future cannot be "known," nor can we "know" what is in the minds of leaders. These things can only be forecast or estimated on the basis of the evidence available and the combined impact of knowledge and expertise. But laying out the evidence and showing the interrelationships that form the basis for the judgments can define the difference between predictions derived through forecasting and predictions derived through fortune-telling.

This distinction does not mean that forecasts always provide a correct answer and fortune-telling an incorrect answer. There will always be forecasts that turn out to be incorrect. The difference is that in forecasts the evidentiary base and analytic logic are transparent.

Analyses of potential developments are based on assessments of factors that together would logically bring about a certain future. These factors are the "drivers" or "linchpins" of the analysis. If one or more of them should change, or be removed, or turn out to have been wrong to start with, the basis for the forecast would no longer hold.

- Identifying the role of these factors in the analytic calculus is a fundamental requirement of sound intelligence forecasts. The policymaker needs to know the potential impact of changes in these "linchpins."

- The consumer especially needs to know if for any of these "linchpins" the evidence is particularly thin, there is high uncertainty, or there is no empirical evidence, but only assumptions based on past practice or what appear to be logical extensions of what is known.

A review of the record of famous wrong forecasts nearly always reveals at least one "linchpin" that did not hold up: the Soviets will not invade Czechoslovakia because they will not want to pay the political costs, especially after having signed the Reykjavík Declaration the previous year; the Soviets will not invade Afghanistan because they do not want to sink SALT II, which at the moment is being debated by the U.S. Senate; Saddam Hussein needs about two years to refurbish his military forces after the debilitating war with Iran and, therefore, will not, despite evidence of motives for doing so, invade Kuwait in the foreseeable future.

- Each of these linchpins was more of an assumption or postulate than an empirically based premise. Each was logical, but each turned out to be wrong.

• In each case, the error was less in the fact that the linchpins did not hold than in the failure of the intelligence products to highlight the extent to which they were assumptions, and the potential impact on the bottom-line judgments if they did not hold.

This approach to analytic tradecraft—facts and findings, and linchpins—forces systemic attention on the range of and relationships among the factors at play in a given situation. Identifying the linchpins encourages testing of the key subordinate judgments that hold estimative conclusions together. Because the premises that warrant the bottom-line conclusion are subject to debate as well as to error, analysts marshal findings and reasoning in defense of linchpins. Finally, this approach helps to focus ongoing collection and analysis: What indicators or patterns of development could emerge to signal that the linchpins were unreliable? What triggers or dramatic internal and external events could reverse the expected momentum?

Implementing Change in "Tradecraft"

For most of the past year the application of these analytic tradecraft principles has been the primary focus of DI supervisors. This has included redesigning the product formats in ways that facilitate customizing for users and that create a natural flow for the "facts, findings, linchpins" tools. The DI's own Product Evaluation Staff has disseminated guidelines that establish these principles as the standards against which products will be evaluated, and as the measure of excellence for evaluating analysts' professional performance. Much progress has been achieved; the principles have begun to take root in the directorate; and change is evident.

The aim, however, is to ensure that this is not allowed to be a passing thing, but rather becomes embedded in the professional ethic of the Directorate of Intelligence. To this end, a "Process Action Team" was commissioned in the latter part of 1993 to study ways to institutionalize these "analytic tradecraft" values in the directorate culture, with particular emphasis on training supervisors and analysts. The team was made up of supervisors and analysts from various substantive areas and echelons, and undertook an intensive training session with outside consultants on quality tools that addressed problem-solving techniques.

• This team's efforts included canvassing nearly 200 intelligence officers to understand their perceptions and expectations on the definition of DI tradecraft and the ways in which it had lasting impact. In these discussions the team gave particular focus to officers who had served in assignments at policy agencies, where they had the opportunity to see firsthand the needs and interaction with intelligence.

• The team also undertook extensive discussions with people from other government agencies, private industry, the media, law and medical schools, and philosophy departments at colleges and universities to identify the systems that had been most effective.

The final report from the team was disseminated to all DI officers and was followed up with extensive oral briefings to DI supervisors and analysts at all levels, as well as to nearly all senior agency managers. The report has been presented to the staffs of the congressional oversight committees.

As a result of the team's findings, the DI has canceled all offerings of the old curriculum of its analyst training courses. A DI Training Board has been established to oversee the complete reengineering of the DI officer training program, for use at all levels including the senior-most supervisors.

The new curriculum is being designed by DI officers detailed to this assignment, and reviewed by the DI corporate management with outside consultants. The courses will be taught by DI managers and analysts, as well as by training specialists, on the theory that teaching is one of the best ways to embed learning. Having managers and analysts involved in training also will help ensure that there is no discrepancy between the training and its application in the production unit. The courses will use real-world cases drawn from past and present issues and products.

• Studying what is good or bad about products from the present work force on issues directly confronted by our current consumers should provide extra stimulus for the application of the principles in the day-to-day work of the directorate.

• Training has the most impact and lasting value when it is part of the common, everyday professional activity of the work force at all levels, when they engage in it together as colleagues.

Finally, rewards and recognition other than promotion must also be brought into line with the professional standards and values that should be encouraged in the work force. A Process Action Team is concluding its study on how we can bring this about and will soon make its recommendations.

Attitudinal or cultural change is not possible unless the desired behaviors are openly recognized and rewarded. In an age of information explosion, bringing value added to the DI's customers will require a blending of skills. Analysts, data organization specialists, visual display experts, research assistants, and others will no longer be able to work independently, but must be organized into a skills team. Synergy and efficiencies in the work process are a must if the DI is to meet demands with a sharply reduced work force.

A Word on "Politicization"

The close engagement of the policymaker-consumers and the more customized products sought through the changes described above have raised a concern about the risk of politicization. Fundamentally, the only guard against politicization lies in the integrity of the supervisors and analysts. Formulating the products for general readership and the distancing of analysts and firstline supervisors from policymakers are not guards against judgments being skewed to fit someone's particular vision.

The tools of tradecraft described above, however, do provide a standard that is inherently resistant to skewing. Conclusions are to be presented as the result of evidence and analysis, not simply as "views." Disagreements must be focused on the evidence and logic, not the judgment that proceeds from them. Conclusions stand on how they are derived, not simply on who made them. If a reader or reviewer who dislikes or disagrees with a given resultant conclusion is to be credible as offering more than a parochial challenge, he or she must be forced to show where the facts or the analytic calculus is wrong or how their own analytic calculus is correct.

• When analytic judgments are fully and demonstrably backed by evidence and the logic is explained, simple assertions of disagreement do not do much for the asserter.

• On the other hand, conclusions not backed by the analytic tradecraft become assertions themselves, and invite the counterassertion from whomever sees the conclusion as unhelpful.

In the majority of cases, the sketchy evidence available can in fact support different conclusions, depending, for example, on the unknowns and the "linchpins." This is what alternative judgments are all about. The intelligence analysts themselves should—indeed, must—be the people to show the alternative outcomes and what are the factors that drive the differences. That is a fundamental principle of good intelligence tradecraft; it is what linchpins are all about.

Experience has forcefully demonstrated that however much policymakers may differ on political philosophy, they react much the same to intelligence reports that run contrary to their expectations or hopes. Unhappy responses from consumers are a natural part of the intelligence territory. No policy official likes to see intelligence that suggests things are going badly for the policy, any more than a coach likes to hear a prediction that he will lose the game. But the job of a football scout is not to turn in a prediction of the score, but to give the coach information useful in formulating a game plan. The same applies to intelligence analysts.

Objectivity is not a matter of who makes the judgment; analysis is not objective simply because it originates from an intelligence analyst, any more than it is automatically nonobjective if it originates from a policy official. Bias is not the private preserve of anyone. Analysts can become wedded to a certain analytic view, just as policymakers can become wedded to a policy view. The principles of tradecraft are the means that help all avoid falling victim to one's own perspectives.

The test of objectivity is how well the evidence is laid out and its reliability exposed, and how openly and carefully the basis for any conclusion is presented. Analysts who are confident that their information is fully laid out and their analytic calculus fully presented have nothing to fear from someone's attempt to find other conclusions. They can let the quality and objectivity of their work speak for itself.

COMMENTS: PAUL WOLFOWITZ

I would like to applaud and comment on two things in particular. The first is Doug's important recognition that the policy process should drive intelligence production and, as such, the policy process should not be seen as a mystery by intelligence analysts. I think that is absolutely right. And my own belief is that the analytic process should not be viewed as a mystery either. Frequently, however, it is made mysterious deliberately.

One definition of the difference between a secret and a mystery, which I have heard attributed to Churchill, is that a secret is like one of those Russian dolls: boxes inside a box, in which eventually you open the last box and inside it you find a secret. A mystery is a series of

Russian boxes in which you open box after box after box until you finally get to the last box and inside there is nothing. That is a mystery. And it seems to me that this is very often what you get from an analyst—opinions backed by mysteries, not facts, not secrets, but nothing.

This tendency on the part of analysts leads to the second thing I want to applaud: the criticism I understand Doug to be making of analysts who say it is their job simply to study all the evidence and give their opinions. This notion that the opinions of analysts are the main product—when often they are not a useful product at all—is a recipe for having analysis ignored.

Perhaps this is revealing a certain arrogance on my part, but I frequently think I am as capable of coming up with an informed opinion about a matter as any number of the people within the Intelligence Community who feel that they have been uniquely anointed with this responsibility. Too often that attitude is a dodge that allows them to conceal ignorance of facts, policy bias, or any number of things that may lie behind the personal opinions that are presented as sanctified intelligence judgments. No one is allowed to question those judgments, especially not policymakers, or, as the argument goes, they will pollute the intelligence process with policy judgments.

I think that this attitude on the part of the Intelligence Community causes a lot of problems. I think that it actually encourages the manipulation of intelligence judgments for political policy purposes. If you can get the authority of the Intelligence Community on your side, you can appeal to authority without having to bother appealing to the evidence. More important, it places great importance on a product that reports the judgments of analysts, which, absent the evidence on which those judgments rest, have limited value to policymakers. It tends to produce turgid National Intelligence Estimates (NIEs), marked by summary judgments in the front, full of carefully balanced sentences ("on the one hand," and "on the other hand"), offering no new facts or reasoning to which any sophisticated reader of the weekly reader would not already have access. On a busy day, they are not even looked at. They may be glanced at because you have to know what someone may say to you at a meeting, citing the judgment of the NIE as an authority. Yet you do not read them expecting to learn very much. An estimate may be a useful weapon in a debate or it may be someone else's weapon against which you have to be prepared to defend yourself, but you rarely read them expecting to learn something new.

The first NIE I ever read was one on strategic forces, introduced with a note by the Director of Central Intelligence proudly congratulating the people who had produced the NIE with only one dissenting footnote. I was appalled. I thought on a subject of this importance, of this uncertainty, that there would be some disagreement. Well, I was a little naive, not realizing how useless such footnotes generally were. I began to see a number of footnotes later on and realized that the footnotes probably had no more analytical standing than the judgments. Once you knew who or what agency authored the footnotes, you knew what they would say; the analysis was largely irrelevant. But the idea that somehow you were saving work for the policymakers by eliminating serious debate is wrong. Why not aim, instead, at a document that actually says there are two strongly argued positions on this issue? Here are the facts and evidence supporting one position, and here are the facts and evidence supporting the other, even though that might leave the poor policymakers to make a judgment as to which one they think is correct. I would have found that kind of document useful; unfortunately, it was far too rare.

This unhappy outcome results partly from the understandable desire to separate intelligence judgments from policy preferences. I will grant that this is a real issue and I do believe that one ought to try to get the facts straight, no matter what your policy preferences. However, if you stop thinking about these products as weapons to be used to win a debate but rather as tools to help develop a policy, the issue becomes much less important. For example, we made enormous use of intelligence throughout the lead-up to the Persian Gulf War, and during the Gulf War. But it was primarily used to figure out how to implement policy, not to debate policy preferences. The policymakers themselves have powerful incentives to get the facts right and not be misled by biases or wishful thinking. We wanted the best possible access to facts so that we could develop the best policy. It was not a matter of having a particular preference for a particular set of facts, it was a matter of having a clear preference for formulating good policy and winning. And I would be the first to say that we got very good support from the Intelligence Community in that case. But I think one has to accept the idea that the analytical process, like the policy process, is not a mystery and should not be treated as one. I think analysts should be brought into the policy process more, and vice versa. The analytical process should not be mysterious; and if it is mysterious, more often than not it is probably because the people doing it are second- or third-rate and cannot defend the judgments they have reached.

I think really first-rate analysis—and I am delighted that I am just reinforcing what Doug has already said—is analysis that lays out all of the facts. It may be that these are all facts to which somebody else had access but the policymaker did not necessarily have. Pulling these facts together, structuring them, and setting out the relationships between them is no mean feat. It is important that analytic products lay out the facts, the evidence, and the analysis rather than simply state conclusions or analytical judgments. One of the most valuable contributions an analyst can make is to put facts together in a new and illuminating way. For example, we had some good analysis (in this case, not from the Intelligence Community, but from Henry Rowen, then-assistant secretary of defense for international security affairs) leading up to the crisis in the Gulf about projections on oil trends and Iraqi oil revenues.

Finally, although it is obvious there has to be a limit on how you do this, it seems to me that encouraging real debate and recording debate where it exists is valuable. This does not mean proliferating debate endlessly, because you will have another problem if you have a product that is nothing but debate. But many of these issues are not certain and it is important to recognize that point. There needs to be some real allowance for uncertainty, and the amount of uncertainty also depends on the time frame you are talking about.

Consider, for example, the NIE in December of 1989 concerning Saddam Hussein's intentions. It would be totally unreasonable to expect an NIE at that time to have predicted what he was going to do. I do not think Saddam himself knew what he was going to do. It is clear that most of the leaders of the Arab world, who had a very large stake in predicting what he was going to do, had no sense of what was coming. On the other hand, I do not think that the NIE's prediction influenced policy one way or the other. I do know that inside the Pentagon, in October or November 1989, we had a big debate about planning for the Persian Gulf. The result of that debate was to change our planning from the scenario of a Soviet invasion of Iran, which everyone agreed was pretty safely out of the question, to planning for an Iraqi invasion of Kuwait and Saudi Arabia. This was not based on someone's prediction that this was an event that was going to happen next year, but rather on looking, for planning purposes, at a five- to ten-year time frame and recognizing the reasonable range of uncertainty about what could happen. We were not going to base our planning on the kind of prediction that people were trying to do in the NIE. We had to base it on a wider range of what was possible: when you looked at the facts, the military imbalances in the region, plus a certain amount of the history of Saddam Hussein and the Iraqi regime, you would have to conclude this was a serious possibility. After all, we were dealing in a world where 10 percent possibility was something we might plan for and, in fact, we did. That it turned out to be 100 percent possible was not foreseen.

Although perfect prediction about the distant future is impossible, one thing that I think one could expect—and here I think the record of the Intelligence Community should have been a little better—is that when the signs started to turn up that the projected scenario regarding Iraqi behavior was not unfolding as we wished (i.e., when Saddam started to make his threats about burning half of Israel, along with a series of other developments) somebody within the community should have said, "Wait a minute, here are facts that we ought to take some account of." Analysis, in this instance, would have usefully pointed to the fact that events were not going in the direction we had expected or hoped for.

I must note, though—and this is etched in my memory—that when we had the NSC meeting on the administration's prewar policy toward Iraq (around September 1989) that the intelligence folks got it right. It was obviously the preference of those writing the interagency policy paper to pursue a course of trying to moderate Iraq's behavior. I was not enamored of that position, but it was hard to argue that the Defense Department had much to say one way or another. So I sat in the back quietly cheering when the president of the United States turned to his key advisers and said, "But we know a lot about this guy Saddam Hussein; can the leopard really change his spots?" And Dick Kerr, then-deputy DCI, sitting in for DCI William Webster, went through a lengthy recitation of facts—facts, not judgments—that were overwhelming in the direction they pointed: this leopard was unlikely to change. I thought this might alter the conclusions of the paper. However, someone then said that we would not lose anything by trying, which may in fact be a true statement. So we went ahead. But the facts were certainly available for anyone who thought they mattered.

In my own experience, the most successful input of intelligence for policy has been when intelligence professionals have been close to the policy process. (I include collectors as well as analysts, because just as the distinction between policy and analysis is somewhat artificial, so also is the distinction between collection and analysis. One of the best analysts on the Middle East that I ever ran into was a collector.) Intelligence provided by those professionals was far more useful than written documents that were carefully sanitized to ensure everybody against all possible critical appraisals that might be drawn two or three years hence. When I was the State Department's assistant secretary for East Asia (EA) in the mid-1980s, we had something called the EA Informal, to which intelligence officers working on the region were regularly invited. They knew what questions were on our minds; we knew what they knew, what they did not know, and when they were just giving us their best guesses.

Similarly, during the Bush administration, the Deputy's Committee (headed by then-Deputy National Security Adviser Robert Gates) always functioned, and I think usefully so, with agency representation. Sometimes we asked the deputy DCI, Dick Kerr or Bill Studeman, for their policy preferences; it was not precluded. But there was no question when they were stating what they thought the facts were to the best of their knowledge. I think more of this kind of interaction would be helpful. I also think it would be helpful to see policymakers more involved in the intelligence production process—even though some in the Intelligence Community seem to think this is a bit like bringing the infidels into the mosque. At the Department of Defense, we started something called the Defense Intelligence Policy Council, which was a serious effort to help our intelligence people get a better feel for what the consumers in the policy areas of the Pentagon wanted. But, frankly, I do not think consumers can reasonably tell you what they want or need in terms of support unless they have an understanding of how the analysis is being done and what the real issues are in allocating collection resources.

COMMENTS: JOHN DESPRES

"The Tradecraft of Analysis" elaborates on Doug MacEachin's proposed solutions to problems (e.g., obsolete methods and inflexible mind-sets) he highlighted in the Working Group meeting. It outlines the main steps that he has taken to change the professional ethic, doctrine, and training of analysts. These initiatives are unprecedented. While they are being implemented, they deserve the benefit of the doubt about their ultimate effectiveness. Although their full effects will take years to materialize, policymakers should begin to see them pay off soon in more valuable intelligence products.

Doug's account of the difficulties in coping with analytical mind-sets reminds me of a second opinion on a National Intelligence Estimate twenty years ago on the Sino-Soviet conflict. It was based on an assessment of the analytical community back then, which was virtually identical to his account of the mind-set of analysts today. In their view, the important thing is for analysts to provide their judgment, their opinion, on the likely course of events—that is what they are paid for. It is not their job to reveal their sources or their methods to policy officials and decision makers who really do not have a need to know how these judgments were reached, but to let the policy community react as it sees fit, or to ignore their judgments if that is its choice. While this oversimplifies, it is a fair approximation of most analysts' attitudes.

Having witnessed a succession of people in Doug's position make similar statements about the situation, I must admit that I have been skeptical that anything short of fundamentally reorganizing will have the intended effect. Yet, I do not recommend radical surgery because I think that what the Intelligence Community does, what the CIA does, and in particular what the Directorate of Intelligence does, is enormously valuable. But it is not strategic intelligence of the sort that has been long sought and rarely achieved.

Without denigrating the importance and the value of what the Intelligence Community accomplished in 1990, which was a key topic of Doug's original presentation, policymakers who use its products need to be more realistic about what the Intelligence Community can do, what it can do uniquely, and what it can do best. Consider its work on Iraq. The administration decided in September and October of 1989 what the policy should be: namely, to try to turn Saddam Hussein into a moderate, to steer him away from a provocative policy of confrontation and deterrence, to get him to earn the status of a leader of a nonterrorist state, and to provide positive inducements, including material incentives, for him to join the civilized world. While this was a reasonable approach, it was not based on an intelligence estimate that weighed other views. Indeed, the NIE on Iraq followed, rather than preceded, the administration's choice of policy; it expressed no alternative views that would alert policymakers to the weaknesses of their assumptions. So, the effect of the NIE coming a month or two later was not merely to ratify the policy decision, but to close the debate and to create a strategic blind spot, making the government more vulnerable to surprise than it otherwise would have been.

This undue complacency about Iraqi intentions was compounded by another estimate, a few months later, on the risks of war in South Asia. This unusually alarming estimate diverted the administration's strategic attention still further away from the Gulf, and toward a South Asian threat that did not materialize.

Of course, even with the benefit of hindsight, strategic uncertainties are still great. For instance, a policy of deterrence toward Iraq might well have been provocative and no less costly or risky. Indeed, it might have complicated the political problem of mobilizing a coalition, especially among the Arabs. Moreover, we may have really dodged a nuclear "bullet" in South Asia. So I am agnostic on the real value of strategic intelligence in this case, even though I do not think these NIEs were close to being right. I also do not believe that the greatest value and the comparative advantage of the Intelligence Community lies in the area of strategic intelligence, or that its deficiencies and failures of strategic judgment are the main measures of its shortcomings. Instead, the Intelligence Community excels at producing tactical intelligence on a daily basis, as well as operational intelligence of enormous value on special occasions in response to well-defined needs.

To perform still more effectively, the community's culture and training should be task- and mission-oriented toward well-defined objectives and feasible analytical tasks that are detached from the policy-making process, along the lines articulated by Doug's paper. When they are done well, as they often are, they provide the best counterweight to the blind spots of policymakers. For instance, notwithstanding the administration's decision in early 1990 to override Congress's designation of Iraq as a terrorist state and the Intelligence Community's rosy view of Iraqi intentions, intelligence on Iraqi terrorist activities, as well as on Iraqi nuclear and special weapons programs, continued to be produced in 1989 and 1990 without serious constraints on the analysts and despite large gaps in basic information. This intelligence provided the elements of a different perception and concept of the Iraqi problem. This kind of intelligence made the policy-making and strategic planning process of the JCS and the rest of the national security community much more resilient and responsive when the crunch came. What was missing was a contrary view of Iraqi intentions and a strategic concept of deterrence. As a result, the administration lacked good options in July for rapidly mounting a show of resolve that could have prevented this crisis from leading to conflict. However, I do not think that the Intelligence Community and analysts by themselves could be expected to anticipate those needs and to detect those shortfalls in policy planning. Indeed, certain shortfalls of that sort are inevitable in every administration.

What kind of people, training, and experience are needed in order to have analysts who are capable of producing good, highly responsive operational and tactical intelligence is a serious question—especially in an organization that has grown too much and too fast. There are two legitimate questions that young people coming into the organization will have: (1) What is their future? (2) How can the career ladder within the Directorate of Intelligence—which has really rewarded short-term assignments, diversity of assignments, and mixing analytical assignments with management assignments—be changed for the next generation? Unless new initiatives put a premium on excelling in the production of intelligence and create an environment to provide more career tracks for people to develop their skills and their expertise in a range of related disciplines and regions over the long haul, the sort of frustrations that the Intelligence Community has now, and that I first encountered twenty years ago, will continue to be with us.

COMMENTS: ABRAM SHULSKY

I agree with almost everything that the previous commentators have noted. I will only emphasize a few points and make an additional comment that goes generally in the same direction. We in Washington tend to focus on reorganizations and wiring diagrams because organizational structures define people's turfs, bolster people's egos, define their titles and so forth, and determine what goes on their resume. But if we look at some of the business literature on reinventing the corporation, we see an emphasis on the culture of an organization, as opposed to its organizational structure. In other words, what people do in reality on a day-by-day basis is much more important than where they sit (i.e., their place in the hierarchy). I think Doug's proposals are largely aimed at changing the culture rather than moving the boxes on a wiring diagram.

A useful example of the relationship Doug wishes to develop between analysts and policymakers can be found in the area of arms control. Historically, this is an area in which the relationship between intelligence and policy-making has been different than it has been elsewhere, and better. Intelligence officers served as members of the arms control delegation and became part of the policy-making process. Although the intelligence representative is doing some things and not others, he or she nevertheless gets a firsthand view of the policy process, gaining insight into what is important to the consumer and what kinds of issues are on the table.

That could be the model to use to change the intelligence analysis "culture." In other words, what we ought to be looking for are bureaucratic forms that enable the intelligence analyst at all levels—from low in the bureaucracy to the Deputy's Committee to the very top—to work closely with policymakers: to attend the meetings, to understand what the day-to-day issues are. That is important, for instance, for tailoring the product to the needs of the consumer at different levels. Intelligence will not be able to do that unless it has a close working relationship with policy. A survey or a questionnaire soliciting the requirements of policymakers will not suffice—an ongoing and continuing relationship is required.

Doug's analogy of the coach who sends off a scout who reports back that "you're going to lose the next game" is excellent. That kind of problem will not occur if the intelligence analyst is actually attending meetings of policymakers, because then the analyst will be forced to focus not on figuring out whether one is going to win or lose, but on what one can do to increase one's chances of winning. When the focus is not on predicting the future—because the whole point of the meeting is, after all, to affect the future—one will be forced to try to spell out what one believes are the key factors that will drive the result, factors that may be manipulable in some ways but not manipulable in others.

This raises the issue of politicization, a very much overstated issue. As Paul Wolfowitz pointed out, politicization can also occur when intelligence and policy are kept quite separate. At a certain point, there is no substitute for backbone or the willingness to be tough; that is true on the policy side as well. Anyone in a bureaucratic situation is going to be faced occasionally with the need to relate facts or express opinions that are not welcomed by one's superiors, and everyone must be willing to do that as necessary.

Another important result of close work between analysts and policymakers is that it will enable policymakers to better understand what the Intelligence Community can or cannot do. This is extremely important; the policymaker must have a sense of what kind of information is really out there, what you can expect to get, and what you cannot expect to get. The *Washington Post* had a beautiful example of the problem on its front page. The headline read: "U.N. Unclear About Origin of Shell in Sarajevo," but the point of the story was that, for technical reasons, it was not possible to provide forensic proof of where the shell came from, although UN officials on the ground were fairly sure that the shell had in fact been fired by the Serbs. The absence of forensic proof did not cast any doubt on the rather clear political and strategic reasoning that led to that conclusion. In general, a policymaker must know enough about the intelligence process to have a sense of when it is reasonable to expect various kinds of evidence to be available.

In summary, if you were to do all those kinds of things, and the many others you mentioned, you will begin to deal with the "culture" of intelligence analysis. If organizational changes are necessary, they are relatively simple to do. But the important thing is the culture, making it clear to the analyst the ways in which he or she is not an academic, but rather is a part of a decision-making process. Making sure that the personal contact is there will help that occur. How superiors will rate the analyst when they do not have a file of written products to look at is going to be a problem, but it should not be allowed to get in the way of this attempt to change the culture.

7

ESTIMATING THE FUTURE?

Joseph S. Nye

As the fates of the Soviet Union, Germany, and recently, the Middle East have shown, no one knows the future. Yet those who set foreign policy constantly make predictions, consciously or not. Will a foreign leader act rationally? Will an allied country be reliable? The consequences of wrong guesses can be catastrophic, and policymakers turn to national intelligence for help. Their need for help continues despite the end of the Cold War.

Intelligence analysts sift through reams of information, trying to sort the accurate from the erroneous; and when not enough facts are available, the analysts estimate what the picture would look like if they had all the facts. Current intelligence—intelligence about current events—is mainly reportorial and interpretive. "Saddam Hussein lambasted the U.S. government again yesterday. He seems to be trying to drive a wedge between Washington and Paris." While the line often blurs, estimative intelligence is more concerned with what might be or might happen. "Is Iraq still hiding weapons of mass destruction?" "Will Saddam still be in power a year from now?" Like all kinds of intelligence, estimative intelligence starts out with the available facts, but then it trespasses into the unknown—the regions where facts are unavailable—or the unknowable—the uncharted future where no facts yet exist. It is no wonder that National Intelligence Estimates (NIEs) are sometimes wrong.

Why take the risks? Why not stick strictly to the facts? One reason is that facts about crucial international issues are rarely conclusive. There is often enough evidence to indict, rarely enough to convict. Yet policymakers are under enormous pressure to make decisions. In some cases, they can wait for more information, but in others, waiting can itself be a decision with irreversible consequences. In the words of a White

Reprinted with permission. A version of this paper, "Peering into the Future," was originally published in *Foreign Affairs* 73, no. 4 (July/August 1994) and first presented on April 12, 1994.

House official, "insight is more scarce than information." To help policymakers interpolate between the available facts, to suggest alternative patterns that the available facts could fit into, to provide informed assessments of the range and likelihoods of possible outcomes—those are the roles of estimative intelligence.

The Cold War Record

President Truman created the new civilian Central Intelligence Agency (CIA) in 1947, but neither it nor military intelligence predicted the North Korean invasion in 1950. Gen. Douglas MacArthur's Tokyo headquarters consistently misestimated North Korean and Chinese behavior. In response, when Gen. Walter Bedell Smith became director of Central Intelligence (DCI) in October 1950, he created a new art form called "National Intelligence Estimates (NIEs)," to be agreed upon at the highest levels in the Intelligence Community.

NIEs are produced by the national intelligence council (NIC), which represents the entire Intelligence Community and reports to the director in his role as head of the community rather than as head of the CIA. (Roughly one half of the NIC's national intelligence officers [NIOs] come from the CIA, one quarter from other parts of the government [State, Defense, Energy], and one quarter from universities or private nonprofit organizations.) The NIC coordinates estimative views from the CIA, the Defense Intelligence Agency (DIA), the four military services, the National Security Agency (NSA), the State Department's Intelligence and Research Bureau (INR), and the intelligence units of Energy, Treasury, and the Federal Bureau of Investigation (FBI). The heads of these organizations constitute the National Foreign Intelligence Board; they review and approve each estimate before it is published and sent to the president and other top officials.

How accurate was the estimative process during the Cold War? It is in the nature of intelligence that successes often remain hidden, while failures become public, so the ledger cannot be balanced until the documentary records are fully available to future historians. Nonetheless, after comparing a series of NIEs with such open sources as the *Economist*, the *New York Times*, and other publications, historian Ernest May concluded that the estimates came out reasonably well. They gave policymakers and their staff information not in the press, and they focused on longer-term questions usually slighted by journalists. Lucid analytic success, however, does not ensure policy impact. For example, pessimistic estimates about Vietnam in the 1960s were analytic successes but were unwelcome by the policymakers; thus they failed to prevent disastrous policy choices.

There were notable failures such as the 1962 estimate that Khrushchev would not place missiles in Cuba, the 1973 failure to foresee the Yom Kippur War, the analytical disarray in 1978 that prevented the drafting of any estimate about the fall of the Shah of Iran, and the 1989 prediction that Saddam Hussein would not make trouble for the next three years. The central estimative issues during the Cold War, however, concerned the Soviet Union. Critics complain that the Intelligence Community consistently overestimated Soviet military strength, but the record is not so simple. While intelligence was good at predicting the development of new Soviet weapons, it was sometimes wrong about the quantity and quality of the weapons produced and deployed. The spurious bomber and missile gaps of the 1950s reflected Soviet deception and exaggeration in the days before reconnaissance satellites. In the late 1960s and early 1970s, intelligence underestimated the buildup of Soviet strategic forces. So the errors were not all in one direction. Moreover, the formal estimative process provided a means for agencies that disagreed with the overall community view to make their alternative conclusions known to decision makers.

Some critics go further. Sen. Daniel Patrick Moynihan has argued that the failure to predict the demise of the Soviet Union led to a decade of wasted military expenditures in the 1980s, and that this should be grounds for abolishing the CIA and giving its functions to the State Department. Again, the record is more complex. The Intelligence Community accurately reported a slowdown in the Soviet economy, although it did not adequately estimate the rapidity of economic collapse. And the questions posed by policymakers were not about some abstract future, but whether even a weakening Soviet economy could support a formidable current military threat. The Intelligence Community estimated correctly that it could.

As for the timing, intelligence analysts were not alone. Almost everyone (including Mikhail Gorbachev) failed to predict that the Soviet Union would collapse in 1991. The exact timing of the Soviet demise was probably an accident of history. If the politburo had picked a less activist and more conservative general secretary in 1985, it is plausible that the Soviet Union would have declined more gradually through the end of the century. And a declining empire with nuclear weapons could have posed a significant military threat. The failure to predict the timing of the collapse of the USSR was common to the global community of Sovietologists—and to most Soviets.

The experience with predicting the demise of the Soviet Union should make one wary of too much consensus and of reducing the number of sources of analysis. It should also make one wary of abolishing the CIA. That would weaken rather than improve estimates by eliminating the community's chief source of nondepartmental analysis. In policy circles, the old adage is that where you stand depends on where you sit. In intelligence, what you foresee is often affected by where you work. The primary duty of departmental analysts is to respond to the needs of their organizations. Diplomats are supposed to negotiate solutions. Even in apparently hopeless situations, they tend to press departmental analysts for the one chance in a hundred that might permit success. Generals are supposed to win battles. Even in hopeless situations, they tend to press their intelligence analysts for estimates of what they will have to face if worse comes to worst. Thus, one type of departmental analysis tends toward optimism, the other toward pessimism. It is not a matter of intellectual dishonesty but of analysts simply doing their jobs.

The best answer to such problems of human and bureaucratic nature is multiple points of view that are brought together in one place, such as national estimates. Then, policymakers can see the sources of differences and make their own assessments. During the Cold War, the CIA provided nondepartmental assessments with which departmental assessments could be compared. Estimates reflected the consensus of the community if there was one; if not, agencies that disagreed with the majority's conclusions could insert their own alternative views. No intelligence agency had a corner on the truth, but this process helped policymakers thread their way between wishful thinking and worst case overinsuring during a long Cold War that was characterized by a dangerous and deceptive adversary.

After the Cold War

The need for estimative intelligence continues after the Cold War, although there is no longer an overriding threat. In a world where rapid change has become the norm, uncertainties abound. The current threats to U.S. security are not entirely new, but they are more diverse. And they are complicated by the "return of history"—the unlocking of ethnic and religious conflicts that had been partly frozen by Cold War blocs. What are the prospects that transnational terrorists will perpetrate another attack like that on the World Trade Center? Where and how quickly will weapons of mass destruction spread? Will economic and social turmoil in Russia or Ukraine lead to the loss of nuclear weapons? Will friendly countries be torn apart by ethnic conflicts and demands for self-determination? What forces and weapons will U.S. troops confront in future peacekeeping or regional conflicts?

Some problems threaten the U.S. national welfare rather than traditional national security. Policymakers also need intelligence about the transnational drug trade, whether foreign governments are using bribes to cheat U.S. businesses, and whether countries are meeting their commitments to protect the quality of the world's atmosphere, oceans, and endangered species. In response, the NIC created a new NIO for Global and Multilateral Issues to develop estimates on such topics.

One problem for intelligence in the post–Cold War world is knowing where to invest a diminishing set of analytic resources. Skilled analysts are needed to deal with new questions, but personnel are being cut 17 percent over four years, and 25 percent over this decade. In such a setting, how many Somali-speaking analysts should be retained? And will the Intelligence Community preserve a surge capacity when CNN or something else suddenly puts the next Somalia on the agenda?

Behind these management issues lies a larger problem: how to understand the structure of world politics that underlies estimative analysis. During the Cold War, the world was bipolar, with most political issues influenced by the USSR and the United States. Today, the structure of power is like a three-dimensional chess game.[1] The top, military, board is unipolar; the United States is the only country capable of projecting global military force. But the middle, economic, board is tripolar. The United States, the European Union, and Japan account for two-thirds of the world economy, and the dramatic economic growth of the People's Republic of China (PRC) may make this board quadripolar by the turn of the century. The bottom board consists of diverse transnational relationships outside the control of governments, including financial flows, drug trafficking, terrorism, and degradation of the ozone layer. On this board, there are no poles.

Greater complexity in the structure of power means greater uncertainty in estimating the future. Polities are often nonlinear in the sense that they are undergoing dramatic change, but such changes have become much more frequent since the end of the Cold War. For example, in the 1980s, if one were estimating the number of nuclear weapons that South Africa would have in the 1990s, one would have calculated what their uranium enrichment plan could produce and answered "six or seven." But the correct answer today turns out to be "zero" because of radical political discontinuities associated with the transition to majority rule and the end of the Cold War. Similarly, if one were to estimate today how many nuclear weapons a country with no nuclear facilities might have in five years, the linear answer would be zero. But there might be a major discontinuity if the country were able to purchase stolen nuclear weapons on the transnational black market.

Another complication for estimators after the Cold War is the increase in the ratio of mysteries to secrets in the questions that policymakers want answered. A secret is something concrete that can be stolen by a spy or discerned by a technical sensor, for example, the number of SS-18 missiles in the Soviet Union or the size of their warheads. A mystery is an abstract puzzle to which no one can be sure of the answer, for example, will President Yeltsin be able to control inflation in Russia a year from now? No one can steal that secret from Yeltsin because he does not know the answer. He may not even be in office a year from now.

Responses to Uncertainty

The NIC has tried to cope with this uncertainty in a variety of ways. Most important is the increased emphasis on alternative scenarios in preference to single-point prediction. Its job, after all, is not so much to predict the future, but to help policymakers think about the future. Since we cannot know the future, it is misleading to pretend we do. On the other hand, if we simply tell policymakers how complex things are, they will echo Harry Truman's request for a one-armed analyst: "no more, on one hand and on the other hand." Analysts owe policymakers a forthright appraisal of the best estimate.

Instead of trying to predict the future, the NIC should describe the range of outcomes that seem possible—including relatively unlikely outcomes—if they would have major impacts on U.S. interests. Further, the NIC should indicate which outcomes are believed to be more likely than others, and why. Finally, the NIC should convey a sense of the absolute likelihood of each outcome, although that is very uncertain ground.

In this connection, rather than use vague words such as *possibly* or *small but significant change*, where feasible the NIC should present its judgments of likelihood as numerical percentages or bettor's odds. This is a controversial approach because it is difficult if not impossible to explain why there is one chance in two or one chance in four. Even so, the policymakers are better served than if they are simply told that something is possible—that's equivalent to telling them there is a 1 to 49 percent chance it will happen, which is not much help to somebody trying to make an important decision. Moreover, if really uncertain about the likelihood of an outcome, or if agencies disagree over that likelihood, the easiest way to depict that to a busy reader is simply to present a range of probability—to say, for example, that there is a 30 to 50 percent chance that it will happen.

After the most likely scenarios have been constructed and presented, the analysts must ask another set of questions before the estimate is done. What would it take for this estimate to be dramatically wrong? What could cause a radically different outcome? This is not the same as doing worst-case analysis. If the most plausible scenarios are pessimistic, the analysts must ask what it would take to produce a favorable outcome. What would such an outcome look like, and how would we know if events were heading in that direction?

Experts often resist this exercise. Because they know their country or region and have already presented all the plausible scenarios, why waste effort on scenarios that are, by definition, highly unlikely? The answer is that such questions help alert policymakers to low-probability but high-impact contingencies against which they might plan. It also informs intelligence agencies about nonobvious indicators about which they should be collecting information.

Perhaps if estimators of Soviet strength in the 1980s had asked themselves explicitly what it would take to greatly weaken the Soviet Union, and what such a stricken colossus would look like, analysts and policymakers would have been more attentive to offbeat indicators and less surprised by the eventual outcome. One of the reasons that Royal Dutch Shell survived the 1973 oil crisis better than other companies is that its planners did not merely do best estimates of future oil prices but also contemplated scenarios of dramatic price changes that were considered at the time to be of very low probability.[2] In the event, prices quadrupled in one year.

Another feature of good estimating is explicit identification of the key assumptions and uncertainties so that the policymaker is aware of the foundations upon which the estimate is based. It is impossible to identify all the assumptions that lie behind the analyses. Everyone assumes that the future will more or less resemble the past; for example, we expect the sun to rise in the east. Some day that will not be true, but it will probably remain true for the time frame of our estimates and we need not mention it. Other assumptions might seem obvious, but nonetheless be worth highlighting. For example, in the

1980s, if one had been estimating Iraq's ability to build a nuclear weapon, one could have explicated the reasonable assumption that Iraq would use only the most modern and efficient techniques to produce fissile material. In the event, U.S. intelligence missed a critical part of Iraq's program, which included electromagnetic isotope separation, a technique that the United States had abandoned as too slow in the 1940s. Had the assumption been explicit, perhaps some analyst or policymaker might have thought to ask what Saddam's program might look like if the assumption were relaxed.

Just as estimates start with a section that highlights assumptions, where appropriate, they end with a section that highlights key uncertainties. After all is said and done, what are the biggest gaps in the NIC's knowledge? This helps not only to alert policymakers to the limits of the estimate just read, but also informs collectors of the needs for further information. In fact, one of the jobs of national intelligence officers is to serve as issue coordinators, to identify gaps in our knowledge, and to provide that information to the DCI and the Executive Committee of the Intelligence Community to help them plan collection programs.

Another way to enrich NIEs is to explore the reasons why agencies hold different views on specific estimative issues. It has long been recognized that providing alternative views is better than suppressing them in favor of vague or ambiguous consensus; yet alternative views have often been presented without much explanation of the basis of the disagreement. Such explanations can be illuminating. Are the facts in dispute? Are agencies and their staff using different conceptual frameworks? Is it a cup-half-full versus cup-half-empty dispute? Policymakers are most helped by estimates that indicate clearly what all agencies agree is known and not known, what they disagree about, and what the evidence for each position is. Indeed, there is no reason why differing interpretations need agency sponsors. In the always foggy estimative arena, analysts within agencies often differ on how to interpret sparse or ambiguous material, and the most responsible thing to do in such cases is to describe the various plausible interpretations and lay out the evidence for each.

As for the problem that there is now a greater proportion of mysteries to secrets in estimative questions, the solution lies in paying more attention to outside and open sources of information. A high proportion of the information needed to analyze Cold War subjects involved secrets that had to be clandestinely collected, while open sources often provided little help. That is still true for closed societies such as Iraq and North Korea. But on many of the key issues outlined above for which policymakers now want answers, clandestine sources may provide only a small (though still useful) portion of the information. Open sources provide context. The combination provides a unique resource that policymakers could not obtain merely from reading journals.

In a sense, intelligence analysts are like people doing a jigsaw puzzle who have some nifty nuggets inside a box, but need to see the picture on the cover of the box to understand how they fit. And those pictures are drawn by outsiders in universities, think tanks, businesses, non-governmental organizations, and the press. National estimates on many subjects today greatly benefit from including the insights of outside analysts. It is important for intelligence analysts to keep up with open literature, but that is easier said than done. As one young analyst described his daily work, "I had no time to read *Foreign Affairs* or talk to academics. I had 800 to 1,100 pieces of traffic to read per day and then write up. I was almost exclusively dedicated to current reporting rather than estimative intelligence. This problem will get worse with downsizing." Managers have to counter this tendency by outside training and by using consultants and conferences. And in estimates, it is often illuminating to describe the range of academic views so that policymakers can calibrate where the Intelligence Community stands. In some cases, this could involve asking outside experts to answer key estimative questions or even to produce parallel estimates.

Innovations and enhancements aside, it does not matter how good the estimates may be unless their contents get into the minds of policymakers. Most high-level policymakers are swamped with information and have schedules that allow them little time to read. They spend their days drinking from a firehose of information. The basic paradox of government is that it rests on a sea of paper, but the higher you go, the more it becomes an oral culture. The finest analytic work that is too long to read, or that arrives when its issue is not on the front burner is likely to be placed in a pile on the back corner of the desk that is reserved for papers too interesting to throw away, but not urgent enough to read now. Every few weeks or months, most of that pile is discarded unread.

To respond to this situation, the NIC has devised two new estimative art forms. Following the example of Britain's Joint Intelligence Council, which produces three-page estimates for the cabinet, the NIC has developed a short "President's Summary" designed explicitly for top policymakers. The complete version of the estimate, with details and justifications, remains a useful tool for staffs and lower levels of policy bureaucracies. Moreover, estimating must be seen as a continuous process. When new developments occur or new information comes in, recipients of estimates are provided with a short memorandum that updates them.

Thinking of estimating as a process requires constant contact with policymakers so that written products are keyed to their agendas. Policymakers are often too distracted to ask for estimates, but they will read or listen if the timing is right. The production of some estimates must be geared to upcoming events such as the visit of a foreign prime minister or a presidential trip abroad. When warranted, estimates or special NIC memos are put on a fast track, and can be produced in a matter of days.

Even efficient and timely publication is not the entire answer. The estimative process involves contact with decision makers before and after publication. The purpose of estimating is not publication, but getting ideas into policymakers' minds. Oral estimating is another important way of doing that. Listenership is sometimes more important than readership.

In short, estimation as a process requires constant interaction between national intelligence officers and policymakers both before and after publication. Such contact raises the red flag of politicization, of consciously or unconsciously crossing the line between objective analysis and statement of policy preferences. The NIOs must be constantly alert to the danger. Fortunately, the taboo against trespassing into policy is so deeply ingrained in the intelligence culture that there are frequent reminders. In addition, estimators often present unpopular information. With particularly sensitive estimates that could undermine a policy or a foreign leader if leaked to the press, the NIC is prepared to limit distribution to a narrow list of people with a need to know, but not to change the nature of the conclusions.

Conclusions

Estimates focused heavily on the Soviet Union during the Cold War. In its wake, policymakers still need estimative intelligence to help them understand the more diffuse and ambiguous threats and opportunities they face. Ideological divisions are less likely to obstruct analysis, but greater uncertainties make analysis more difficult. The greater the uncertainty, the greater the scope and need for estimative intelligence. But the task is not simple prediction. Estimators are not fortune-tellers; they are educators. Rather than trying to predict the future, estimators should deal with heightened uncertainty by presenting alternative scenarios. To be useful, estimates must describe not only the nature and probability of the most likely future paths, but they must also investigate significant excursions off those paths and identify the signposts that indicate we are entering such territory.

Estimates are ways of summarizing what is known and structuring the remaining uncertainties. Sometimes they will be wrong; sometimes, even if correct, they will be ignored. Sometimes, as in the case of the 1990 estimate that correctly predicted the violence in former Yugoslavia, policymakers can draw a variety of conclusions about whether to intervene or not. Often estimates will be unpopular when they cast doubt on preferred options or put awkward new issues on the policy agenda. But properly conceived and effectively presented, estimative intelligence can help policymakers make better choices in a future that will contain a more complex mix of threats and opportunities.

8

THE INTELLIGENCE INDUSTRIAL BASE

Robert Kohler

T he future of the industrial base that supports and sustains the nation's intelligence collection programs of the United States is an issue of great importance that, unfortunately, has been largely ignored. Ever since the fall of the Berlin Wall, the return of the Eastern Bloc to freedom, and the collapse of the Soviet Union, a central issue of debate has been the role of the Intelligence Community in the new world. Increasingly, this debate has centered around the appropriate size of the community's budget. Lacking a crisp answer to the question: "What is the appropriate role for the Intelligence Community in the future? The community's budget has continued to be cut, and the cuts have fallen disproportionately in the critical area pertaining to the development and acquisition of technical collection systems.

These disproportionate cuts have occurred not only as a result of a lack of an overall community strategy, but also because development and acquisition budgets are easy to cut. These cuts do not require government employees to lose their jobs, but people in industry do. This simple statement is not a complaint. I believe that the industry that supports intelligence has a role equal in importance to that of government organizations, and that its health needs to be considered in that light. The reality is, there are jobs in industry—that support intelligence—as important as those in government, but this fact is being overlooked in the effort to downsize the Intelligence Community and cut its budget.

The basic proposition of this essay is that the intelligence industrial base is the heart of U.S. intelligence supremacy and is the major reason that U.S. intelligence is the premier intelligence system in the world. The base consists of a constellation of companies and people that has grown and evolved over the past four decades to develop, design, build, operate, and maintain the technical systems the nation has used to

This paper was first presented on December 8, 1993.

collect and analyze intelligence. The technical systems produced by this industrial base have been a key component of the strength that enables the United States to assert and protect its interests around the world.

Unfortunately, the intelligence industrial base has been and continues to be the victim of indifference and neglect. Since 1990, the five major companies that develop collection systems for the Intelligence Community have reduced their work force involved in these programs by nearly 75 percent, a loss of employment for about 20,000 people, and the number continues to rise. By comparison, in the "white world" (i.e., nonsecret) space business, the reduction has been approximately 20 percent, percentage-wise far less a reduction than that experienced by the Intelligence Community. So, although it is true that the community's budget has suffered cuts less severe percentage-wise than that of the Department of Defense, the community's contractors, its industrial base, have been severely hit.

The intelligence industrial base is part of the larger defense industrial base, which is also in the throes of a major upheaval. The source of this turmoil is the significant drop in defense spending. In the 1993 Defense Authorization Act, Congress directed the Department of Defense (DoD) to lead an interagency study of the defense technology and industrial base, including a financial analysis of key sectors and a study of areas where DoD is dependent on foreign producers. The report was due September 30, 1993, with recommendations derived from the study due March 31, 1994. But the draft report was rejected by senior Pentagon officials because it did not look closely enough at how the commercial sector (i.e., non–defense related industries) could function as an alternative to dwindling capacity in some portions of the defense industrial base.

Clearly, the system is not functioning properly. One of the problems is that there are too many government-imposed regulatory and bureaucratic barriers to the effective and efficient management of programs in industry. A notorious example was pointed out by Vice President Al Gore in his report "Reinventing Government." During the Persian Gulf War, the Air Force offered Motorola $10 million to supply 6,000 two-way portable radios. However, the company could not comply with federal cost accounting rules on such short notice. As a result, the air force had to ask the Japanese government to buy the radios and donate them to the United States. I agree with the vice president that when we have to look to a foreign government to save us from our own procurement regulations, especially during an acute international crisis, then reforms are needed.

The picture is not entirely bleak. There are a few officials, most prominently William J. Perry, who have indicated their interest and concern about the future of the defense industrial base. In an interview in *Aviation Week and Space Technology*, Dr. Perry, then deputy secretary of defense, stated that "Our [DoD's] role should be giving accurate and credible information to the defense contractor community on what their market is going to be for the next six or seven years."[1] The Department of Defense is taking steps, as it did with its "bottom-up" review of defense requirements, to provide the information necessary for companies doing business with DoD to make strategic plans with few illusions about the future. The point is that DoD is trying to rationalize its industrial base, while the Intelligence Community is not.

There is a view that if the critical DoD industrial base is protected, then the intelligence industrial base will be protected as well, but that assertion is not valid. In the DoD study, the industry that supports intelligence is not being treated separately from the defense industrial base. This overlooks the fact that the intelligence industrial base is very different from the defense industrial base in that its work and product are more specialized, which imposes "special" problems and cost burdens on the intelligence industrial base. If these differences are not recognized, and if the core competencies and critical technologies are not protected, then the nation runs the risk of losing these capabilities forever.

The Role of Intelligence

Any conversation on the role of intelligence starts by trying to answer the question: Where does intelligence fit in the post–Cold War world? Prior to the collapse of the Soviet Union, the role of intelligence in the security of the nation was clear. In the 1990s, the targets, and hence the role for intelligence, are uncertain. Redefining the role of intelligence and its value to national decision makers is a difficult and, as yet, unresolved task. Much of the intelligence debate has focused on the appropriate size of the organization and budget of a restructured Intelligence Community. The contractor world that supports it, however, has been ignored. Industry should not be immune from cuts or the downsizing that must occur, but industry must be downsized in a way that makes sense. This will only be done if it is understood that the industrial base that supports intelligence is as important as the government base.

As an example, the industrial base that supports the National Reconnaissance Office (NRO) is one of the country's most important national assets. Quite simply, without the creativity, energy, and skill resident in industry, there is no NRO. Yet, NRO decisions are made with little thought given to the people, capabilities, and technologies that support this element of the Intelligence Community. Thousands of industry employees who have supported the NRO for years have been laid off and their critical skills lost. Many of these people and skills have been lost forever as people choose to leave the industry altogether rather than face continued career uncertainty.

THE IMPORTANCE OF SATELLITE RECONNAISSANCE

How important is satellite reconnaissance to U.S. national security? Historically, this fundamental question was answered clearly and decisively with satellite reconnaissance being accorded the highest national priority in terms of resources, attention, and focus from the national security leadership. Today, however, it is unclear just how important those efforts are and how they rank against other intelligence programs and activities. Also, because NRO programs typically involve large expenditures of money when compared with programs of other elements within the community and, as a result, tend to stand out within the budget, they have become an easy "cash cow" to be milked to cover cuts made elsewhere in the intelligence budget. But, just because the trade-off is easy does not mean it is the right thing to do.

But, why should we care? After all, most satellite programs were designed and built to collect intelligence on the vast, closed areas of the former Soviet bloc. With the collapse of that target, what is the need? I believe that NRO programs are still vital to U.S. national security. Hardly a day goes by that there is not a new trouble spot or conflict somewhere in the world. Such conflicts might or might not expand into major regional or international crises, but as the world's only superpower, the United States can expect to be involved politically or diplomatically. Some of these crises will expand to the point where the United States will need to apply military force to achieve important security objectives. If U.S. military forces are to be committed, they will require a thorough understanding of the enemy forces they will face and the operational terrain. Satellite reconnaissance remains the fastest, most accurate, and easiest way to provide such information from anywhere in the world.

THE NEXT WAR

The worldwide coverage and rapid responsiveness offered by satellite reconnaissance are becoming increasingly compelling attributes. Both allies and enemies will be less constant, and the location and type of crisis will be much less predictable. Within the last dozen years there have been significant crises in the Falkland Islands, Grenada, Panama, Kuwait, Bosnia-Herzegovina, and Somalia. Most of those situations involved the commitment of U.S. military forces or resources, and yet how much attention was being paid to those areas even mere months before the respective crisis flared? Where will future crises originate— Pakistan, North Korea, Kashmir, Burundi? Regardless, only satellites provide the capability to cover the world today and be ready to focus on the crisis of tomorrow. There will also be instances where access to territory of interest to the United States is temporarily denied for political reasons or as a consequence of a crisis or conflict. A robust, flexible National Reconnaissance Program is the strongest capability to address such challenges.

More often than not, the crisis of the future will find the Intelligence Community playing "catch-up." Yet, the community will be trying to "catch up" with fewer, less capable systems; fewer, costlier weapons; and an industrial base (if current trends continue) that does not have the critical mass to respond quickly to unexpected needs. Because the community will be getting a late start and will be uncertain about its objectives in the early stages, there will be a high premium on information collected from satellites, as well as their ability to collect in a "panic." Much of this "panic" collection will be against those radars, communication systems, and electronic devices that are coming to dominate the battlefield. To support military operations effectively and provide maximum protection to U.S. forces, we must control the "high ground" of information. That goal is best achieved through satellite reconnaissance.

Human intelligence (HUMINT) collection has an important role to play in providing needed information to national policymakers; there are certain kinds of information that can be collected in no other way. But HUMINT is typically very labor intensive, requiring a considerable network of resources to support even a limited number of agents, and the time frame to acquire a new and reliable source of intelligence can be lengthy. HUMINT also requires an agent to "get in close" to the target in order to collect the relevant information, with all the attendant vulnerabilities. Satellites, on the other hand, offer the ultimate standoff capability, collecting the needed information from outer space without putting people, either U.S. intelligence officers or their agents, in harm's way. HUMINT, when focused appropriately, is invaluable, but it cannot serve as a substitute for timely, global satellite reconnaissance.

Ensuring the continued existence of a capable National Reconnaissance Program is in the U.S. national security interest. The challenge will be to maintain that system, and the industrial base that produces it, in the face of massive cuts in defense and intelligence spending. Most agree that some programs of the past deserve to be cut. The concern, however, is for the future. The international environment is changing ever more rapidly, and the national leadership will require an intelligence collection capability that can respond to those changes. As standing military forces are reduced, an even greater burden is placed on intelligence to guard against uncertainty and to give greater warning time of future crises. Cuts in intelligence that weaken that ability could be considered reckless.

Robbing Peter to Pay Paul (and Save Paul's Job)

As deep as the reductions to the Intelligence Community have been, the cuts have fallen disproportionately on the investment accounts of research, development, and procurement. Organizationally, those cuts have hit hard at the NRO. While it is relatively easy to discuss the NRO and understand it in this context, all the community's research and development (R&D) and procurement accounts have been similarly cut for the same reason. So, across the board, one must ask, "Why?" I believe it is because within the National Foreign Intelligence Program (NFIP) there is a bureaucratic imperative to protect within the community the civilian manpower growth of the past two decades, even as the military cuts its force structure and industry proceeds with massive lay-offs. Any new initiative is held hostage to maintaining base programs, which form a cocoon around the manpower growth of the past.

The vast manpower growth in the Intelligence Community needs serious review. It is no longer acceptable to cut the R&D and procurement accounts, and put the onus on industry to make the personnel reductions, rather than consider a "reduction in force" across the NFIP. Certainly there are reductions to the procurement accounts that make sense, but they should be made because the programs are no longer needed, not to protect Intelligence Community manpower. The following example is instructive. The National Security Agency (NSA), in an effort to protect its civilian employees, has started an aggressive plan to bring work "in-house" and reduce the amount of business it does with industry. In October 1993, a senior NSA official stated that in the past contractors enjoyed 85 percent of NSA's total business, but today it is about a fifty-fifty split between contractors and in-house personnel.

Most observers believe that the ratio will continue to decline during the next few years with less and less work going to industry. The NSA official thought, however, that the pendulum would swing back the other way over time. That may be true, but how much capability within industry will be lost, never to be retrieved? More important, how much technology needed for the future will never be developed or invented because of lack of government business? Moreover, past experience demonstrates that the government can neither match nor maintain the technical expertise that industry counts as one of its greatest assets.

Preserving Unique Programs

To maintain a strong satellite reconnaissance program, steps must be taken to help sustain the unique industry capabilities that make those programs possible. The Defense Department is already moving ahead to preserve what are referred to as "defense-unique" programs: that is, maintaining capabilities for which there are no commercial equivalents, such as nuclear submarines, armored vehicles, and fighter/attack aircraft. DoD is limiting its efforts to special cases where, first, the technology is unique to the nation's defense; second, it is critical to defense; and third, it is not being supported in the private sector in any way. Those are valid criteria, and the exact same effort needs to be undertaken within both the National Reconnaissance Program and the rest of the Intelligence Community.

There is an entire class of technologies truly unique to NRO programs. If those technologies and suppliers are not protected and nurtured, the capabilities those technologies support will simply disappear. As in the case of defense programs, the Intelligence Community must develop some criteria to determine "intelligence-unique" technologies worthy of support. For example, the technologies should be spearheaded by NRO requirements, developed with NRO funding, be much more advanced than unclassified or DoD technologies, and be unlikely to receive funding from any other source. Examples of critical future technologies worthy of support are large deployable structures; large, lightweight optics; data compression algorithms; and multispectral focal planes.

In addition to critical technologies and the companies that supply them, there is also a need to preserve critical skills for the future. There will be a need for specific systems engineering skills such as system concept definition, data analysis/understanding, and architectural configuration development; cleared development engineers to handle antenna and feed design; and manufacturing integration and test personnel for areas such as optics and large antennas.

Where important and needed technologies are likely to be developed by other sources such as Advanced Research Projects Agency (ARPA), National Aeronautics and Space Administration (NASA), or commercially, then no National Reconnaissance Program funds should be used. But where there are no commercial or other governmental options, then an investment of intelligence resources would be advisable. To facilitate the protection of that technology, the Intelligence Community should also consider establishing "Centers of Excellence," where companies join together to work on specific programs and technology in order to sustain their expertise and business.

THE FUTURE IS NOW

The Intelligence Community must also reserve some resources to plan for the intelligence collection systems of tomorrow. Most of the systems now in orbit are based on technology developed in the late 1960s and 1970s. We are exploiting the fruits of investments made twenty years ago; my question is: Twenty years from now, what systems will we be using, and based on what R&D investment? Where are the technological breakthroughs, like electro-optics, going to come from if adequate funding for R&D is not provided in the near term?

The Intelligence Community cannot choose the critical technologies and skills or make investments of dwindling resources blindly; it must develop a strategic plan that identifies the top-level requirements of the future and then describes the core programs and activities needed to satisfy those requirements. The next step is for the NRO to decide how it can best meet those requirements and, most important, to articulate the competitive advantage of satellite collection versus other forms of collection in fulfilling those needs.

THE VALUE OF SATELLITE COLLECTION

The clear competitive advantage of the past—only satellites can penetrate "closed societies"—is largely gone. The most important contribution the NRO can make to the debate over apportioning intelligence resources is to articulate crisply and simply the competitive advantages (and disadvantages) of satellites compared with those of other forms of collection. In industry, this generally results in one or two fundamental strategies: you have a unique product that everybody wants, or you have the best value product on the market, that is, the product that has (in the customer's eyes) the highest quality for the most reasonable (not always the lowest) price.

For a long time, the NRO fit neatly into the first strategy. It provided a product that was unique, could not be obtained in any other way, and people were willing to pay to get it. Now, however, the National Reconnaissance Program actually fits into the second strategy—best value—which is much more difficult to determine and measure. The NRO can demonstrate quality: images that are of sufficient resolution to permit accurate interpretation and analysis. They can demonstrate quantity: so much area covered and reports issued. But the issue of determining best value remains daunting, especially when comparing satellite systems with other forms of collection.

There are historical examples of instances where intelligence made seminal contributions to U.S. national security, but how can they be assigned a value? What was it worth, in real dollars, to know that the Soviets were stationing offensive, nuclear-capable missiles in Cuba? What was, and still is, the value of being able to monitor the status of Soviet ICBM fields and missile test ranges for over thirty years? What price can be assigned to the information that Saddam's forces were still in place and facing forward as the left flank of the coalition's military force executed its pincer movement? These are but a few examples, ones that can be mentioned openly—there are also many occasions when intelligence collected from satellites was decisive, and yet the circumstances are and must remain classified.

"I'll Know It When I See It"

Analysis by anecdote is not a completely satisfactory methodology, but it is hard to imagine a better alternative. Too few guns, tanks, ships, or planes is a relatively straightforward matter to evaluate, but how do you assess too little intelligence? How many policies will fail, how many resources will be squandered, and how many lives will be lost if there is insufficient intelligence? There is no way to tell, before the fact. Perhaps as former Supreme Court Justice Potter Stewart defined pornography— "I know it when I see it"—you will know the value of intelligence when, for example, you look at the image. It is impossible to characterize the value and utility of information before it is received. The value of intelligence must be considered ultimately an issue of philosophy and history, not of engineering and accounting. There is one fundamental question: Can the president and the national leadership be adequately informed on the state of the world without the unique capabilities of satellite reconnaissance? I believe the answer to that question is a firm "no."

The discussion above does not mean that reductions are impossible. Redundancy, overlap, and waste in intelligence as in other areas of government should be reduced, but carefully and prudently. In the haste to make reductions, care must be taken to maintain the critical mass of skills and technology that make the U.S. satellite reconnaissance system possible and that will enable the Intelligence Community to address the issues and problems of both today and tomorrow. Some in Congress and elsewhere say to go ahead and cut the programs and technology—if they are needed in the future, we will simply pay to reconstitute the capability.

This logic is flawed. First, if the capability is cut, then it will not be available to address today's problems. Maybe that is a trade-off you are willing to make. Second, however, if you determine that you do need the capability in the future, it may well be unrecoverable because the people with the needed skills are no longer available and the companies and facilities no longer exist. There is also a third, more intangible, problem. Many capabilities have been developed over time, in an evolutionary process; how do you account for the capability that will never be developed or the invention that will never be made because the structure that supports those efforts is gone?

Besides regional and politico-military problems, the revolution in technology will pose its own challenges. For example, there are nearly forty major world suppliers of telecommunication systems, some of which have 20,000 channels using digitals pulse code modulation (PCM). Additionally, users have moved rapidly to assimilate new technologies, including facsimiles, spread spectrum, cellular telephone, electronic mail, computer-to-computer data transfers, fiber optics, and others. It will be up to the Intelligence Community and the industrial base that supports it to provide the wherewithal to recognize, collect, process, and disseminate information from these and other new technologies. Historically, the community has been up to the task, but can those capabilities, especially in the private sector, be maintained in the face of an unmanaged decline in resources?

It's Not Too Late—Yet

Is the intelligence industrial base doomed to extinction? The answer is: Not necessarily, but we are getting close. There is no guarantee that it will survive; just because it has thrived in the past does not mean that it will survive into the future. Until recently, the industrial base was taken for granted, even as it has been bled to maintain personnel levels elsewhere in the Intelligence Community. The good news is that it is not too late, although damage to the critical skills and technology base has been inflicted.

When will it be "too late"? If the present trend continues, there will come a time—be it next year or a decade from now—when the intelligence industrial base loses its coherence and effectiveness. There are some steps, however, that can be taken to reverse the negative trends and ensure a continued, vital technical industrial base to support the satellite reconnaissance program.

I have already suggested several steps that government should take to maintain the industrial base: the Intelligence Community should prepare a strategic plan describing what capabilities are needed and what technologies need protection; the NRO should state the comparative advantages of satellite programs; the Intelligence Community should define and implement criteria to determine which technologies and skills will receive exceptional support and set up Centers of Excellence to nurture that support; and the NRO should reserve some resources for advanced R&D and program development.

There are additional issues that should be addressed by the Intelligence Community. First, because there is less of a market for satellite reconnaissance systems in government, the government should allow contractors to market and sell certain of those systems to other countries, especially in the areas of imagery and remote sensing. The size of the potential market is unclear—estimates range from hundreds of millions of dollars per year to a few billion per year, according to *Space News*. Several companies, including Itek, Orbital Sciences, GDE, and Lockheed are actively exploring that market. At a hearing before the Senate Intelligence Committee on November 17, 1993, however, the Intelligence Community indicated that it was considering entering the market to sell satellite imagery in order to control its dissemination.

As the president of Itek said of the prospect of competing with the CIA to sell imagery, "It would be the death knell for a commercial imaging market." Frankly, it is time for the U.S. government to put up or shut up. In speech after speech, pronouncement after pronouncement, the government has claimed that economic competitiveness and support to the U.S. economy is one of its highest priorities. In March 1993, Secretary of State Warren Christopher gave a speech where he stated that the first pillar of foreign policy is that it "should serve the economic needs of the United States." In a September 1993 speech,

National Security Adviser Anthony Lake proposed a "strategy of enlargement," which would be rooted in the strengthening of the U.S. economy. More recently, Secretary Christopher testified to the Senate Foreign Relations Committee that "our national security is insepara- ble from our economic security." The point is obvious: you do not "serve the economic needs of the United States" by foreclosing a multimillion- or billion-dollar foreign market to U.S. firms, especially when there are foreign firms with competing systems and technology. Either clear away the obstacles so that U.S. firms can seize the market (and, at the same time, help to preserve the intelligence industrial base) or stop all the rhetoric about how important it is to help U.S. firms be competitive.

Second, the government should reduce the burden of security regu- lations and requirements, which impose considerable costs on contrac- tors and inhibit the accessibility of technology developed in government-funded programs to commercial users. Saving even a frac- tion of the millions of dollars spent now every year on security will be progress.

Third, it would be useful for the government to initiate a new "Team B" exercise to conduct a thorough analysis of the intelligence budget. The original Team B was a group of nongovernment experts estab- lished in 1976 at the urging of the President's Foreign Intelligence Advisory Board to conduct an independent assessment of Soviet mili- tary capabilities and intentions. It is as important today to take an inde- pendent look at the U.S. intelligence budget, including requirements, spending priorities, investment strategies, and R&D, as it was to look at Soviet military activities in 1976. It would serve the administration well to appoint a panel of respected, recognized, nongovernment experts knowledgeable about all aspects of intelligence to carry out a "bottom-up" review of the intelligence budget.

The intelligence industrial base, which has been the foundation for the nation's most advanced and capable intelligence collection system for over twenty-five years, is not necessarily "doomed" to extinction. However, it will not survive unless government and industry work together to face the problems posed by new budget stringencies and the resulting management challenges of the post–Cold War world.[2]

9

DENIAL AND DECEPTION: THE LESSONS OF IRAQ

David Kay

This chapter will provide a discussion of Iraq's deception and denial activities designed to cover its weapons programs. For analytical clarity, these activities have been separated into four separate, but overlapping, layers:[1] political, procurement/acquisition, facilities and activities, and inspections.

I would like to recall briefly what was discovered by the post–Persian Gulf War inspections in Iraq. First, we found an immense military production establishment that was producing or striving to produce a broad range of chemical, biological, and nuclear weapons, as well as missiles capable of delivering them. The nuclear program alone involved investments amounting to at least $10 billion. Second, we were surprised by the progress that Iraq had made toward obtaining nuclear explosive devices. At the time of the Gulf War, the Iraqis were probably only eighteen months away from their first crude nuclear device and no more than three to four years away from more advanced weapons. Third, the amount of foreign assistance and technology that fueled the Iraqi arms program was truly staggering.

Iraq is a prime example of the fallibility of international inspection and national intelligence when faced by a determined, clandestine proliferator.

On April 18, 1991, Iraq submitted to the United Nations Special Commission on Iraq (UNSCOM) and the International Atomic Energy Agency (IAEA) details of the quantities and locations of its chemical, biological, ballistic missile, and nuclear materials stockpiles. This listing, which was required by the terms of Security Council Resolution 687 and was designed to provide the baseline for the inspection activi-

This paper was first presented on May 3, 1994.

ties that were to dismantle Iraq's weapons of mass destruction, was signed by President Saddam Hussein and accompanied by a letter from Iraq's foreign minister, Ahmed Hussein. This declaration acknowledged nearly 10,000 nerve gas warheads, 1,000 tons of nerve and mustard gas, 1,500 chemical weapon bombs and shells, and 52 Scud missiles with 30 chemical and 23 conventional high-explosive warheads. Iraq, however, denied that it had nuclear materials that fell under the resolution or any biological weapons.

While this declaration was eye-opening with regard to the Iraqi chemical weapons stockpile and its acknowledgment of chemical warheads for Scuds, it was widely acknowledged at the time—and subsequently confirmed by on-site inspections—to be seriously misleading in the nuclear, biological, and missile fields. It was also soon discovered to be a serious misstatement of the size of the Iraqi chemical weapons arsenal as well. Rolf Ekeus, chairman of UNSCOM, on July 30, 1991, informed the U.N. Security Council that inspectors had already found four times more chemical weapons than the Iraqi government had declared (46,000 chemical shells as compared with 11,500 declared, and 3,000 tons of chemical agents as compared with 650 tons declared). By October 1991, inspectors had found 100,000 chemical shells and bombs—almost ten times the number initially declared.

On the nuclear front, the scale of deception and denial was even greater. Iraq's initial declaration (April 19, 1991) avowed that it had no proscribed nuclear materials. This was amended on April 27 to acknowledge that it did have 27.6 pounds of high enriched uranium, 22 pounds of low enriched uranium, and a peaceful nuclear research program centered on the Tuwaitha Nuclear Research Center. All this had been reported to the IAEA before the war. Subsequent inspections, however, found an altogether different program. Iraq in fact had, beginning in 1981, embarked on a clandestine uranium enrichment program using three different methods (electromagnetic isotope separation, the so-called Calutron method; chemical enrichment; and gaseous centrifuge enrichment). At the time of the invasion of Kuwait, it had begun the start-up for an industrial-scale enrichment process using Calutrons and had acquired the material, designs, and much of the equipment for 20,000 modern centrifuges. Design, component testing, and the construction of manufacturing facilities for actual bomb production were well advanced. It was subsequently determined that more than 20,000 people were employed in Iraq's clandestine nuclear weapons program.

Political

According to Dr. Jaffar dhia Jaffar, the scientific leader of the Iraqi nuclear weapons effort, in the wake of Israel's June 1981 successful attack on the Osirak research reactor, Iraq launched an internal review of the future course of its nuclear activities. This review concluded that a major effort should be made to develop a uranium enrichment capability and that this program should be clandestine while Iraq overtly complied with the terms of the Nuclear Non-Proliferation Treaty (NPT). In these internal deliberations, as described by Dr. Jaffar, the deciding factor in this decision was the desire of the military and security services not to attract any undue attention to Iraq's developing nuclear program. It was believed that any attention would complicate procurement and development efforts. The argument ran: "Let Israel believe it destroyed our nuclear capacity,[2] accept the sympathy being offered for this aggression, and proceed in secret with the program." If one accepts this account as broadly true of the internal Iraqi discussions in the autumn of 1981 as to how to proceed with its nuclear activities, then by its own admission the program was rooted in a fundamental deception as to Iraq's NPT undertaking.

Throughout the 1980s Iraq played an active role in the IAEA's various programs, welcomed agency staff to its Tuwaitha Nuclear Research Center, sought and received technical assistance, and was a frequent member of the agency's Board of Governors. Iraq was not a silent member of the IAEA, leading the demands for international condemnation of Israel's attack on its safeguarded reactor and pushing for international protection for peaceful nuclear facilities against military attack. Iraq repeatedly emphasized the peaceful and safeguarded nature of its nuclear facilities and contrasted its openness to inspection with Israel's refusal to sign the NPT.[3] Ironically, Iraq played a leading role on the board in 1985 in praising and ensuring the continuance and eventual expansion of a program to introduce more rigorous evaluation of IAEA programs. The ultimate irony is that Iraq's IAEA governor had, in fact, as chairman of the Iraq Atomic Energy Commission (IAEC), presided over the initiation and large expansion of Iraq's nuclear weapons program in the early 1980s.

The strength of the Iraqi denial and deception program is that it was anchored in a fact—the Israeli destruction of the Osirak nuclear reactor. Moreover, this reality was reinforced by the accompanying sympathy that this attack engendered in the West and the desire of those who carried out the Osirak attack, as well as those who admired the technical skills demonstrated in the attack, to believe that the attack had dealt a decisive blow to the Iraqi nuclear program. The prevailing view can be seen in a Congressional Research Service study at the time. The study, which concluded:

> Iraq's long term potential had been reduced by Israel's bombing of Iraq's large research reactor. The assistance which that reactor might have provided now will not be available until it is rebuilt. . . . It seems unlikely too that Iraq's own industries will be able to design and build a reprocessing plant, an enrichment plant, or a nuclear power station for many years to come. . . . [Any future undertaking would have to] be kept secret for several years so that other countries would not have an opportunity to take countermeasures. While the success of such an undertaking cannot be ruled out as impossible, it nonetheless appears to be improbable. In summary, Iraq's potential nuclear weapons capability at the outset of the 1990s would still be small, assuming that it does not get access to engineers and technicians experienced in the production of nuclear weapons materials.[4]

Outside the nuclear arena, throughout the 1980s, Iraq skillfully played on the fear in the West and on Iranian fundamentalism in the Persian Gulf region. Iraq's portrayal of itself as a secular bulwark against the wild mullahs of Tehran provided an effective rationale for its large arms buildup. The fact that much of this took place during the course of Iraq's war with Iran, when most Western governments provided assistance despite their professed neutrality (and often domestic legislative prohibitions against military assistance), provided a cloak against too close scrutiny of Iraq's arms buildup.

Procurement/Acquisition

The physical scale of Iraq's arms program is what has astounded most observers. The facilities were large, well designed, amply furnished with the latest technologies, and often constructed with foreign assistance. For the nuclear program alone it is easy to identify more than twenty-five major facilities. What is less clear is the multilayered deception efforts that Iraq applied to avoid the unmasking of this program as it was being assembled. These deception efforts consisted of, at least, nine major thrusts.[5]

COMPARTMENTALIZATION AND MULTIPLE
PROJECT CODES

Iraq's nuclear weapons program was heavily compartmentalized and managed through a complex system of multiple and shifting project codes. Not only did various elements of the project teams generally not know the total program, they often did not know the real purpose of their own work. Firms, international as well as indigenous Iraqi manufacturing facilities, would often be approached to manufacture components without being told the use that was to be made of these components. In the case of Iraqi manufacturing facilities, plans and material would be delivered by the IAEC with instructions to produce a set of components. After production was completed, the items and all scrap or unused material would be taken back by the IAEC. Many of the large pole magnets for the Calutrons were produced in Austria by a state-owned firm and then shipped to Iraq—half by trucks through Turkey and half by ship through Hamburg. The Austrians did not ask the purpose of the magnets and the Iraqis did not volunteer the information. Much the same story applies to the high-quality copper that was used to wrap the magnets. It was produced in Finland to Iraqi specifications and sent by ship to Iraq. In both these cases—and in many others—the Iraqis did not even have to go through the motions of creating a cover story with the operating rule of the commercial world being "don't ask, just sell."

Project codes, another example of good tradecraft, were an integral part of the Iraqi deception effort. Petrol Chemical Project 3 (PC-3), the overall project code for the Iraqi nuclear weapons program, became widely known after the Persian Gulf War, but that misses the reality of the Iraqi use of project codes. Iraq used multiple, constantly shifting, and overlapping codes for individual components of all of its arms program, and these numbered in the hundreds. It became clear during the course of the post–Gulf War inspections, where the codes were a constant source of confusion, that the codes had presented a real obstacle to national intelligence services trying to track the Iraqi program. There was more than one occasion during the course of an on-site inspection when several of the governments that were providing intelligence support to the inspections would openly disagree on which element of the Iraqi weapons program a particular code related to. It is important to remember that the codes were used not only for the Iraqi nuclear program but also for all of its most sensitive weapons programs.

During the inspections, the project codes were a nightmare as inspectors tried to relate documents, invoices, shipping crates, Iraqi declarations, and actual physical facilities. This relatively simple deception technique must have proven equally frustrating to analysts trying to decipher the Iraqi weapons program before the war.

MISDIRECTION AS TO PURCHASER AND END USE

Most export control regimens do not attempt to block all exports to a given country; rather, they try to control exports so that specific institutions, for example, the military, or other potentially harmful programs, such as chemical weapons programs, do not benefit. While there is a list of items related to nuclear weapons that the London Suppliers Guidelines decree should not be exported to non–nuclear weapons states, the bulk of exports fall into the uncertain category of dual-use items. A high-speed, computer numerically controlled machine tool may be used, for example, to produce truck engines for a civilian automotive industry or gas centrifuge rotors for a nuclear weapons program.[6] The more modern and industrialized the economy, the wider the possible permitted uses for almost any import. To further complicate matters, it is up to the importer to identify the user and uses for any imports, and to a lesser extent to the exporting firm or its agents to confirm these facts.[7] Very seldom are on-site checks made either before, or after, sales of dual-use items. All in all, the export control system is a system ripe for abuse and deception, and Iraq understood the weakness of national export control regimens.

During the course of the UN inspection after the Persian Gulf War, it became clear that the University of Baghdad, the Ministry of Industry, petrochemical projects, and many other seemingly innocent purchasers had been only shells for the Iraqi nuclear weapons program. Falsified end uses were routinely declared, and in most cases the stories did not have to be terribly clever because—until Iraq lost the Gulf War—they never had to withstand any type of check after the item was received in Iraq. This stratagem worked particularly well for Iraq during the 1980s because parallel with a clandestine weapons program there existed a very large conventional military program that, by and large, was not the subject of Western export controls, and a booming civilian economy based on Iraq's oil revenues and loans from Gulf states.

BUY-IN TO FOREIGN MANUFACTURERS

Iraq also used another deception strategy that is particularly hard to monitor in a world that places a premium on international freedom to trade and invest and, indeed, a world where governments compete to attract foreign investment. Iraq invested in legitimate foreign firms that either manufactured equipment useful for its clandestine weapons program or that could legitimately order such equipment purportedly for the firm's own use. The most publicized case of this type was the Iraqi acquisition of the British firm Matrix Churchill, a small, struggling machine tool producer that was facing severe financial problems in the mid-1980s. Iraqi investors were viewed as saviors coming to the rescue. Over the years, Matrix Churchill provided not only a valuable source for illegal exports of high-performance machine tools but also a useful cover for ordering products from other firms for later transshipment to Iraq.

MIDDLEMEN AND FRONT COMPANIES

In building up its weapons program, Iraq benefited from its ability to use a complex network of middlemen and front companies. Some of these were purely creatures of the Iraqi weapons program, but others were creations of smugglers, traders, and fast-buck artists that swarm to wherever there is money to be made. Modern electronic communications and the opening up of so many borders has made this a particularly powerful deception technique when money or material needs to move across borders without undue notice of its origin or destination. The Gulf region is particularly fertile ground for such operations as new wealth reinforces the long tradition of smuggling and avoiding government attention.

MULTIPLE PURCHASES

On first examining the Iraqi weapons program one is struck by how much the Iraqis spent procuring foreign material. This "shop until you drop" mentality had several origins. As a deception strategy it worked on a rather profound understanding of the way export controls are administered and how intelligence services interpret information. In seeking to purchase export control–sensitive items, Iraq often placed orders in quantities that were below the size that triggered controls. The Iraqis believed that this would avoid controls and, even if detected, would signal that their program was in the early stages of development and hence not of great concern. They also understood that the discovery of one procurement channel would most likely lead to a reaction of "we have caught them and covered that source" and not trigger an intensive search for other pathways to obtain the same item. Iraq learned early that an effective deception can be based on a defeat or a loss in its procurement efforts—much faster than "the victors" learned that every victory in stopping an illicit shipment contains the seeds for self-deception in curtailing other procurements.

Multiple purchases of the same items were also central to the very nature of the Iraqi nuclear weapons program. If correctly understood, it could have raised serious alarms about that program well before the Gulf War. Iraq was engaged in a crash program to acquire nuclear weapons, roughly modeled on the Manhattan Project of World War II. Research and development activities for uranium enrichment were running parallel with construction of large production facilities. For example, the large facility at Tarmiya (designed to produce highly enriched uranium using the electromagnetic isotope separation [EMIS] process) was constructed as Iraq built its first small EMIS machines. Similarly, a very large facility to produce thousands of gas centrifuges at Al-Furat was being constructed before Iraq had decided upon the ultimate design of the type of centrifuge to be built. In such a crash program—particularly where the government rules by terror—any material bottlenecks would have serious consequences. Iraqi officials attempted to ensure against such bottlenecks by multiple purchases on the theory that even if several procurements failed, the weapons program would go on unchecked. It was better, from the Iraqi perspective, to spend money for supplies that were not needed than to not have supplies when they were needed and have the program grind to a halt.

SYSTEM INTEGRATION IN IRAQ

Many of the equipment items required for the production of weapons of mass destruction and advanced conventional arms are legally exportable so long as they do not contain particular attachments, for example, laser alignment systems, flow-forming mandrels of the specific dimensions associated with gas centrifuge rotors, and so on. The principle involved is that without such attachments the equipment can only be used for tasks either associated with permitted military applications or civilian uses. Additionally it was believed that even if states like Iraq managed to obtain the restricted attachments separately they would be unable to successfully integrate them with the legally obtained parts to form the more capable equipment. The general assumption was that countries like Iraq lacked the system integration skills needed to merge research and development work on a process like Calutrons or centrifuges with the civil construction of a production facility, the equipment installation, and the process engineering—all of which are critical steps in making a uranium enrichment facility operational.

Iraq successfully exploited the weakness of these assumptions. Computer numerically controlled machine tools that could not be exported legally from the United States with laser alignment systems were exported without them only to be mated with them later in Western Europe and Iraq. Iraq also demonstrated considerable skill in project management and system integration, particularly in its EMIS program.

Systems integration is a powerful deception technique. The focus of collection efforts inevitably must be sharp enough to exclude most of the large trade and technology flows that go into even a mid-level industrializing economy, and yet most weapons programs are composed of a lot of very innocuous items, which take on their deadly character only when combined in very specific ways. If intelligence collection efforts are unable to detect the purpose of imports at their most vulnerable stage (i.e., when borders are being crossed), then a very heavy burden is placed on national technical collection efforts and human intelligence to detect the actual integration of these items into weapons production systems, which occurs mostly inside buildings in secured areas.

GOOD TRADECRAFT

Iraq applied a lot of good tradecraft to its efforts to disguise the clandestine weapons program. Invoices routinely had their supplier and banking transfer agent blacked out or completely cut out. Wooden shipping crates, as soon as they arrived in Iraq, had the shipper and destination blacked out or physically chipped out. Iraqi scientists who traveled abroad used false identity and travel documents. These techniques and similar ones identify, above and beyond the usual fog of analysis, the problems of detecting the true purpose, size, and state of development of the Iraqi programs.

COMPETITIVE COMMERCIAL NEGOTIATIONS

Iraq was able to use the strong desire of Western providers of technology to make sales both to conceal the true purposes of its efforts and to extract a considerable amount of proprietary information from Western companies without any compensation. A classic example of this is connected to Iraq's efforts to obtain technology for the chemical enrichment (Chemex) of uranium. There are two suppliers in the world of chemical enrichment technology: one is Japanese, the other French. In the mid-1980s Iraq initiated preliminary discussions with both and indicated a desire to acquire a uranium enrichment capability using the Chemex technique. After preliminary exploration, the Iraqis decided to concentrate on the French process. The inspection teams learned during the postwar inspections that a strong factor in Iraq's decision to abandon discussions with the Japanese was that the Japanese process required exotic resins that have few other uses, and Iraq was worried that the large-scale importation of such resins would signal the scale of its uranium enrichment program.

Iraq's negotiations with the French firm stretched out over several years. The course of these negotiations took on a familiar pattern. Iraq would indicate it needed only a little more technical information on which to make a decision; the French would reveal more proprietary data and the cycle would begin again. The French firm was particularly anxious to make a sale because the process had yet to find its first customer. Finally, after the French firm had revealed essentially all of the technical details concerning its Chemex process, Iraq announced that it had concluded that the process was too expensive and was abandoning all interests in pursuing it. The French believed that Iraq had given up on this process; Iraq started its own clandestine development of Chemex.

Many of the natural forces of the commercial world—competition among suppliers, protection of proprietary customer information, reluctance to admit that a deal has been lost, lack of a basic counterintelligence perspective in most commercial enterprises—can actually help a proliferator's deception effort.

LARGE INDUSTRIAL AND CONVENTIONAL MILITARY PROGRAMS

The scale of Iraq's industrial and conventional military programs—the conventional military program of the 1980s is estimated by Iraq to have cost $110 billion—made it almost impossible for any intelligence service to keep abreast of all the commercial discussions, imports of material and technology, and new construction that were under way and that might have some relevance to clandestine weapons capability. It would be foolish to assert that the conventional military program and the large civil economy investments were part of an Iraqi deception effort. However, it would be equally foolish to miss the fact that these investments aided the deception effort. In all but a few countries, such as the isolated North Korean regime, it is essential to recognize that the "noise" of normal commercial activities and conventional military programs may provide ready cover for clandestine programs. This is particularly true for chemical, biological, and missile programs, which share many of the characteristics of innocent undertakings.

Facilities and Activities

Just as deception played a great role in Iraq's purchasing and acquisition efforts, deception also played a significant role in Iraq's attempts to conceal the actual purposes of facilities and activities.

FACILITIES

Iraq understood the deception advantage of hiding a clandestine program in plain sight. Its major declared nuclear research center at Al Tuwaitha was also the initial center of Iraq's clandestine nuclear program. Al Tuwaitha was visited every six months by IAEA safeguard inspectors who announced, at the conclusions of such visits, that there was no sign of diversions of nuclear material. The inspectors gave a general clean bill of health to the facility; two deputy director generals of the IAEA and many staff members visited Al Tuwaitha, all of whom indicated that they saw no suspicious activity. In addition, selected Western scientists were invited to the facility. This openness was carefully controlled. The IAEA inspectors were only allowed to visit portions of three of the almost one hundred buildings at Al Tuwaitha, and the IAEA staff and Western scientists were guided through chosen labs and held their meetings in the center's conference building. While the restrictions on the movements of these visitors could have been viewed as a warning sign, they were not recognized as such by most of the visitors at the time. The safeguard inspectors were routinely subjected to such restrictions in almost every country they visited, and it is only since the Persian Gulf War that this has begun to slowly change. The other visitors were controlled with "busy" schedules, generous hospitality, and cultural tourism. One of the IAEA deputy director generals, a former defense official of an Asian country, assured me prior to my first inspection in Iraq that he had toured all of Al Tuwaitha and that there was nothing at all there related to uranium enrichment or a weapons program. While there was no doubt self-delusion involved in some of the assessments of the peaceful nature of Al Tuwaitha, Iraq deserves credit for the skill with which it controlled visitors, as well as for the clever layout of the facility itself. The placement of the buildings, the visual screening provided by trees, and a careful routing of the internal road system made it very difficult for any visitor without access to overhead intelligence to accurately understand the size of the center and the relationship of buildings.

UNDERSTANDING THE PHOTOINTERPRETERS/ ANALYSTS ALGORITHMS

The Iraqis demonstrated on numerous occasions their accurate understanding of the limitations of U.S. technical collection systems and of how data gathered by such systems were interpreted.

The catalogue of techniques used by the Iraqis to thwart these systems includes construction of buildings within buildings (Tuwaitha); deliberately making buildings designed to the same plans and for the same purposes look different (Ash Sharqat and Tarmiya); hiding power and water feeds to mislead as to facility use (Tarmiya); disguising operational state (Al Atheer); diminishing value of a facility by apparent low security and lack of defenses (Tarmiya); severely reducing off-site emissions (Tuwaitha and Tarmiya); moving critical pieces of equipment at night; and dispersing and placing facilities underground.

All of these techniques, and others, vastly complicated the job of understanding the nature of the Iraqi nuclear weapons program. At the same time, they provide at least a partial answer as to how a program so large could have been so incompletely understood by the world's intelligence communities.

PERSONNEL

The Iraqi nuclear program involved at least 20,000 personnel, many of whom had training and contacts abroad. This was a potentially large source of leakage of information on the aims and direction of these activities. Iraq faced this problem and adopted a series of deception practices designed to limit any such loss.

First, Iraq managed its flow of personnel to ensure that students were not sent to the same universities and countries. This had several advantages. Training in most scientific disciplines follows different approaches in different countries and provides access to different networks of information. This is particularly true in the various engineering and science disciplines that most concern a nuclear weapons program. For example, in the United States Iraqis could not learn about the operations and techniques involved in focusing X-rays, because that information is classified. However, this information could be obtained in Great Britain, Germany, or Japan, where it was part of the general physics literature. By dispersing students, Iraq also made it more difficult for any one country to fully appreciate the breadth of technical skills being built up in Iraq. And this dispersal of students made it more difficult to track individual Iraqi scientists. Concerns with privacy and academic freedom, as well as being a low collection priority, has meant that few countries collect systematic data on foreign students and seldom share it with other countries. For example, although one senior Iraqi scientist's entire university training, from undergraduate to doctorate, had been in the United States, and his first job had been at a U.S. nuclear power plant, the Intelligence Community was unable to come up with any data or pictures on this key individual.

Second, Iraq moved from an almost total dependence upon foreign training in the 1970s to almost totally indigenous undergraduate and master's level training, and even credible doctorate-level training in some fields, in the 1980s. This vastly complicated the task of accurately addessing the talent and direction of Iraq's scientific infrastructure. It became clear during examination of Iraqi weapons laboratories that they kept abreast of the latest scientific work in English, French, Russian and, German. By contrast, few resources seemed to have been devoted in the West to tracking the theses and other work being produced in Iraqi institutions.

Third, Iraq purposely followed strategies designed to ensure that the purposes of scientific visits would not be easily discerned. False names and passports were used, the purpose of visits and requests for training were misidentified to sound innocuous, and the employer was misidentified to avoid any connection with the IAEC or the military.

A final barrier to leakage of information from the staff of the nuclear program was a set of fringe benefits and punishments that discouraged those who knew important details of the Iraqi program from divulging information. First, the staff of the IAEC received an automatic draft exemption from the Iraqi army—and this was at the time of the bloody Iran-Iraq war. Second, salaries were consistently kept above the announced government salary scale. Other benefits, including financial bonuses and access to travel and foreign goods, were also substantial. Although the benefits were good, the "severance package" was horrible in its brutality. Those who attempted to defect and were caught, or those who showed any sign of lack of loyalty to the regime—including not reporting on family members who were disloyal—were brutally executed, in many cases, in front of their families.

Inspections

As a member of the NPT, Iraq was subject prior to the Gulf War to routine—roughly once every six months—IAEA safeguard inspections of its declared nuclear material. These inspections took place at Tuwaitha Nuclear Research Center—the only site that Iraq declared as having nuclear materials. Because Tuwaitha was the initial center for Iraq's clandestine nuclear program, it was important both that these inspections not inadvertently stumble upon weapons activities and also that Iraq appear to be fully cooperating with the IAEA. Inspections were also the key to the postwar unraveling of Iraq's program for development of weapons of mass destruction. In both the prewar and postwar phases, deception and denial activities played a significant role in trying to limit the utility of inspections. The deception and denial activities can be separated into six major thrusts.

FAT AND HAPPY INSPECTORS

Under the IAEA safeguard procedures, a country is allowed to designate the inspectors that it will accept to inspect its facilities. This provision, which had originally been insisted upon by some Western European states who desired to limit what they thought would be commercial espionage by Japanese-national inspectors, turned out to be a major brake on the integrity and efficiency of the safeguard system. Iraq consistently accepted only inspectors from the then-Soviet Union, East bloc allies, and Africa. Not only were Soviet inspectors presumed to be more controllable, given their nation's close military arrangements with Iraq, but they also were the beneficiaries of a quirk in the IAEA pay system that made inspection missions highly profitable. Soviet inspectors had to turn over their salaries to their government, which kept most of it to cover the cost of providing their housing in Vienna and "other expenses" and deposited the balance into a ruble account of no use to the inspectors while in the West. But there was one exception. Soviet inspectors were allowed to retain all of their per diem allowance received while on official travel. Thus, the less a Soviet inspector spent on lodging and food while on inspection missions, the more he had in hard currency to spend on goods unobtainable at home. Iraq was a particularly profitable mission for inspectors because the official conversion rate of the Iraqi pound before the Gulf War was artificially high, and consequently the UN per diem rate was substantial.

Soviet, East bloc, and many inspectors from the developing world were widely known to seek out the cheapest available accommodations and to enjoy official entertainment as a money-saving strategy. The Iraqis exploited this desire by providing cheap accommodations, at a considerable distance from the nuclear research center at Tuwaitha, and hosting late evening official dinners for inspectors. The result was that the inspectors were often weary, but happy at the money that they were saving and not inclined to do more than the limited and minimal official inspection tasks. To do more would have been to risk that Iraq would refuse to accept an inspector with the consequent loss for the inspector of valuable income.

During the first round of postwar inspections, the Iraqi authorities continued to try to delay and reduce the coverage of inspections by suggesting long and pleasant lunches, late dinners, and sightseeing visits to some of the interesting archeological sites several hours from Baghdad.

THREATS AND INTIMIDATION

During the postwar inspections, Iraq moved from positive inducements for easy inspections to physical and verbal threats and intimidation. Inspectors were awakened with telephone threats; obscene and threatening notes were slipped under hotel doors; hotel rooms were ransacked; verbal abuse on the street and at inspection sites became common; and on several occasions inspectors were physically attacked by outraged Iraqi "civilians," UN vehicles were bombed and tires slashed, and shots were fired over the heads of inspectors as they photographed Iraq's secret uranium enrichment equipment. The Iraqi authorities made it clear to UN and IAEA authorities which inspectors they found acceptable and which they desired not be sent to Iraq again. Formal letters of censure were sent by Iraq to the UN and the IAEA concerning some inspectors, and the Iraqis demanded that no Americans be allowed to lead inspection missions. It would be easy to dismiss most of this except that it did have an impact. For a while, Americans were not put in charge of missions and some inspectors reported that the IAEA leadership sought to soften the tone of its inspection presence.

MONITOR INSPECTORS AND PROCEDURES

Both before the war and during the postwar inspections, Iraq carefully monitored inspection procedures and adapted its deception activities accordingly. During the course of the fourth postwar inspection, the Iraqi national safeguard head—who was responsible for ensuring that national nuclear safeguards were applied—appeared and during the course of a four-hour meeting repeatedly bragged that he had applied everything he had learned from his earlier job as an IAEA safeguards inspector to ensure that his former IAEA colleagues did not detect the clandestine nuclear weapons program during their routine inspections. In great detail he described the dual books, limited access, keep-the-inspectors-happy strategy that Iraq had used.

During the postwar inspections, the Iraqis engaged in active bugging of the hotel, meeting rooms, and office spaces used by the IAEA and the UN. Local drivers and maintenance personnel often admitted that they reported—per the direction of Iraqi security authorities—daily on inspectors' activities. Neither the UN nor the IAEA provided their staff with any training in counterintelligence or communications security. Although vigorous attempts were made to show how such lapses were seriously hindering effective inspections—and several embarrassing cases where IAEA "surprise" inspections became known in advance—this remained an uphill battle against an entrenched mindset that failed to recognize the problem.

MISDIRECTION

The inspections after the war began with the old IAEA cooperative inspection model of asking the Iraqi authorities to take the inspectors where they wanted to go. During the first inspection Iraq used this routine to keep the inspectors away from sensitive sites. When this same tactic was tried during the second inspection, the inspectors responded by using handheld Global Positioning System (GPS) instruments and current intelligence data, including very accurate line drawings of Iraqi weapons sites. This hindered but did not stop Iraq's effort to misdirect the inspection effort at every stage.

COVER STORIES

Cover stories were another form of misdirection. Some of the cover stories that Iraq used to attempt to shield its clandestine program were quite elaborate. Tarmiya, one large site of Iraq's massive uranium enrichment effort, was said to be only a high-voltage transformer testing facility; the Palm building where much of the testing for the Iraqi Calutrons was done was only an air force truck repair and radar testing facility; the first Calutrons seen by inspectors were only scientific mass spectrometers, and on and on. Some cover stories were clever and required a great deal of scientific and inspection effort to penetrate; some may have never been identified as false.

When cover stories were penetrated, Iraq would abandon them in a controlled fashion that tried to indicate that minimal disclosure was complete disclosure. The first admitted separation of plutonium was said to be the only separation—until another larger separation was uncovered by inspectors. Denial of any centrifuge activity was followed finally by an admission of a small centrifuge enrichment program, which was said to be all there was—until a massive program was discovered by inspectors. Even a penetrated cover story served a useful purpose of allowing another opportunity for Iraq to claim that it had turned over a new leaf and was making a full and final disclosure of its secret activities. More than ten such "full and complete" disclosures have been made, and yet the UN remains unconvinced that the various clandestine programs have been fully disclosed.

Destroy/Shield

Before the first inspectors entered Iraq after the war and later when the inspectors began to close in on important elements of the Iraqi nuclear program, Iraq began to systematically destroy facilities so that their true purpose and state of development could not be identified. At the Tuwaitha nuclear research center, the large Calutron test facility (80 by 120 meters) had escaped all damage from the coalition bombing but it was completely leveled by Iraq and covered with dirt before the first UN inspector entered the site; laser and centrifuge test facilities (also at Tuwaitha) were similarly destroyed leaving uncertainty as to how much progress Iraq had made with these programs. In the north, near Mosul, at Al Jesira where UCl_4 and UF_6 were produced to feed the uranium enrichment program, two substantial buildings were leveled by Iraq and one was doused with thick layers of epoxy paint to make all sampling efforts impossible.

One reason that many of the early inspections in Iraq became confrontational is that Iraq made it impossible to obtain easy answers as to how far its program had proceeded. Faced with a massive denial effort and forceful deception, inspectors had little choice but to adopt a search strategy that would take account of Iraq's moves. This required the inspectors to move to sites without prior notice, go after documents, make greater use of technical intelligence methods, and assert a healthy skepticism of all Iraqi claims.

The Future of Deception and Denial in Shielding Clandestine Nuclear Programs

There is an important question that remains in the wake of the discoveries of the extent of the Iraqi clandestine weapons programs and the role that organized denial and deception played in shielding these programs: Is Iraq only an exceptional case or is it a prologue to a period in which denial and deception activities gain even greater importance in shielding clandestine programs? Although this question deserves more systematic treatment than can be provided here, there are a number of factors that point to a growing availability of deception capabilities to states that have clandestine operations to shield.

First, it must be acknowledged that the necessary technical ability to conduct deception operations is spreading widely from bastions of military power in the West and the East. The technical manuals and personnel of the former Soviet bloc are available at modest cost. Beyond that, the technology revolution that is driving Western economies is making available deception techniques that are better than the best available at the height of the Cold War. Environmental control technologies today are capable of reducing off-site emissions to levels that are undetectable except by the most sensitive analytical methods. Government efforts to preserve the environment are driving these techniques into the marketplace and lowering their cost. Even the world of entertainment, assisted by widely available computer technology, is introducing techniques of deception that with little additional effort can serve a clandestine weapons program.

Second, the scale of the Iraqi program—large, expensive, and a dedicated weapons cycle—may turn out to be a thing of the past and representative of the character of future weapons programs. The industrial base of many middle-sized developing countries is such that a modest chemical and biological weapons program could be easily accommodated within their open civilian infrastructure, without the construction of significant dedicated facilities. Even in the nuclear world, the civilian nuclear infrastructure of countries such as Taiwan and the Republic of Korea, and most of Western Europe could easily and quickly produce a small number of crude nuclear weapons with little new construction and few warning signatures. The 1990s mark the beginning of a period of virtual proliferation where capabilities are generally available and the real question becomes one of motivation and intentions. In such an environment the task of intelligence collection and analysis becomes harder as the requirements for denial and deception become easier.

10

ANGLETON'S WORLD: LESSONS FOR U.S. COUNTERINTELLIGENCE

William Hood

There has probably been as much written about James Angleton as about anyone who has served in the CIA except, perhaps, Allen Dulles. Some of this literature is straight. Unfortunately, however, much of what may come to pass as history is unfair not only to James Angleton and the DCIs for whom he worked and who supported him, but to the agency, and to history itself.

It is not my purpose to argue the various operations and cases that have been so widely tossed about in recent intelligence literature. The only way anyone can plausibly discuss a secret operation is after a thorough study of the files. It is the nature of the intelligence business that even if all the files were read, a single cable arriving the following day could necessitate a reevaluation of all the preceding material. The most that can be done here is to suggest some of the things that may have influenced Angleton's approach to his work and to try to put some of that work into focus.

James Angleton was born in 1917 in Boise, Idaho. In the years before World War II he went with his family to Italy where his father, a well-known American businessman, represented an American company. Angleton attended an English public school, Malvern College, traveled in Europe on vacation, and worked one summer in an automobile factory in France. He returned to the United States and graduated from Yale in 1940. As Professor Robin Winks learned, Angleton was not much of a scholar, but he was one of the founding fathers of *Furioso*, a remarkable undergraduate literary journal. Edward Applewhite, a Yale classmate, recalled that Angleton's knowledge of modern poetry was such that Professor F. S. C. Northrop credited his discus-

This paper was first presented on September 14, 1993.

sions of poetry with Angleton as having inspired the analysis of art that is at the heart of the professor's major book, an unusual level of credit to be given to an undergraduate by a well-known academic. After Yale, Angleton completed more than a year at Harvard Law School before entering the U.S. Army as a private in 1943.

Some critics have ascribed significance to Angleton's middle name, Jesus, and have suggested that because it reflected his mother's Mexican origin, it embarrassed him. A simpler explanation of why Angleton abandoned his middle name is suggested by the experience of a mutual friend, and former colleague, who entered another English public school. In his first interview with the headmaster, the boy was advised to anglicize the pronunciation of his name. He took this advice, retaining the anglicized pronunciation until he retired from the Central Intelligence Agency (CIA) and returned to his family's wine business.

After completing basic training in 1943, Angleton had a choice between Judge Advocate Officer Candidate School (OCS) or a job in the Office of Strategic Services (OSS). Despite his interest in law, Angleton chose the new and more exciting venture. After OSS training in Washington, D.C., Angleton was posted to London, working in X-2, the counterintelligence arm of OSS. Within a few weeks, he took over the Italian desk in the X-2 headquarters on Ryder Street.

X-2 remains the least well known, least publicized component of OSS, and few of the people most vocal about Angleton have shown much knowledge of it. Angleton's experience in X-2 is at the root of his intelligence career, and some knowledge of that organization is essential to understand him. X-2 was the only component of OSS that had sustained access to a significant portion of the ULTRA product, which included deciphered German intelligence messages. The fact that ULTRA was one of the most tightly held secrets of the war shaped every aspect of X-2. Clearance for access to ULTRA traffic was granted on a very strictly interpreted need-to-know basis. Neither rank nor seniority had much to do with that determination.

Once cleared for access to ULTRA, the working levels of X-2 personnel were almost totally isolated from the other components of OSS in London, and in the European theater of operations. Even in the X-2 headquarters in Washington, only a few of the most senior officers were cleared. In addition, the only place one could be "indoctrinated" (the MI-6/X-2 term for having been cleared for ULTRA) was in London. The British controlled all access to ULTRA material, and had to approve the security of any American who was indoctrinated.

Because of ULTRA, X-2 units operating in the field had private communications with the London headquarters. This traffic was handled by the X-2 communications staff and seen only by indoctrinated X-2 personnel.

I was in uniform when I joined OSS in London, by way of the armored force and military intelligence. After signing a half-dozen forms and oaths at OSS headquarters on Grosvenor Street, I was told I was assigned to X-2. That sounded appropriately mysterious, and after a considerable wait, I asked where I was to report. This provoked a huddled conference in the corner of the personnel offices. There was another wait until a spokesman was selected to inform me that I could not be told where I was to report. For a mad moment I thought this was a test. If I could not discover where I was to work, I clearly was not the man for such an elite outfit. As it turned out, I was eventually told to follow an armed officer courier on his afternoon patrol from Grosvenor Street to the inner sanctum.

This is a true story. Obviously, many OSS officers knew where the Ryder Street offices were and who worked there, but the incident was a near perfect illustration of the sound, but sometimes ludicrous, aspects of secrecy. As such, it made a lasting impression on me, as it certainly must have on young Angleton.

X-2 worked more closely with the British than any other OSS component that I know about. We shared the Ryder Street premises with components of both MI-6 and MI-5—separate offices, but in the same building. There were a few English secretaries in some of the X-2 offices, but no American secretaries in the British shop.

These were counterintelligence operations staffs engaged in the extremely sensitive supervision of the penetrations of German and Italian intelligence, exploiting double agents, apprehending new agents, and rendering support to the deception operations that protected every important military initiative in the theater.

One of the X-2 functions was to clear all OSS agent recruitments, which involved checking the identities of prospective agents against ULTRA holdings and usually consulting other less sensitive British files. It should be noted that the OSS had no counterintelligence files when it began work.

The clearance procedure was not without serious problems. OSS operatives with no knowledge of ULTRA and far removed from London could see little reason to ask such a distant headquarters for approval to approach a low-level agent. A few rugged individualists (of the "just tell me what I'm supposed to do and let me get on with it" school) sometimes refused to cooperate at all; others were reluctant to allow the British a glimpse of their activity. The problem intensified when there were no collateral data to support the ULTRA information. To protect ULTRA, some clearances for would-be agents had to be denied on grounds too flimsy to satisfy some of the more aggressive OSS field operatives.

X-2 also conducted more routine research into the organization, personnel, and practices of Axis intelligence on the basis of data from ULTRA and masked by material from less highly classified sources—prisoner of war interrogations, double agents, military sources, and the various allied services. (When Germany surrendered and Walter Schellenberg, chief of Amt VI, RSHA—the Nazi foreign intelligence service—was brought to the United Kingdom for interrogation, he was shown a chart of his service that had been drafted by X-2 London. After studying the chart for some time SS Standartenfuehrer Schellenberg admitted ruefully that it was clear his interrogators knew more details of his organization than he did.)

In sum, X-2 came to signify total security, near total compartmentation, private communications open only on a very strictly interpreted need-to-know basis, agent clearance responsibility; a special relationship with the British, and above all, exclusive access to a superior source. The access to this source was the basis for X-2's position. The source was not a single superior agent, or even a stable of such agents, but a source so important that not even its existence could be disclosed.

In my opinion, this experience and the overall excellence of X-2 had a decisive impact on Angleton's view of how counterintelligence should be conducted and organized, and traces of this are apparent throughout his career.

It is difficult to recreate the atmosphere that existed at the time Angleton was in London and Italy. However obvious it may seem to those who were involved, the driving factor was—in the often repeated phrase of the time—"There's a war on." Until early 1944 very few were entirely sure how or when the war would end. In some informed quarters there was still concern about Hitler's secret weapons. Those serving in a headquarters were very much aware that comrades and friends at the front were being shot at, and that those behind the enemy lines were in even greater peril. This knowledge fueled the work habits and, to a degree, limited other activity.

Although accepted by many as fact, it is not true that Angleton was tutored in counterintelligence by Kim Philby. At the time they both served in the United Kingdom, Philby was responsible for the Iberian Peninsula. Angleton's activity in London was focused on Italy, and on learning all he could about what he called "the business." There was very little, if any, need for liaison between the Italian and Iberian desks. I was never aware of any tutorial relationship between any X-2 people and their British opposite numbers at that time.

In addition, Philby was heavily occupied with his own more immediate activities—funneling intelligence and counterintelligence of the highest order to Moscow, doing his MI-6 job well enough to ensure his reputation and future in the British service, and protecting his own security. Such time as Philby had to flesh out the Russian files on OSS personnel might more plausibly have been devoted to the more senior staff. Eventually commissioned as a lieutenant, Angleton was less important than Norman Pearson and other senior X-2 officers. For example, Winfield Scott, who had the more important German/Swiss/Austrian desks, was considerably senior to Angleton and remained in London as chief of station after the war. If in 1944 and early 1945 Philby foresaw the creation of the CIA and Angleton's role in it, he was indeed farsighted. But there can be no doubt that by the time Philby was assigned to Washington in 1949 Angleton was a prime target for cultivation.

Angleton has been cited as having "given away the store" in his dealings with Philby. Despite the fact that this is taken as gospel, and similar judgments repeated in much of the literature, I have never seen any reference to exactly what he may have given away, or indeed what Angleton may have learned from Philby. Curiously, almost nothing has been written about Philby's strenuous cultivation of other CIA personnel, many of them senior to Angleton, others less experienced in dealing with wily liaison officers, and all working in areas of considerable interest to Soviet intelligence. Nor has much been written about Philby's cultivation of senior Federal Bureau of Investigation (FBI) personnel. Liaison with the bureau was also an important part of Philby's work for both the British and the Soviets, as well as for his own protection.

The Albanian operation is sometimes mentioned in this context, but even the open literature argues that this sad activity was compromised from the outset, and was known to Philby in detail long before he left England for his post in Washington. If the Albanian operation was compromised in its early stages, it seems extremely doubtful that the KGB would have bothered an agent as sensitive as Philby for details.

Angleton has sometimes been described as an anglophile. This may be, but, in my view, time spent attending a British public school at that time did not necessarily lead to anglophilia any more than Angleton's experience in his early days in X-2 in Italy might have increased such an attitude.

Many of those who worked closely with the British during the war came away with the clear—and understandable—impression that the British considered their own interests first and always, and that it was up to the United States to protect its own equities. Angleton coped with this much more skillfully than some early American operatives.

By 1945, British intelligence policy was being shaped for the postwar world. One objective was to establish a kind of liaison hegemony in Europe and elsewhere. By the time Angleton got to Italy, X-2 was in a bruising tussle with its British opposite numbers. Angleton won the fight in Italy; OSS lost it in some other areas.

By the time he was named Chief X-2 Italy, Angleton had attracted General Donovan's attention, who was also thinking about postwar intelligence. In 1947, when Angleton left Italy, the Italian station was recognized as one of the models for stations to come, and was ranked as high as Dulles's Swiss station.

In Washington, Angleton served briefly as personal assistant to Director of Central Intelligence (DCI) Admiral Hillenkoetter, moving from that assignment to a key position in what became known as the Directorate of Operations (DO).

It should be remembered that most OSS procedures were improvised under the pressure of World War II. These worked adequately in the circumstances, but could scarcely be expected to serve what had become an established government agency. After the passage of the 1947 legislation establishing the CIA there was much to be done to formalize procedures for the most routine activities—relations with other government offices, the civil service, Department of State, Department of Defense, the FBI, Bureau of the Budget—and in the process, to protect the equities and independence of an agency unlike any that had ever existed in Washington.

Angleton's work in this area reflected his lifelong interest in the law. He was active in establishing and codifying liaison procedures and practices, agent clearance procedures, operational reporting requirements, and other practices and disciplines that are now taken for granted within the CIA.

Writing on secret intelligence operations presents more problems than most outsiders appear to realize. Until recently the absence of original documents available for study meant that research depended heavily on the not necessarily accurate news reports of compromised secret activity, defector accounts, old-boy memoirs, interviews with former insiders, congressional testimony, and earlier books based on all of the above. Thus many of the errors in the early literature are repeated unchallenged until they have attained the stature of truth, such as Angleton being tutored by Philby, Angleton giving away the store, the mad mole hunter, the daffy paranoid, and on and on.

In the absence of documents, the problem of source evaluation becomes critical—not necessarily impossible, but difficult. One recent author spoke enthusiastically of his sources as an elite group, dedicated, hardworking, the finest officers in the agency; but from inside the agency, they were not much different from everyone else—some were outstanding officers, others perhaps average.

No Washington sportswriter would base his evaluation of the Redskins exclusively on the team members' opinions of one another and the team itself. A wise writer might try to factor in the locker room comments of the Dallas Cowboys as well. In the absence of an objective standard of performance, such as the final score in the Super Bowl, the problem of evaluating inside comments becomes even more critical. The New York City Ballet's dressing room remarks on the Bolshoi are fascinating for an outsider, but in my experience are not without an unmistakably subjective flavor.

What is true of ballplayers and the ballet—and perhaps even the faculties at Yale and Harvard—is equally true of secret intelligence. From area to area, from function to function, perhaps even from generation to generation, jealousy, resentment, and sometimes simple self-serving pettiness flavor evaluations of performance.

Many writers slip swiftly past the fact that Angleton enjoyed the confidence and respect of an impressive list of DCIs for whom he worked. Hillenkoetter, Dulles, Smith, McCone, Helms, and Schlesinger were all strong supporters, and Angleton could not have made his way with these men by anything but exceptional performance.

The author of one recent book erroneously dismissed as extraneous Angleton's relationship with Israel. During memorial services for Angleton in Israel, two monuments were dedicated, huge stones with bronze plaques engraved in English and Hebrew. One is on a hillside a few miles from Jerusalem and the scene of a major battle in the early days. The other is in a park near the King David Hotel in Jerusalem. The ceremonies were attended by the surviving chiefs of Israeli intelligence and various public figures. A future prime minister dedicated one monument. I know of no country that has given such public recognition to a foreign intelligence officer, indicating that Angleton's relationship with Israel was significant.

The more important issues raised in recent books are that important areas of operations were brought to a standstill by Angleton; that for some time defectors were turned away as dispatched agents; that some officers' careers were thoughtlessly ruined by Angleton's paranoid search for traitors within the agency; and that Angleton was responsible for the jailing of a controversial defector. Let us dispose of this last charge first.

The decision to hold Nosenko was made by the operations division responsible for his handling. Angleton was opposed to it, and won a retraction of the allegation that he was responsible from a national news magazine. This is covered in detail in an article by Samuel Halpern and Hayden Peake.[1]

As for the other allegations: A senior FBI man has told me that in the 1960s he served with an interagency team that examined numerous CIA stations for the White House. Discussions were concentrated on agency operations against the USSR. Not once was any complaint raised that Angleton was hampering anyone's operations.

Later, in the 1970s, this officer was attached to the President's Foreign Intelligence Advisory Board (PFIAB). In this capacity he was again a member of a team that visited several CIA field stations and participated in discussions at the CIA in Washington. There was never a hint of complaint against Angleton.

Much of what some sources have attributed to Angleton in allegedly bringing CIA operations against the Soviet Union to a halt was in fact the timely tightening of operational security within the division itself and the pruning of numerous operations that, however long-lived and time-consuming, had never proved productive. I say "allegedly" brought to a halt because at the time to which the allegations apply there were in fact a variety of operations going on, new activity was being initiated, and defectors were being welcomed.

I do not recall any critic pointing out that, although the counterintelligence (CI) staff under Angleton was responsible for approving or disapproving proposed operations on security grounds, the division chiefs had the right to appeal the CI staff's decision to the deputy director for operations (DDO). If the division chief was not satisfied with the DDO's decision, he could appeal directly to the DCI. If either the DDO or the DCI agreed that the potential value of a proposed activity outweighed the probable risks, the approval would be granted regardless of the CI staff position.

One former DCI could not recall any such appeal ever having been made to him. The CI staff was a staff. Like other agency staffs it had influence, but no command function beyond the staff itself. It had no responsibility for promotions or the assignment of personnel. It was subordinate to the DDO.

The notion that the so-called mole hunt began when Major Golitsyn opted out of the KGB is manifestly false. The counterintelligence components of the FBI, CIA, and the Department of Defense were well aware that Soviet intelligence services had been active in the United States almost from the time of their inception. The open literature provides a good notion of what had gone on—Chambers, Massing, Bentley, and many others, all catch the spirit of the prewar years. The classified files are even more revealing.

From its beginning, Soviet intelligence compiled an outstanding record of recruiting and running penetration agents. The British/American deception of German intelligence and the General Staff in World War II is well known. Less recognized is the fact that the Soviet services also were masters of deception. In the eyes of some experts, the Soviets were steps ahead of the Allies in this field.

In 1950, the Korean War brought a considerable expansion in personnel to the CIA and to other intelligence organizations. Many who were recruited by the CIA had extensive foreign backgrounds. An FBI man stated the problem plainly: "How in hell do you do background checks on someone abroad?" There are of course means of checking, but these are not nearly as effective as what can be done domestically. Klaus Fuchs is a good example of the problem.

When the personnel expansion ceased, security offices in many agencies were able to look more deeply into the background of the newly recruited staff. This is something less than a mole hunt, and more nearly an updating of security clearances—a procedure that all agencies conduct as a matter of routine.

In the days of ULTRA the problem of background checks abroad was at the root of the British insistence that anyone being cleared had to have been born in the United Kingdom, and of a family with at least two generations of residence there. British security imposed a similar requirement on OSS personnel.

This concern with security was no less pressing after the war. The success of the Soviet services in penetrating foreign intelligence and security organs was sobering. The potential for disaster was immense. The United States was the principal enemy of a world power that had a vast nuclear arsenal and that was ruled by an elite whose concept of international relations was hardly Wilsonian.

Published data show Soviet penetrations of almost every foreign intelligence service of possible interest. Many of these penetrations went to the core of the target organizations. Defector testimony before Congress shows repeated instances of agents doubled against Western services, sometimes by Soviet allies—Czechoslovakia, Cuba, Poland, and others. In view of this evidence, would it be so unusual for a chief of counterintelligence to be concerned with the security of the service he is charged with protecting?

Any intelligence chief who assures a president or prime minister that the country's service is not penetrated is ignorant of intelligence history. The most he might say is "As of now, I have no reason to believe that my service is penetrated, but before the echo has died away someone, somewhere, might be arranging to commit treason."

It is hard to imagine that the alleged symptoms in James Angleton were apparently so easily detected by journalists and others that went unnoticed by Donovan and five directors—Hillenkoetter, Smith, Dulles, McCone, or Helms.

Anyone reflecting on Angleton's career should keep some of his less heralded accomplishments in mind. He effected the centralization of counterintelligence in the CI staff, a concept to which the agency has now returned; he made it clear that collection operations and even covert action programs cannot exist without strong counterintelligence support, a principle that has also been embraced; he showed that counterintelligence analysis and review must take historical context into consideration; and, in the face of serious problems, he kept liaison with the FBI on an even keel.

Angleton could be cantankerous and cross-grained. He abused his body, refused exercise unless it was in a trout stream, and kept eccentric hours. He maintained friendships with an extraordinary range of people around the world, and was a loyal and compassionate friend. He thought longer and more deeply about his trade than anyone else I knew. He was a dominant figure in his world for decades.

But mistakes were made: He should have left a better written record; he overvalued certain sources; he focused too narrowly on European problems; I think he allowed himself to become too isolated late in his career; he might have participated more directly in the CI training programs; perhaps he should have stepped aside at some point, but, for better or for worse, that was not in his nature.

Allen Dulles popularized the term *tradecraft* and used it to describe the practices and principles of secret operations. American trainees take courses in tradecraft; the Russians study *conspiracy*. Conspiracy, with its slightly sinister overtones, lies closer to the inner reality of espionage and counterespionage.

Call it tradecraft or conspiracy, Jim Angleton had the deepest understanding of it of anyone I have ever known. Where others might contribute a thought or two to an operational discussion, Angleton would add a full dimension. One did not have to agree with his every analysis to appreciate the power of his imagination and his complex grasp of operations.

One night after a performance in Paris some years ago, a musician was reminiscing about a friend, an alto saxophonist. One of those at the table, emboldened by the drink that was flowing, pointed out that some of the jazzman's recollections seemed to be contradictory. Buck thought for a moment and said, "Yes, of course, but what you have to remember is that he surer than hell could play . . . and was a fascinating bunch of guys." He might have been talking about Jim Angleton.

COMMENTS: JAMES NOLAN

I first met Jim Angleton in the late 1960s. I have often thought about it and wondered why he paid any attention to a young bureau supervisor and why we became friends. I am not really sure, except I do know that we shared one thing, a passion for counterintelligence. As I reflected on his relationships with other individuals from the FBI, particularly those with whom he remained close friends for all of his life, it seemed to me that all of his FBI friends shared his passion for counterintelligence.

I do not think one can begin to understand Jim without understanding the total commitment he made to counterintelligence. It was the overriding thing in Jim's life. Yet, despite his total commitment to counterintelligence, he made mistakes, just like everyone else.

As to the question of the penetration of one's own service, I do not think that there is anything more difficult with which to deal. If you read the literature about Jim, you would believe that his deep concern about the penetration of the CIA was based solely on a fragmentary report by one defector. This is nonsense.

All of us who have been involved in this work know that information on possible penetrations comes all the time. Such information comes, for example, from double agents who have been told by their foreign intelligence service handlers not to worry about getting caught—that they will know if the FBI or CIA becomes suspicious of them. Such information also comes from recruited foreign intelligence services officers who, while they have no personal knowledge, have heard stories in their training courses of great penetrations of Western services. Such information comes in bits and pieces, fragments; it is rarely a single lead. It may also come from analyses of our own cases that have failed. Thus, the idea that Jim accepted a single piece of defector reporting and began a twenty-year hunt for penetration of the CIA is solely for the writers of fictionalized biographies.

There are also the cases that those who focus on what they call Jim's paranoia of penetration always seem to neglect to mention. I mean of course those cases of actual penetration of the CIA (and the OSS before it) that are in the public record. By omitting any discussion of Larry Wu-Tai Chin, who as an employee of the CIA from 1952 until 1981 regularly supplied CIA information to Chinese intelligence; or Karl Koecher, a Czechoslovakian illegals officer who successfully penetrated the CIA; or of Barnett, Moore, and Howard, three CIA officers who provided data to the Soviets, Jim's concern that the agency might be penetrated might seem paranoid. With these cases before the reader, Jim might appear to have a reasonable basis for concern.

Then there is the nonsense that he could not make friends after having been betrayed by Philby. Jim had a host of friends. He had poker friends, fishing friends, and poetry friends. He had such friends because he was a fascinating and interesting person. He was interested in everything. He would know the life history of a waitress who served him. The second time she served him, he would be inquiring about her children and what each one was doing. It was probably all recorded in his tiny handwriting on the back of a matchbook.

The books about Jim, particularly Mangold's, are not biographies but rather indictments. They take every case they can find and take the most critical view of it. For example, Mangold writes: "Of all of the KGB and GRU defectors who were recruited by the FBI and CIA to risk their lives in the dangerous world of double agent operations"— his language is a wonderful illustration of his grasp of CI—"none was more shamefully treated than the one the FBI called 'TOPHAT' and the CIA 'BOURBON.'" Mangold then goes on to accuse Jim Angleton and Bill Sullivan of General Polyakov's compromise and execution. Mangold states that it was their disclosures to Edward J. Epstein in 1977 that resulted in Polyakov's arrest.

It is possible that the KGB, without any other help but the Epstein disclosure, finally detected Polyakov in 1990. But it seems much more likely that Edward Lee Howard in 1985 was the source of Polyakov's final undoing, as he was surely the source for the undoing of others of whom Jim Angleton had no knowledge.[2] Mangold's book does not even mention this possibility; rather, it is all Jim's fault.

Before we make damning judgments about the decisions of the senior counterintelligence officers of the 1950s and 1960s, we need to put ourselves into the world Bill Hood was describing: a world in which virtually every Western service was penetrated and where we were constantly receiving information that the CIA and the FBI must be penetrated. Documented Soviet successes in recruiting U.S. government officials, combined with decrypted KGB traffic (the VENONA material) and information provided by a Soviet source, reasonably reinforced concerns about the CIA's own vulnerability. I do not know what the standard was then before one took action to transfer or even remove from service a suspected employee. That standard was obviously not "probable cause"—for with probable cause one could have secured an indictment. It was obviously some degree of suspicion. All of us who were faced with having to make such difficult decisions would like to think our actions were based on "reasonable suspicions." But our first responsibility was to make certain that our services were safe and it was that sense of responsibility that I believe drove Jim in these cases.

Finally, as to Jim's contributions, he had the aura—the charisma—that made counterintelligence important to decision makers. In making counterintelligence important in the CIA, he also raised its stature in the FBI. He had a great belief that counterintelligence was a career. That expertise required long study and indoctrination and he did not accept the myth that all CIA officers or FBI agents were counterintelligence officers. Such myths did not stand up for long in discussions with Jim. He recognized the size and sophistication of the Soviet intelligence threat and he had the capacity to draw both allied services and the FBI into coordinated actions in response. Someday perhaps someone will write a fair biography of him, but no one has done so yet.

COMMENTS: SAMUEL HALPERN

In preparation for this discussion, I sat down and tried to make a list of all the myths that have appeared over the years about James Angleton. I found myself coming up with a good-sized book and decided against doing that. Instead I will talk particularly about myths that I have some personal knowledge of or personal involvement in, particularly during my seven years as executive assistant to three DDPs, now called DDOs, starting with FitzGerald, Karamessines, and about three or four months with Bill Colby. Those of you who know my work in intelligence know that I concern myself with facts, dates, and above all, something called chronology, the importance of which was impressed upon me by my professors as I studied to be a historian. It was doubly reinforced in me by Jim Angleton for dealing with intelligence work.

I met Jim Angleton in 1948, when he was special assistant to Col. Don Galloway, head of the CIA's clandestine service, the Office of Special Operations, which was engaged only in gathering intelligence clandestinely by human sources, and in counterintelligence.

I was a young case officer in the Far East Division, and was running an agent in a liberal left trade union in Southeast Asia. One day I was suddenly summoned to Jim Angleton's office. I had never heard of him before, so I stopped in my division chief's office on the way and told him I was going down to see someone named Jim Angleton. My division chief said to let him know what happened when I got back. When I arrived at Jim's office, he immediately read me the riot act about crossing lines with his labor operations and ordered me to cease and desist forthwith. I argued back that since I did not know he had any operations to begin with, I could not know about, or be responsible for, crossing any of his lines. (I did not know then about Jim Angleton's connections with the AFL-CIO's Jay Lovestone.) And as for stopping my operation, I told him that only my division chief could so direct me; Angleton said he would arrange that. I reported all this to my division chief, who said for me to keep doing what I was doing until he told me otherwise. Actually I never heard another thing about it and I continued the operation for several years. So much for Angleton's alleged power over people and operations.

Another myth is that there was no counterintelligence at all before Angleton became chief of the CI staff in 1954. This is not so. CI continued without a break from the days of X-2 in OSS under Jimmy Murphy, into SSU, then in CIG, and finally into CIA when Staff C (for counterintelligence) was under the direction of people like Dick Hawes and later Bill Harvey. The CI staff under Angleton began in 1954, two years after the merger of OSO and OPC (the covert action arm of CIA). CI as a function was always there; it never disappeared.

One overall myth is the alleged power of Angleton to start or stop operations, acting as some sort of éminence grise who could make things happen with the lift of an eyebrow or of a little finger. That is nonsense. I saw enough of that in the seven years I was in the DDP's office. He did have a say about what was done and what should not be done, but staff and division chiefs could, and often did, win time and time again on their operations.

For example, there was the 1954 agreement with the British regarding Southeast Asia, forty years ago. Times were different then than they are today in Southeast Asia. Frank Wisner, then DDP, had the idea of aligning British foreign policy with that of U.S. policy, particularly with regard to Vietnam. At that time there was a question as to whether the United States would support Emperor Bao Dai or a new man, Ngo Dinh Diem. President Eisenhower sent an old army friend of his, Gen. Joe Collins, to Saigon to find out which man the United States should support. Collins recommended supporting Bao Dai, which the CIA people in Saigon thought would be a horrible mistake, as did the DDI's people in Washington, the State Department, and those in the operations side who had chosen Diem. The State Department wanted allies, and particularly wanted support from the British and were having difficulty getting it. Wisner devised an arrangement with the British that permitted them to align their policy with that of the United States throughout Southeast Asia, not just Vietnam. When Wisner reported this to the then–assistant secretary of state for East Asia, the latter was absolutely amazed and could not understand how Wisner had done it.

Throughout all the negotiations in late 1954, Angleton opposed this new arrangement. He did not trust the British then, particularly after some of the events that had happened, and argued against the entire effort, including arguing with Allen Dulles about it; in every case he lost the argument. He was not influential in this case and his views were ignored.

The point I am trying to make is that while Angleton had his say he was not always the winner and did not always have his way. In 1955, for example, I drafted a policy message concerning relations with the intelligence and security services of two friendly countries. The cable was to be released by the DDP and the DCI. I tried to get the CI chief or his deputy to initial-off as coordinating on the cable. Neither person was available and I was under orders to get the cable to the DDP as soon as possible. When I got the cable to the DDP he never asked me why there was no CI staff coordination on the cable, and he was directed by the DCI, by means of a telephone conversation, to release the message. The DCI did not inquire about the views of the CI staff. When the confirmation copies of the cable were distributed the next day, Angleton's deputy called me in high dudgeon to remonstrate with me about the lack of CI staff sign-off. I said that I could not find him or Jim, and that the DDP wanted the cable out. I asked him if the CI staff wanted to change anything or add anything to the message. He said no, it was a fine cable, but that the CI staff should have coordinated its release. So much for bureaucracy. But neither the DDP nor the DCI was concerned about the lack of CI input by Angleton or his staff.

This mention of cables leads to another myth: that Angleton received a copy of every cable in or out. Without commenting on other elements of the CIA, with message facilities that Angleton might not even have been aware of, he certainly never received copies of all clandestine service messages. He also never got his own communication channel that he wanted so badly. Nor for that matter did he get his own field representatives abroad with direct communications to him bypassing the line divisions. That was something he fought for and never won. CI staff could not get copies of all messages because the CI staff was cut out of many activities. CI was not, for example, given any messages with Prescribed and Limited distribution, a mechanism that was worked up with the Cable Secretariat in the late 1950s. This distribution system was authorized by the DDP in each and every case that required a special hold-down of dissemination of the messages. The area division or staff, deemed to be the action unit, got the action on the messages, with additional distribution decided on a case-by-case basis by the action unit and the DDP at the start of the activity. The Prescribed and Limited system was a means of tailoring cable distribution for each activity that needed it. This system was used for messages processed by the Cable Secretariat attached to the office of the DCI. All the area division and staff chiefs had a privacy channel within the limited distribution system, with the DDP getting copies of all messages and the DCI getting copies whenever the Cable Secretariat thought the DCI should get them. The CI staff often was not on the distribution list of Limited distribution cases. This procedure was never questioned by three DCIs.

In addition, when assigned to the office of the DDP in 1966, I created the restricted handling cable system wherein messages were processed directly with the office of communications, bypassing the Cable Secretariat. This system was revealed by the Church Committee in its 1975 and 1976 reports. The action unit and the DDP were the only units to get copies of all messages and there was no further distribution of restricted handling messages except by the action unit. In no way did Angleton or the CI staff get copies of all messages.

This leads to another myth: that Angleton was known as "No Knock" because of his alleged ability to enter the DCI's office at will at any time. First, Jim Angleton was a gentleman, and would never barge in on anyone without permission. Second, the secretaries just outside the door of the DCI shielded the DCIs from intrusion.

Other nicknames such as "Mother," which I never heard in all my years in intelligence, may have come from the book *Orchids for Mother* by Aaron Latham. That and the alleged description of Angleton's office with a fireplace and two wolfhounds may be great theater, but has no relation to reality. As for the myth that Angleton's word was law, in addition to the points raised above, there was the case of Angleton and the Sino-Soviet split of 1959. Even before Golitsyn defected in December 1961 (or in January 1962 depending on the source), Angleton held in 1959 that the split was a fake and a sham. Angleton's view was disregarded by most, although a few senior officers agreed with him. No action, however, was taken on it. Even on his own staff, the chief of the international communism branch derided it both to Angleton directly and to the rest of the clandestine service. That man was Lothar Metzl, the expert on all things dealing with communism. I repeat this simply because it shows Angleton's lack of superpower or super influence over agency activities.

A new myth is in the making. A new book is being published calling Angleton an "Israeli Mossad Man." Elizabeth Bancroft's latest issue of *Surveillant* brought to my attention this book by Terry Ellsworth, a Yale graduate of the class of 1965, which says that Israeli intelligence has manipulated the CIA since the 1940s as a result of Angleton's having the Israeli desk. In my opinion, Angleton's handling of the Israeli desk was exemplary, but as with many good things it lasted too long. Despite his being responsible for the liaison aspects of Israeli intelligence, he also produced some excellent unilateral information about Israel. Angleton was not a Mossad man.

The myth also exists that Angleton single-handedly provided funds for Israel to carry on activities in Africa. This is false. Angleton never had such funds. Any such program would have been fully approved by the National Security Council approval mechanism at the time. Such a program would have let the Israelis carry out effective activities helping in African areas with the American hand concealed, as a true American operation should.

One subject not on the myth list is that of CI operations being penetrated by the opposition. The example is a disclosure made in 1987 by a Cuban DGI defector that the DGI had actually run many, if not all, of the alleged Cuban agents that were run by the CIA in recent years. This was in effect another series of operations run by the DGI and the former Eastern bloc countries allied with the former Soviet Union. Some former CIA officers, including a former deputy chief of the CI staff after Angleton's tenure, have said that Angleton's insistence on studying the old Soviet Trust and similar operations was a waste of time; but maybe Angleton was right after all. It is quite possible that if the Cuban agents recruited by the United States had been reviewed by Angleton's staff as required by regulations, the CIA might have been saved from its later embarrassments. During the 1960s, when I was on a Cuban operation called Operation Mongoose and its follow-on names, these Cuban operations were exempt from getting the usual CI staff approvals before recruitment of agents. It will never be known if that was a procedural mistake, because the possibility exists that we paid a high price for not going by the book.

I could go on with other myths such as Angleton having jailed Nosenko, which he did not do, although he did not object vigorously, but it was not his decision to make; or his control of travel behind the Iron Curtain; or what DDP FitzGerald might have done if he had lived; and the "ors" could go on. The agency needed and still needs, in my opinion, a "doubting Thomas." Angleton served that purpose for too long a time, but the function is a necessary one. Remember that during Angleton's tenure there was no penetration of CIA at upper levels abroad, which was his area of responsibility. He cannot be charged with failure on those operations from which he was kept away. In my view, at the moment the best all-around study of Angleton to date is found in Robin Winks's *Cloak and Gown*.[3] Until Bill Hood or someone similar writes a biography of Angleton, Winks will have to do.

11

THE FBI'S CHANGING MISSION

Patrick Watson

The topic of this chapter is the Federal Bureau of Investigation's (FBI's) counterintelligence mission in the 1990s. The year 1990 brought dramatic changes in the world and the bureau has done a lot of thinking about the future of counterintelligence and how to keep the FBI's role in counterintelligence relevant to the issues and threats the United States faces today and will face in the future.

The best way to understand where the FBI is today is by first discussing where it has come from. The FBI's Foreign Counterintelligence (FCI) program in the decades following World War II was very much in tune with the national security policies of the United States as set out, for instance, in NSC-68 and guided by the general strategy of containment. The bureau's essential FCI mission was to meet the threat posed by the intelligence activities of the Soviet Union and its allied states in the United States.

The result was a very focused FCI effort. The vast majority of the bureau's resources were deployed against the states within the Soviet bloc. Far fewer resources were directed at targets outside that group of countries. As a result of this focused effort, the FBI developed an expertise with respect to these countries' intelligence activities that served the United States reasonably well during the Cold War.

While the emphasis placed on the Soviets and their allies was appropriate and fully justifiable, it left the FBI somewhat blind to other intelligence activities that were occurring in the United States. If these activities came to the bureau's attention and were thought to be sufficiently serious, the FBI would investigate them, but the overall focus of the FBI's FCI program—and the dedication of resources within that program—was on a limited number of nations.

By early 1990, however, it was clear that the world had changed radically and that the bureau needed to rethink its FCI program. Just as

---

This paper was first presented on March 24, 1992.

the political, military, and economic realities of the past dictated what the FBI's counterintelligence policy would be, so, it was concluded, would the political, military, and economic realities of the 1990s. The defeat of Germany and Japan in World War II opened the way for Soviet expansion and led the United States to develop its policy of containment. The demise of the Soviet empire will undoubtedly result in a similar revolution in the international security environment. But what precisely this new world order will look like is difficult to predict. As the president said in a speech at the CIA in November 1991, "This is not the end of history." We stand at the threshold of a new era.

The political changes in the countries of Eastern Europe and the resulting decline in the intelligence threat they posed caused the FBI to initiate an internal review of its FCI program and strategy. That review produced a number of findings and generated several new concepts, which have been pulled together and subsequently called the National Security Threat List (NSTL). The NSTL provides a sensible strategy for the FBI's FCI program now and in the future.

In conducting this review, one of the first conclusions reached was that there were still some countries in the world that posed strategic intelligence threats to the United States. Although the list of those countries was growing shorter and shorter, there were countries that still sponsored terrorism and were still actively engaged in extensive hostile intelligence activities directed at the United States. In short, the FBI identified a number of countries as ongoing threats and targeted them much as it had done during the Cold War.

A second phenomenon the bureau took note of in its review was the rise in nationalism. To a far greater extent than before the end of the Cold War, countries were using their intelligence capabilities to support their own, narrowly conceived, national interests. As the bipolar world ceased to exist, and the alliances associated with the competition between the Soviet Union and the United States became less of a factor, an increasing number of countries became more aggressive in their use of their intelligence services to pursue their particular security and economic agendas.

In addition to what the FBI could determine through its counterintelligence activities, the review also took into consideration the findings of the larger U.S. national security community. The FBI took into account the National Security Strategy prepared each year by the president and his administration; Presidential Strategy for CI in the 1990s, studied and implemented in National Security Review 18 and National Security Directive 47; and other documents that set out the president's priorities for intelligence collection. Then the question was posed: What is it that the FBI does as a counterintelligence service that is relevant to these national security concerns? How, in short, could the bureau's FCI program support the national security policies of the United States?

Upon completion of the review at headquarters, the findings were discussed with field office executives in a series of meetings at the FBI's academy at Quantico, Virginia. The result was the NSTL.

The NSTL combines two elements. First, it includes national security *issues* that the FBI has concluded need to be addressed no matter where the threat comes from or what country is involved.[1] Second, it includes those *countries* that pose a continuing and serious intelligence threat to U.S. security interests. (The FBI maintains a classified list of these countries.)

In considering which states should be put on the country-specific threat list, the FBI considers four criteria. The first criterion is the level of intelligence or terrorist activity a country is involved in. This is based on what the FBI and the rest of the Intelligence Community actually observe. The second criterion is the targets of the activity. Are they, for instance, targeting U.S. interests, programs, plans, or citizens? Third is an assessment of the actual capability of a country or group for intelligence collection or terrorist activity (i.e., their infrastructure for collection). While a country or group may be targeting U.S. interests, what is the likelihood that they can, in fact, conduct effective operations? The fourth criterion is: What is our political, military, and/or economic alignment with that country?

Based on these factors, the FBI develops a list of countries that pose a significant intelligence threat to the United States. This list is given to the attorney general for consideration. In addition, discussions are held with the relevant elements within the Department of State. Upon the completion of these discussions and a review, the attorney general makes the final determination as to what countries will be placed on the Country Threat List.

A similar process was involved in developing the Issue Threat List. First, after reviewing key national security documents and considering information provided by other elements of the Intelligence Community, the FBI identified seven categories of foreign intelligence activity that were deemed to be significant threats to U.S. national security interests. The creation of this list refocused the attention of the FBI's counterintelligence program and enlarged its perspective to include the entire world. With regard to activities described in the Issue Threat

List, the FBI will be looking at any and all countries that are engaged in intelligence activities related to these issues.

The first issue on the Issue Threat List concerns foreign intelligence activities directed at U.S. critical technologies. These are technologies designated as critical by the President's National Critical Technologies Panel. This was an area the FBI thought was important to address based not only on what the bureau has observed, but also on what the FBI has been told by the rest of the national security community. These technologies were judged to be key to the future economic and military well-being of the United States.

There are a number of government documents listing "critical technologies." The key lists used by the FBI are the White House–created panel report published as the National Critical Technologies List and the Department of Defense Military Critical Technologies List.

What does this new emphasis on technology mean to those in the counterintelligence business? In part, it means a different approach from that of the past. The approach is no longer limited to investigating the officials and official establishments of communist countries. This change in FCI priorities has moved the FBI closer to the world of security and countermeasures, a world that the bureau has in the past stayed apart from.

Further, this new focus on critical technologies requires that the FBI actively reach out to U.S. companies involved in such development so that the FBI can better understand what specific foreign intelligence collection efforts are being directed at them. The FBI must combine that understanding with its knowledge of how intelligence organizations operate, and focus its counterintelligence resources accordingly. This is different from the traditional FCI method of keeping tabs on intelligence officers and tracking them to the target. The logical target of foreign intelligence collection is identified and counterintelligence activity initiated to determine whether or not collection is occurring.

The FBI no longer makes the assumption that only communist countries will engage in intelligence activities inimical to U.S. national security interests. Any country that is engaged in intelligence activities directed at U.S. critical technologies will be a target for investigation. Given the breadth of this task, the FBI cannot perform alone. The bureau must reach out to the rest of the Intelligence Community to acquire whatever information and expertise are available to support its efforts in addressing this issue.

The second issue on the Issue Threat List is foreign intelligence activities directed at collecting proprietary information and technology of U.S. corporations. This is information and technology, the loss of which would undermine the country's industrial strength and position in the world's economy even though the information or technology has not been specifically identified as being critical to U.S. national security. Potentially, this substantially broadens the scope of activity that the FBI might be involved in. However, as a practical matter, given how CI operations are actually conducted, much of what the FBI will do in this area will be in response to foreign intelligence activities detected through established coverage of foreign intelligence organizations and their agents as well as contact between the FBI and the private sector.

The third issue listed is clandestine foreign activity in the United States. This is an issue that was generated from within the FBI. It simply means that if a country has an intelligence presence in the United States that is engaged in clandestine activity, then the FBI should know what it is up to. In this regard, over the past year, the FBI has begun looking at the intelligence activities of countries that were not given much attention before. The point is, if a foreign nation has an intelligence officer in the United States who is not in liaison with the U.S. government, then the FBI has a responsibility to determine the nature of the intelligence activities that officer is engaged in.

Of course, there are clandestine activities that countries can be engaged in within the United States that are not directly targeted at U.S. interests. The question is: What should the FBI's role be in monitoring this kind of activity? Should the bureau be concerned if an intelligence officer from one country attempts to recruit an intelligence officer from another country? As a practical matter, the FBI has to be concerned with such activities, if only to identify the scope of those activities. The amount of resources the FBI applies to a given activity will depend upon what impact the activity has on U.S. national interests. But to say that the FBI should allow an intelligence service to operate in the United States without any monitoring by the FBI is something that the bureau is not willing to accept. The United States needs to know what foreign intelligence services are doing in the United States.

The next item on the Issue Threat List is foreign intelligence activities directed at collecting information relating to the U.S. defense establishments and the related activities of national preparedness. This is a traditional counterintelligence concern frequently involving violation of the espionage statutes.

The next issue of concern is foreign intelligence activities involving the acquisition or proliferation of weapons of mass destruction and their delivery systems. This issue is currently receiving a great deal of attention in the Intelligence Community as a whole. For the FBI, the question is: What should its role be in addressing this particular issue? The FBI has initiated investigations involving the issue of proliferation.

The sixth issue on the Issue Threat List is foreign intelligence operations that target U.S. intelligence and foreign affairs information and U.S. government officials. This, again, is a traditional FCI concern. Any intelligence service or country involved in such activities will be investigated. This issue is listed here to reiterate the bureau's continuing responsibility in this area.

The final item on the Issue Threat List is foreign intelligence activities involved in perception management or "active measures" operations directed at the United States. This is an issue that causes concern in some segments of the public. They worry about the FBI's definition of *active measures* and they worry about what the bureau's role is in countering such activities. For the FBI, the issue is relatively straightforward. If a foreign intelligence service is attempting to manipulate American public opinion or the government by clandestine means, then a counterintelligence investigation is justified.

The FBI is aware that when it gets involved in these types of investigations it is often perceived to be treading on the edge of the First Amendment and First Amendment freedoms. Yet, the adoption of the NSTL has not changed the fact that the FBI will and must operate under the attorney general's guidelines with respect to FCI investigations of U.S. citizens. On December 31, 1991, the attorney general signed a new set of guidelines that incorporated the NSTL. This was done after consultation with the Intelligence Community, the NSC, and the intelligence committees of the House and Senate.

With respect to the NSTL, we no longer live in a world where the FBI can afford to focus FCI efforts on a handful of countries. The bureau must operate in a security environment in which countries that previously were either aligned with the United States or that posed no strategic threat may now be engaged in intelligence activities that run counter to U.S. national interest, and this includes economic well-being. This is uncertain territory and figuring out precisely how the bureau as a counterintelligence service will address these various issues will take time.

For example, because the NSTL sets as a task the protection of key technologies and proprietary information, the question naturally arises: What about industrial espionage? Industrial espionage is not now covered by the NSTL. This is not to say that industrial espionage is of no interest to the FBI; to the extent that federal statutes are violated, it is a bureau concern. Moreover, there is increasing interest in expanding the definition of property to include intellectual property. If this happens, the bureau's role in investigating interstate transportation of stolen property would expand accordingly. Yet, both industrial espionage and intellectual property rights, while important concerns and potentially subjects for FBI investigation, are not counterintelligence issues. When the FBI speaks about counterintelligence, it is really talking about responding to organized, clandestine efforts of foreign governments or groups.

This general uncertainty about FCI is fueled by the demise of the Soviet Union and its empire. Now that the government in Moscow is no longer the military threat it once was, has not counterintelligence become less important? Certainly, before, there were counterintelligence investigations that concerned the potential survivability of the United States. One only has to think about the case of John Walker to realize how critically serious his espionage was. If the Cold War had turned hot, the information he and Whitworth provided the Soviets could very well have had a decisive influence on how such a war turned out. In this sense, FCI investigations like that of Walker's did concern the survivability of the nation.

If one thinks the role of counterintelligence is only to address that kind of threat, then one might conclude that the role for counterintelligence will diminish in the 1990s. However, I am convinced that counterintelligence has a broader role. There are other foreign intelligence activities that are a threat to the national security interests of the United States and that, in the long run, have an impact on the nation's ability to maintain its position as a preeminent military power in the world. Furthermore, the country's economic well-being—described even back in the 1950s as a key element in the nation's security posture—has taken on renewed importance as we use this respite from superpower competition to consider the long-term requirements for keeping the United States strong. In short, while these issues might not go so directly to the survivability of the United States as espionage cases, these issues nevertheless concern the extended survivability of the United States as a power in the world and are important to the immediate national security interests of the nation. In these areas, counterintelligence still has a role to play.

It is also necessary to mention the kind of resources the FBI will need to implement its NSTL strategy. The political and military realities that will be faced in the 1990s are not set, so the precise FCI capability that will be required is hard to predict. It is certain, however, that there is a need to maintain such a capability. Intelligence collection efforts continue to be mounted by a significant number of countries and directed at a wide range of targets. In certain respects, what the FBI does as a counterintelligence service will not significantly change. The difference will be in how these traditional techniques are applied to reflect the new challenges as set out by the NSTL.

Not only is the FBI going to have to maintain its counterintelligence capabilities, but also it will need to improve them in certain areas. One such area is analysis. If the FBI is going to come to terms fully with the significance of foreign intelligence activities and determine their impact on U.S. national interest, the FBI will need increased analytic support. Such support will be key to focusing our FCI resources intelligently. The benefit of solid analytical support is something the bureau has recognized for some time and has been working to improve. In addition, the FBI's base of information is going to have to be much broader than it has been in the past. As a result, the bureau will need to reach out more than it has in the past to other parts of the Intelligence Community to acquire the kind of information it will need to properly focus its FCI operations. In an era in which there will probably be fewer resources, they must be used more wisely and in a more focused manner.

There was a time when the practice of counterintelligence involved applying all available resources to monitoring the activities of a limited number of hostile nations. In the 1990s the threat will come from many different directions and the enemy will not always be apparent. Entering this new era will require the FBI to develop better assets, a better intelligence base, and a better analytical capability so that investigative capabilities can be focused where they are needed most.

In summary, the FBI has been attempting to construct a counterintelligence program that will be consistent with the national security interests of the United States and be able to respond to an uncertain future.

Looking at a new world order that is in the process of developing, the challenge is to develop an FCI program that stays relevant. The hope is that the NSTL will provide the foundation for a strategy that is flexible enough to address today's concerns and to meet future threats.

12

COVERT ACTION: NEITHER EXCEPTIONAL TOOL NOR MAGIC BULLET

Roy Godson

I n the absence of a clear and present danger, covert action (CA) is likely to remain a controversial instrument of foreign policy. Throughout much of U.S. history it has been viewed as an exceptional tool of statecraft and often used as a tool of last resort.

For many contemporary scholars, commentators, and public officials covert action basically consists of secret government, dirty tricks, dirty wars, and other activities generally viewed as incompatible with an open and democratic foreign policy. Proponents of this view generally believe covert action should be banned altogether, or used only as a tool of last resort. This came to be the dominant view in the U.S. foreign policy establishment in the mid-1970s; it is still prevalent.[1]

For others, covert action remains an exceptional tool of statecraft because they regard it as a substitute for policy—doing what you can when diplomacy will not work and military action is too dangerous, doing something when everything else has failed, or doing *something* rather than doing (or being accused of doing) nothing.[2]

But there is an alternative view of covert action—one that views CA as a regular instrument of statecraft designed to achieve, or assist in achieving, specific national security objectives. From this point of view, covert action is not an exceptional tool to be resurrected when almost all else is likely to fail. It is not to be used more or less by itself—uncoordinated with, or unsupported by, diplomatic, military, and economic measures and public diplomacy. Nor is it to be used as a substitute for policy when government is uncertain of its objectives

This paper was first presented on October 29, 1992.

and unable to develop a coherent strategy, or is unwilling to defend its policy publicly.

When U.S. covert action was used in the late 1940s and early 1950s in Western Europe, the objectives were relatively clear: the Truman administration was willing to defend them and Congress was supportive. There was what some have referred to as a covert action annex to the Marshall Plan and NATO,[3] coordinated with the diplomatic, economic, and military components of this strategy. This is not to say that every major covert action program at that time was blended perfectly or adequately into U.S. policy or that U.S. policy was always well thought out. It was not. But, taken as a whole, covert action in Western Europe was accepted within policy-making circles as a regular adjunct of the policies being elaborated.

To specify a time when CA came to be regarded as a regular tool of U.S. policy is not to say that there should be more or less use of covert action in the 1990s. Nor is it to say that CA should be used in the absence of a consensus over foreign policy goals or the means necessary to implement these policies. It is only to underscore that there has been little debate about the utility of covert action as a regular instrument in the post–Cold War world and how best to maintain an effective covert action capability.

To explore this view of CA, this chapter first defines covert action and several of its key characteristics, then briefly considers circumstances when covert action has been and can be a useful instrument. It seeks to illustrate what happens to states that blend covert action effectively into their strategy and to those that do not. It then briefly explains why the instrument remains controversial and why the capability to use it has atrophied. Finally, it discusses what can be done to help ensure that the use of CA is effective, rather than a self-fulfilling prophecy of futility.

What Is Covert Action?

The most recent official—and public—word on covert action is found in the Intelligence Authorization Act of 1991, which defines CA as "an activity or activities of the U.S. government to influence political, economic, or military conditions abroad, where it is intended that the [U.S.] role . . . will not be apparent or acknowledged publicly."[4]

Congress has wrestled with the problem of definition for almost two decades, mostly in an effort to specify what the executive branch must report to Congress before it can undertake a covert action. The

Intelligence Authorization Act of 1991 is the most recent iteration of a process of definition that began with the Hughes-Ryan amendment to the Foreign Assistance Act of 1974. No other government in world history has sought to undertake this task, or to emulate the contemporary U.S. effort.[5]

On a broader scale, because covert action is not confined to governments, it can be defined as the attempt by a government or group to influence events in another state or territory without officially revealing its own involvement.

Seeking to influence others is a natural part of politics and foreign policy. Indeed, it is almost synonymous with them. And while pursuing these activities, people and governments rarely reveal exactly what they seek to accomplish or how they intend to do it, nor do they acknowledge publicly their every major action. Their actions are to one degree or another secret or disguised, and they use a variety of traditional instruments (e.g., diplomacy) without publicly acknowledging government activity. Covert action to some extent can be distinguished from these activities, but it is difficult to do, as repeated congressional efforts from 1974 to 1991 can attest.

Covert action is a uniquely American term of art that came into use after World War II. The term is not typically used (even in translation) by most other states, although this does not imply that these states do not engage in what we call covert action; many do. The point is that most states do not make a sharp distinction between overt and covert behavior and few single out a special category of covert behavior. While some may create special components within the bureaucracy to deal with some aspects of covert tradecraft, they often regard the exertion of influence, with varying degrees of secrecy, as a more or less normal component of statecraft.

The purpose of secret action is the attainment of defined political, military, or economic objectives, usually by supporting friendly forces and impeding an adversary's forces. There are generally four types of secret activities that can be used or denied in order to enhance one's own objectives or to impede those of an adversary:

• *Political action*. This may involve supporting and coordinating agents of influence and others involved in high policy circles. It may also extend to important nongovernmental fields such as labor, youth, intellectual, and religious movements.

• *Propaganda*. This includes providing information, guidance, equipment, and money to individuals and groups to promote a given objective, and can involve the print media, as well as radio or television.

- *Paramilitary activity.* This form of CA can range from support for terrorists and assassins to resistance movements, insurgents, and other unconventional forces. It also includes aid to forces seeking to counter or impede any of these activities. (There is no general agreement as to just where covert paramilitary assistance becomes secret "special operations" or covert military assistance.)

- *Intelligence assistance.* In addition to regular "liaison" with other intelligence services, this type of CA involves providing assistance to the intelligence services of another group or government to achieve specific political purposes. Assistance may involve training for personnel, material, technical assistance, or the passing of information to assist or direct the recipient.

For many governments, the principal covert action component will be part of the intelligence service rather than a separate bureaucracy. There are several reasons for this. First, there is administrative convenience. The secret bureaucratic arrangements for CA are almost identical to those of positive collection and CI (i.e., secret offices, communication systems, funds, people, agent recruitment, and handling). Many of the same facilities and bureaucratic arrangements can handle all these functions. Second, there is an important symbiotic relationship between CA and the other elements of intelligence. CA depends upon both collection and analysis to identify opportunities and to accomplish its purposes. It also depends on CI for protection. Conversely, a CA operation often produces special information (i.e., it contributes to collection and, in turn, to analysis) while it also provides special opportunities for CI.[6]

Efforts to covertly influence the policy or actions of another nation or entity (i.e., covert action) are not carried out only by the Great Powers among themselves or to harass and bully lesser states. It is a common aspect of statecraft, practiced by many states, great and small, and often by nongovernmental actors such as multinational corporations, trade unions, religious movements, and international criminal cartels.

Advantages of Covert Action

History is replete with examples of the advantages accruing to states with covert action capability—that is, of states that have used covert action in accordance with well-coordinated policy, usually conceived as covering an indefinite, and probably extended, period of time. History also illustrates what happened to states that did not use or did not have the capability to use CA effectively.[7]

To cite just a few Western examples: covert action was a major supplement to the diplomatic and military strategy of Queen Elizabeth I during the latter half of the sixteenth century. CA played an important role in maintaining her on the throne, keeping England Protestant, and preventing Spain from becoming the dominant power on the continent. Another example was the use of covert action as part of the strategy of the French in the eighteenth century to weaken England, France's principal rival. Indeed, France's use of covert action is a key factor in understanding how the American colonists broke free of the British empire.

CA has also played an important role in the critical struggles of the twentieth century. While covert action did not assure victory or lead to defeat, it was a significant tool of statecraft at key junctures. For example, it was one of the techniques that Britain used effectively in World War I as part of its strategy to move the United States away from a policy of neutrality, to acquire U.S. munitions during U.S. neutrality, and then to lead the United States into the war on the Allied side quickly and effectively in 1917. The British used covert action again for similar purposes in the early 1940s.

Following World War II, the United States and other Western states used covert action effectively as part of their overall national efforts initially to contain Soviet influence in Western Europe and later to help bring about the demise of ruling Communist parties in Poland and Afghanistan.

History is also replete with examples of the difficulties that beset states that did not effectively blend CA into their strategy. For example, the reverse side of the British success in gaining U.S. support in World War I was the failure of Imperial Germany to prevent effective U.S. entry into that war on the side of Britain and France. In no small measure, this failure was the result of Germany's decision to engage in submarine warfare against neutral (i.e., U.S.) shipping on the high seas and, equally dramatic, its attempt to involve Mexico in a plot against the United States (the Zimmermann Telegram). However, Germany's failure to keep the United States out of World War I was also a product of an ineffective covert action program aimed at U.S. officials and the general public, despite the relatively fertile ground for such a program. At the war's start, the American public was generally suspicious of European conflicts and hard-pressed to understand how such conflicts were relevant to their country's security or well-being. In addition, a significant percentage of Americans were of recent German descent. To its disadvantage, Imperial Germany was unable to capitalize on this opportunity.

Hitler's Third Reich also covertly sought to take advantage of U.S. isolationist opinion to keep the United States out of the war, which began in 1939. But the Nazi effort was shot through with ideological misjudgments and was apparently blatantly inept. Even then it was a close call. Had not the Japanese attacked Pearl Harbor, and the Nazis in turn declared war, and had not Britain mounted its own campaign to influence U.S. opinion, President Roosevelt would have had a very difficult time bringing U.S. might to bear on the conflict in Europe.

Britain and the United States have not been spared policy and CA failures. For example, in World War I, the British sought initially to keep Russia in the war after the overthrow of the czar in 1917. The CA part of the effort apparently was done mostly through an inexperienced operative, the novelist Somerset Maugham. Somehow Maugham was single-handedly supposed to keep Alexander Kerensky, then head of the provisional Russian government, in power. Little thought seems to have been given to how such a big purpose was to have been achieved by such paltry means. If that were not enough, at the same time British military operatives were working against Kerensky.[8]

After the Bolsheviks seized power, the Allies again sought to influence Russian affairs by trying to overthrow Lenin. Anglo-American efforts involved overt diplomatic moves and military intervention, as well as covert plots that continued into the early 1920s. All failed miserably, partly because of a policy failure in London (the British refused to commit sufficient forces to their military intervention), and partly because Bolshevik counterintelligence outwitted the British and U.S. operatives working on Soviet soil[9]—as they were to do repeatedly in subsequent decades.

For more than thirty years after 1947 the United States, to one degree or another, tried to overthrow many ruling Communist parties—and failed, through varying combinations of failed policy, failed intelligence, failed counterintelligence, and failed covert action.[10]

The United States also failed at times to overthrow lesser foes. Chile is an example. At the end of the 1960s, Richard Nixon, apprised of the looming possibility of the election of a quasi-communist government in Chile, in effect, dismissed the threat. But, as that threat became increasingly real in the fall of 1970, after Allende failed to win outright and the election was thrown into the Chilean Congress, Nixon ordered that he be stopped. This was the "magic bullet" conception of CA. Although the CIA station chief warned that this was too little, too late, the president insisted.[11] The CIA then tried and failed, and as a result the reputation of the United States in Chile and elsewhere in the world suffered.

Nor was the U.S. reputation enhanced in the wake of the invasion of Panama in 1989. U.S. political leaders were willing to go to war, but either unwilling or unable to use effectively what almost certainly would have been much less bloody covert action to remove General Noriega.[12]

This review of successes and failures is at odds with the view that covert action—even when successful—is of only marginal significance. This was the view put forward by Gregory Treverton in one of the few high-quality studies of the subject. Treverton was a principal investigator for the Church Committee and a member of the recent Twentieth Century Fund Task Force on Covert Action and Democracy. His book concludes: "seen in the long light of history most successes of covert action look small, ambiguous and transitory."[13] Treverton believes this also holds true for other powers that have utilized the instrument since World War II, such as the Soviet Union and Israel.[14]

Treverton provides almost no substantiation for his view of the Soviet and Israeli examples. More important, his analysis of U.S. covert action is flawed primarily because the public historical record is more complex than he acknowledges. Significantly, he dismisses in one or two paragraphs the U.S. use of covert action to contain communist power in Western Europe after World War II. He focuses most of his material instead on the U.S. spectaculars to overthrow governments (i.e., the coups in Iran in 1953 and Guatemala in 1954, the Bay of Pigs, the attempt to overthrow Allende, and the Iran-contra affair). His book, written in 1986, treats U.S. policy in Afghanistan only in passing and makes almost no reference to the then-unacknowledged covert action program in Eastern Europe in the 1980s.

It is true that the record of U.S. policy and covert action in the postwar period was mixed. However, the historical record for this period of U.S. history, for other periods of U.S. history, and the experiences of other Western and non-Western states, do not lead to the conclusion that the covert action instrument was of only marginal significance throughout. Moreover, even if one accepts for the purpose of argument that it was of only marginal significance, did covert action fare any worse than other nonmilitary instruments of statecraft such as public diplomacy, economic assistance, or even regular diplomacy?

American Use and Capabilities Today

In the 1990s, the United States does not have a strong CA capability and well-ingrained tradition of its use as a normal element of policy formation and implementation. There are several reasons. The first is the nature of the U.S. polity. The United States differs from totalitarian and authoritarian regimes, and to an extent from other Western liberal democracies, in its attitude toward the use of clandestine instruments. The prevailing view for much of the country's history has been that clandestine intelligence activities, particularly counterintelligence (CI) and CA, are regarded as exceptional activities.

The major, but by no means exclusive, exception to this general perspective occurs when the nation is clearly perceived to be threatened. In these circumstances, the United States will often engage in silent, and not so silent, warfare. Notwithstanding these exceptional circumstances, however, a bias in U.S. opinion (both popular and elite) against the clandestine arts has been the norm. This is usually explained by reference to democratic principles and to the need for accountability—although even those explanations may have their real bases in the strain of populist suspicion of government that runs strongly through U.S. history.

Following the War of Independence and the founding of the republic, the United States was more or less at peace. President Washington apparently downgraded U.S. intelligence from the full-service capability that he had created during the Revolutionary War. Its democratic government established and at peace, the United States saw little need to maintain such an intelligence capacity. Thereafter, except when the United States felt threatened by war or armed conflict on its borders, U.S. presidents showed little concern for intelligence and only episodic interest in what is today called covert action.

The two world wars of the twentieth century brought sharp increases in support for intelligence. Many of the measures adopted during World War I lapsed in the years between the wars, to be revived with energy, new organization, and new procedures just before and during World War II. These were mostly dismantled by the United States when it was assumed that the peace achieved in 1945 was to be the norm thereafter. Not long after, beginning in 1947, many were rebuilt when the president believed the United States faced military and political threats of unprecedented size and scope, and of indefinite duration.

Over a twenty-year period, from Truman through Eisenhower, Kennedy, and Johnson, covert action came to be viewed generally, if not always, as a useful instrument in the U.S. policy of containment. In the fall of 1947, it was viewed as an ad hoc necessity to complement economic and military tools. Gradually, however, top policymakers in the executive branch and Congress came to view CA not as a last resort—between doing nothing and "sending in the Marines"—but as something for more routine use in policy implementation. As part of containment strategy, it was no longer a "magic bullet" to pull U.S. chestnuts out of the fire, or to carry the full burden of U.S. policy, or to substitute for a panoply of diplomatic, military, and economic efforts.

Instead, the National Security Council (NSC) authorized covert action programs designed to (1) contain the spread of communism in the noncommunist world by supporting governments threatened by communist takeover, by strengthening noncommunist political and military forces, and by countering Soviet propaganda; and (2) weaken communist regimes on their own terrain by supporting resistance movements inside their territory, and by weakening the loyalty of their citizens through radio broadcasts, leaflets, and Western literature.

The U.S. government did not view this as "dirty tricks." It was not manipulating people to do what they did not want to do. On the contrary, within the Intelligence Community, the covert action people were regarded as the "do-gooders," helping foreigners who wanted to do more than would be possible without U.S. aid. The United States mainly provided unacknowledged moral, political, and material support to those leaders of democratic political parties and nongovernmental forces who wanted to remain outside the communist orbit, and to those within it who wanted to undermine communist rule.

The regular use of covert action to support a particular policy, in this case containment, was exceptional. Covert action was not so well institutionalized in Washington that the Departments of State or Defense or even the CIA leadership believed that it should be a regular adjunct to other aspects of policy as were diplomacy, economic and humanitarian aid, and overt information programs. Most U.S. government bureaucracies were in fact unenthusiastic supporters of covert action. They tolerated it, although they at times vented their frustration by leaking details of covert action programs. But outside of the Cold War, they did not believe covert action had much to offer in pursuit of U.S. interests. They were also averse to the power and resources available to the CIA's deputy directorate for plans (DDP), over which they had so little practical control.

As the years went on, covert action came to be viewed as the special preserve of just one bureaucracy, the CIA—and even there it was not universally welcomed. State, Defense, CIA, and the White House sometimes planned and approved operations involving more than one agency. But on the whole, covert action was left to the DDP's specialists.[15] Over the decades, the rest of the U.S. government tended to make covert action the CIA's exclusive business.

The Defense Department, except during actual wars (e.g., Korea and Vietnam), was usually little involved in CA except for logistical and cover arrangements. Although initially the State Department was involved at the top in helping to design overall covert action plans, it became less and less involved over the years in the planning and actual implementation of operations. Senior State (as well as military) officials almost always participated in the NSC's covert action approval process, and at times provided logistical and cover arrangements, but covert action itself was outside their preserve. That was something the CIA did. Most Foreign Service officers, even many ambassadors, knew little about what the United States was doing, and rarely worked tactically with the CIA in an orchestrated manner, combining covert tools with overt mechanisms.

In the 1970s, first with President Nixon's policy of détente, and then when President Carter declared that the United States was inordinately fearful of communism, the country's political circumstances began to be perceived differently. The result, with regard to intelligence, was a sharp reduction in resources and the abandonment of the symbiosis necessary for a full-service intelligence system. By the late 1970s U.S. intelligence capabilities were such that the president and Congress became concerned about U.S. intelligence weaknesses. President Reagan, believing from the outset that the United States faced increased military, paramilitary, and political threats, subsequently further changed policy and sought to increase U.S. intelligence capabilities, including those related to covert action and counterintelligence.

The lesson is clear: If the United States feels threatened, there will be more resources for and attention to intelligence, and the scope of intelligence operations will be broadened; but if threats appear to be diminished, less use will be made of, and fewer resources will be available for, intelligence. It follows that there will be a decline in the regular use of, and thus capability for, covert action.

In addition to the nature of U.S. government and the perception or lack of perception of danger, another factor that accounts for the decline in the use of and capability for effective CA was the bureaucratic struggle within the CIA itself. At its founding, most of the CIA's principals were reluctant to undertake the function, but because the State Department and the Department of Defense (DoD) did not want it, the Office of Policy Coordination (OPC) was assigned to the CIA under State Department guidance.[16] Gradually this changed.

The ethos that veterans of the Office of Strategic Services (OSS), particularly Allen W. Dulles as director of central intelligence (DCI) in the 1950s, put in place at the CIA remained dominant for two decades. Dulles ensured that analysts, collectors, covert action operators, and counterintelligence were supported, and that they collaborated, even if not always harmoniously. The full-service ethos was dominant within the CIA.

By the 1970s, however, bureaucratic pressures within the agency and the breakup of the foreign policy consensus outside it led new CIA leaders to make important changes in the power and relationships of the various elements, and gradually to change that bureaucratic ethos. Under a succession of DCIs, the major covert action and counterintelligence components were downgraded. In turn, analysis and technical collection became dominant and there was little integration of the elements of intelligence.[17]

To these influences were added the pressure of the constant struggle since the 1970s between the executive and legislative branches of the federal government over the (some would call "imperial") powers of the presidency, particularly with regard to foreign policy. The consequences with respect to intelligence are well known: From the congressional perspective, oversight of intelligence activities was an important political and constitutional imperative; from the executive's perspective, intelligence was seen as an instrument that was supposed to be directly responsive to the president, but over which Congress had striven successfully to expand its say.[18] The form and practice of intelligence in the United States and CA, in particular, reflected this evolving institutional struggle.

But the history of policy and covert action in the 1980s, especially in Central America, shows that the decline of covert action in the U.S. government can also be traced to additional factors. Perhaps the most important was the lack of presidential leadership (i.e., a lack of capacity on the part of recent presidents to formulate policies and to force opponents to oppose them on the merits). Presidents sometimes have chosen covert action as a substitute for well-thought-out policy, as a half-measure when they were unwilling to mobilize the means to achieve clear-cut ends and then to force the issue. One of the most attractive features of half-measures is that they enable the president to feel that he is doing something even when it is not enough to achieve real results.

It is no wonder that the bureaucracies within the executive branch have reflected the contradictions that presidents have been unwilling to resolve. If the president supported a certain operation—but without putting his own prestige on the line—and Congress was believed to oppose it, CIA professionals understandably were reluctant to put their own relations with Congress on the line for the sake of that program. While there were a few exceptions in William Casey's CIA, by the late 1980s few, if any, CIA officers believed that the regular use of covert action was rewarding for the United States politically or, for themselves, personally.

Therefore, the U.S. capability for covert action has declined since the 1960s. The U.S. government downgraded its covert action infrastructure, or as it is sometimes called, the CA plumbing.

A covert action infrastructure has various components. To oversimplify, it consists primarily of various types of people and of various kinds of material resources. The people are prepared and trained to operate covertly even before the "balloon goes up." Some of the people are full- or part-time CA professionals. They may be CIA employees or American or foreign "contract agents" (i.e., people with other real jobs or special skills such as journalists, trade union officials, and so on) who have been hired secretly for full- or part-time work by the CIA. They are hired because it is believed that they know how to get the job done. They know who's who in a given foreign country and how to get access to and influence them. In addition, some of the people in the infrastructure are local agents or assets—foreign political, military, or intelligence operatives; media personnel; and trade union or religious leaders who collaborate on given projects. These assets, or agents, may or may not receive money.

Starting in the late 1940s, the United States built up a large human and material infrastructure. Probably it was too large and inefficient, and certainly it had far too little CI protection. In the late 1960s, the infrastructure began to be downgraded.[19] Few CIA officers or full-time contract agents specialized in covert action. The asset base at home and abroad also declined.[20]

Even before the Church Committee hearings in the mid-1970s, the executive branch imposed restraints on the CIA. In the mid-1970s, under congressional pressure, the CIA voluntarily agreed to another series of unilateral restraints on the use of various professions in the United States, either for cover or as a recruitment pool for agents. The full list and the constraints on the use of Americans—and even foreigners—have not been made public. Reportedly, the list included U.S. journalists, educators, religious leaders, as well as certain categories of government employees, such as current and former Peace Corps employees. The United States was thus deprived of current and future opportunities for using the cover that key professions within the private sector could provide.

Prudent Principles for Successful Covert Action

There has been little effort in contemporary discussions of security in the post–Cold War world to overcome these self-imposed weaknesses in U.S. statecraft. Some, however, try to "square the circle." The circle is the traditional prejudice against covert action and the contemporary restrictions surrounding both the executive and legislative branches' assent to covert action. The square is the dangerous world in which we are likely to continue to live. We are witnessing the reassertion of historical pressures that were only temporarily stilled or, rather, muffled by the East-West conflict. These forces are not necessarily benign.

While the direct survival of the United States may no longer be threatened since the demise of the USSR, the United States is not as relatively powerful as it was during the past five decades. This relative change has taken place in a world very different from that of the Cold War. The large-scale stability of the Cold War (with all its risks) was, historically speaking, unusual. Today's regional instability and even "ungovernability" are closer to the historical norm. For example, the area from Central Europe to the Yellow Sea, a vast area populated by hundreds of millions of people, is in varying degrees of turmoil. The world, as the authors of the 1990s version of the Church Committee's Final Report described it, is indeed "a dangerous place in which threats to the United States, its interests, and its citizens continue to exist."[21]

The resultant circle and square are an impossible fit. When they are combined with the failure of the chief executive to formulate coherent policy and fight his battles in support of his policies, the result is largely paralysis. But even in the present atmosphere of executive and legislative struggle, this paralysis can be ameliorated if basic prudent principles of successful covert action are followed.

The first principle is that CA should be one part of a policy that has been well thought out. Ends, with means reasonably calculated to achieve them, must be thought through. This cannot be emphasized too strongly. Covert action is a policy tool. It is not a substitute for policy. It must be designed to support policy—not adventures. This means that it must usually be conceived as covering an indefinite, and perhaps extended, period of time. As noted above, such was the conception of Elizabeth I in weakening Spain and the Catholics in the sixteenth century. It was also that of the French in supporting the American Revolution to weaken the British in the eighteenth century, and the United States at the time of the Marshall Plan.

To repeat: Covert action is not a substitute for policy. It is generally counterproductive when used by a government that has not really decided what it wants to do, but wants "to do something," yet is unwilling to make a sustained commitment of resources and political capital to carry out its policy. Examples of the latter were Great Britain and the United States, first following the Russian revolution, and then again after World War II in dealing with ruling Communist parties from the late 1940s to the 1970s. The two Western powers did not want to just sit idly by, but they could not decide exactly what they were willing to do. In lieu of an effective policy, half-hearted covert action seemed a reasonably risk-free option.

Covert action is also not a magic bullet, nor is it an exceptional tool to be used by itself when almost everything else has failed. Its use in either of these fashions is not responsible leadership, but rather surrender by a government to pressures upon it. There may, of course, be occasions when a Trojan horse operation, an assassination, or assassination prevention can change the internal balance of power in a targeted state, or even the external balance (e.g., as the assassination of Hitler probably would have done), but such circumstances are rare. To be effective, covert action must usually be coordinated with and supported by diplomatic, military, and economic means. Policymakers must be sensitive to these realities.

Covert action is one of a number of instruments that can be used when it is clear that policy objectives cannot be achieved exclusively by, or as effectively with, exclusively overt policy means. It is absolutely essential, however, that the risks and difficulties of the covert action be carefully weighed. Such were British operations when they sought to bring the United States into World Wars I and II, and those of the United States in support of both the Marshall Plan and NATO.

To enunciate these principles is not to argue for more or for less covert action. It is a call for use of the instrument when a government, even a democratic government, is clear about its policy and willing to defend it. A democratic government should not, as a rule, embark on foreign initiatives unless it is willing to mount a public campaign for them and unless there is a reasonable chance of gaining support for its policy. The general goals and the overall means reasonably calculated to achieve them should be laid out for the people in a democracy.

To develop and articulate and defend objectives publicly does not mean that the government must spell out its covert action programs. But, as a rule, those programs should be consistent with policy. If they are, even if leaked or small mistakes are made, they will not lead to public displeasure and government disarray—as they did in the United States in the Iran-contra affair in the 1980s.

But policy must rest on something more than the calculated aims of presidents and their advisers—congressional and executive. The second principle of prudent covert action is capability-in-being. To lurch forward at the last moment to find the people and to develop the techniques that will fulfill the policy is a necessary characteristic of an emergency mobilization, not of preparedness. For example, with the general decline of U.S. covert action capability, in particular the loss of trained personnel over more than a decade, the CIA was hard-pressed to respond to the Nicaraguan problem. A retired military specialist from the Special Forces who had taught at Fort Bragg was brought in to train the Contras. Out of touch with current attitudes, he wrote a manual that indirectly advocated assassination. In the early 1960s this would not have caused a great stir, but in the early 1980s it was political dynamite. It caused harm to the Contras, to the case officers who hired him, and to the advocates of U.S. aid to the Contras. This mistake could have been avoided if the president had had a capable infrastructure to start.

Another example is the Middle East in recent years. The United States has done little to ensure that it has a cadre of Arabs, Iranians, Palestinians, and others opposed to radical states and groups that target U.S. citizens and interests in the region. As a matter of routine, the United States has not covertly helped pro-Western elements in the region the way the Soviets, Libyans, Iranians, and others recruited and aided their friends in an unacknowledged manner, and in the way the United States did in Europe and the developing world in the 1950s and 1960s. So when the United States needs political operatives to help in the struggle against, for example, terrorism, nuclear proliferation, narcotics, and radical Islam in the 1990s, it finds itself with few political assets. Indeed, when the United States has been moderately successful in the region, as in the struggle in Afghanistan in the 1980s, it was not because the United States had many people to do the CA job. Rather, the United States was able to join in a covert coalition with others. According to the man who ran the war for a time inside Afghanistan (and inside the USSR), the Pakistan Intelligence Service benefited from U.S. (and other) money, training, equipment, and intelligence. But it was the Pakistanis, rather than the Americans, who did the work inside Afghanistan.[22]

Hugh Tovar, an OSS veteran, a generalist CIA case officer, chief of the CIA's covert action staff in the late 1960s, and one of the most perceptive commentators on the CIA's "halcyon days," said in 1988:

If the need for CA initiatives should burgeon . . . a rapid and effective expansion of the infrastructure would be difficult to effect. . . . I see no way to circumvent this problem except to begin to work into the system people possessing the special skills and knowledge that would allow them to cope successfully with current requirements and later rise to the occasion when new CA initiatives are in heavy demand.[23]

The prejudice against covert action, which currently permeates the U.S. government, should not dictate the future.

Still another lesson is pertinent. As stated at the outset of this chapter, the relationship of covert action to the rest of intelligence is, for the most part, symbiotic. Covert action should be integrated not only with policy, but with the other elements of intelligence—collection, analysis, and counterintelligence—as well. Obviously, covert action planners and operators should be beneficiaries of the end products of collection and analysis. Collectors are in contact with many people who by virtue of their position and status are not only valuable sources of information but are also the movers and shakers of society. Also, to avoid duplication of recruitment efforts and competition for assets, it is useful for the collectors of intelligence to work very closely with covert action operators. Many an intelligence agent is also potentially a natural covert ally. There is a natural symbiosis between collection and covert action, and former practitioners have pointed out that some of the best collection operations have benefited from covert action.

Similarly, covert action benefits from good analysis—especially if it is "opportunity analysis." Spotting opportunities and vulnerabilities in the foreign society provides a natural guide to covert operators. Analysts who know who is who, who wants what, and who is vulnerable to what political, economic, and military pressures are invaluable to operators.[24] For example, merely knowing that there are ethnic and religious tensions in a given region is not enough. The operators need to know the strengths and weaknesses of the key players, what motivates them, and what opportunities there are to influence them.

This is not to say that analysts should be tied too closely to the covert action operators. If they are, there is a danger that they will become involved and committed, and thereby lose the advantage of "objectivity." Covert action managers need to harness the analysts while at the same time keeping them at a distance.

Another advantage of close collaboration between analysts and covert action is that sometimes the analysis itself can be used in actual operations. For example, the analysts' description of the venalities of terrorists, their corruption, weaknesses, and machinations can be used to discredit them. Analyses—in a sanitized form—can also be passed to foreign leaders to shape their perceptions of the world, much as the British did in the United States prior to U.S. entry into World War II.

Covert operators also need good counterintelligence; if they try to work without it they will be in trouble. They must know if their foreign allies are genuinely loyal to the causes that they espouse, or if they in fact are double agents of other intelligence services or private groups.

There are pros and cons to placing responsibility for covert action in the same bureaucracy with the other elements of intelligence—the United States and Great Britain have had experience with both. For the moment that is a secondary issue. The primary issue is to restore covert action to its place in the symbiosis essential to an effective full-service U.S. intelligence capability.

In sum, the world is likely to remain a dangerous place. There are almost certainly circumstances where the United States will want to covertly help friendly forces and hinder adversaries. The fate of the United States may not be at risk, but as history demonstrates, the United States is likely to have an advantage if it has the ability to covertly influence conditions abroad and a disadvantage if it does not.

To enhance and protect its interests, the United States must first consider covert action a normal instrument to be blended together with other tools of statecraft. If it does, then it will be only natural to maintain the necessary skills and infrastructure for its effective use. If covert action is regarded as exceptional, the skills and capabilities for its use will not be maintained. Then, when the instrument is used and found to be ineffective, this will merely confirm the predictions of the exceptionalists. Finally, covert action must not only be coordinated and blended in overall policy-making and implementation, it must be blended with the other elements of intelligence. The effectiveness of this secret instrument will be enhanced if its operational security is protected through sound counterintelligence, and the secrets of others are exploited through opportunity-oriented collection and analysis. The country needs no less.

COMMENTS: RICHARD KERR

What is covert action? The following have all been used to describe covert action: a vital element of U.S. policy; an anachronism in the "new world"; an impossible task given the intrusiveness of oversight and the inability of the executive to keep secrets; an essential tool to affect events in an unruly world; inconsistent with democratic values; an action between a diplomatic note and the use of B-52s.

Covert action encompasses a wide range of activities: from the training of foreign intelligence services to conducting a low-intensity war. It has been the source of major problems between the executive and Congress and the origin of much of the criticism of the CIA.

It is time to assess covert action in the context of a changing world and with clear recognition of its value and limitations. Covert action needs to be better defined. Some of the activity now categorized as covert action should be handled as the normal business of foreign policy. New procedures should be established for control of those actions that truly require congressional oversight. To avoid covert action being the center of foreign policy debates, Congress needs to be better briefed about U.S. foreign policy. It also is necessary to more clearly define the role of the U.S. military and other government elements in covert actions.

Several principles should guide any consideration of covert action:

• It is difficult if not impossible to keep a major covert activity secret— and secrecy defines whether an activity is covert or not. This is primarily a problem of executive discipline.

• Any major covert action aimed at changing a government, supporting or fighting an insurgency, or conducting a long-term and expensive effort to change the behavior of a country must have bipartisan support. It also must be "approved" in some formally established executive and congressional process.

• Although covert action should be an integral part of policy development, it often is used as a last resort after conventional foreign policy mechanisms have been used and have failed.

• Successful covert action requires a clear policy objective and patience, and should be attempted only as part of a full effort to use all the instruments of foreign policy. It is not a good tool to be used alone.

Why Is Covert Action Needed?

Covert action will be necessary in this increasingly complex and contentious world. The United States inevitably will want to affect events in a particular country or region. It will want to change the behavior of a country, support an embattled "good guy," stop proliferators, interdict drugs and weapons, or stop a terrorist act. Diplomacy, the threat of military action or actual use of military force, and overt persuasion through the media or organizations such as the National Endowment for Democracy (NED) are preferable methods. Nevertheless, there will be occasions when overt means are insufficient and the objective is too important to just give up.

How to Do It?

First, the definition and approval process for covert action should be reviewed. Covert actions must be separated into several different categories with a different set of approval procedures for each category. For example:

• Activity intended primarily to assist a foreign government to improve its capability to counter terrorists, to be more effective in counternarcotics programs, or to protect its leadership should not be considered covert action. (This does not mean that there should be no oversight of these activities by Congress. Such activities should be reported to Congress and defended as part of the normal process.) Attempts to help a country improve its ability to assist in areas that the United States believes are important to its interest should not be viewed as sinister.

• Activity aimed at supporting well-established policy such as countering illegal trafficking or terrorism should be placed into a new category that allows executive action without going through the current approval process in which presidents sign formal findings authorizing covert programs. Many actions involving U.S. intelligence and law enforcement should be done on the basis of standing executive authority. Review of these activities by Congress is necessary but committees are not good risk-taking organizations and are not capable of making operational decisions. If Congress does not have a role in approving operations and only reviews performance, it is imperative that the executive have effective internal control procedures.

• Activity aimed at changing governments, the behavior of governments, and other such politically sensitive actions requires some type of "finding" process, but the current process must be improved. Over the past dozen or so years Congress has used the covert action approval process as the way to debate foreign policy decisions by the executive. On some issues Congress was opposed to the policy but did not have or choose to use another forum to debate the issue. Sometimes policy has not been well articulated or did not exist. There is no simple solution to this problem and all of the above will occur again. But some of the more destructive fights can be avoided by better communication and better procedures.

Implementation of Covert Action

A single organization is needed to coordinate covert action programs—the CIA or a successor. It is less clear that the CIA must execute all covert action programs. It is time to assess the role of the U.S.
Special Forces and other elements of government in activities that are
now in the category of covert action. The CIA probably does need to
maintain the infrastructure for moving people and equipment in secret,
and it also will need to maintain generic capabilities to provide support
to covert activity. One of the major tasks may be to demystify covert
action and accept that using all the tools at the disposal of the government—secret or not—to further well-defined U.S. objectives is a moral
and correct objective. Often secrecy is intended only to protect the sen-
sitivities of a foreign country. Secrecy also is intended to protect the
means of support and the people involved. It should not be intended to
hide the policy of the United States.

The Role of Intelligence Analysis

In this new and more complex world it will be necessary to use analytic
capability as an integral part of U.S. operational activity. Ethnic, tribal,
regional, and religious conflicts present more complicated challenges
than in the past, when allegiance to the West or to the East often
defined the problem. Also, the type of analysis required in dealing with
the new set of problems—proliferation, terrorism, and counternarcotics—is different and much more investigative and actionable than
traditional intelligence analysis.

   One danger in mixing the analytic and operational sides of intelligence must be recognized. Those conducting operations cannot objectively evaluate how well they are doing. Some separation must exist,
but interaction is essential to make sure that action is consistent with
understanding.

COMMENTS: ERNEST MAY

Dick Kerr approached Roy Godson's arguments from the future; as a
historian, I approach them from the past. While I take issue with some
of Roy's arguments, I differ primarily in my emphasis. Differences in
emphasis, however, can produce important differences in inference
and recommendation. I would emphasize more the points with which
Roy begins than those with which he concludes.

   In his typology, I classify myself as an "exceptionalist" of both type A
and type B. While I would not go so far as to contend that covert action

is incompatible with democracy, I do think covert action is not easily accommodated by the U.S. democratic system. And while I would also not contend that covert action can be a substitute for policy, I do view it as an alternative worth consideration primarily when, as Roy puts it, diplomacy will not work and military action is too dangerous.

Roy says, in effect, that there are three requirements for covert action: (1) a coherent policy by a government that has decided what it wants to do; (2) a well-coordinated policy (i.e., well-planned diplomatic, military, and economic measures to go in tandem with covert measures); and (3) covertness—ability to keep the government's role not apparent or at least not publicly acknowledged.

I believe that the United States is not constituted to meet any of those three requirements. I say "constituted" because I do not mean simply that it is ill-equipped or ill-organized or temporarily ill-disposed. I mean that the basic political structure is not constituted to produce, except in conditions of extraordinary emergency, the three conditions stipulated.

The U.S. Constitution was intended to make it very difficult to define national interests and hence to specify the goals for coherent, well-coordinated policies. The Framers did this because they had experienced something like the Elizabethan system. They had seen state interests defined by those in seats of power, and they had not liked the results. They thought that state interest defined from on high had not accommodated the interests and sensibilities of particular localities and individuals. They designed a political system that made wide consultation a precondition of designating any interests as of overriding common concern.

It is harder in the United States than in any other major nation, now or in the past, to be able to say: "This is our national interest. We should and will commit our resources to pursue it. We will, if necessary, fight for it." Among other things, the Constitution requires that any formal engagement be endorsed by the president and two-thirds of the Senate. It further requires that the president and majorities in both houses of Congress agree on any commitments of resources—and do so again every single year.

The U.S. political system is designed not only on the premise that delineation of a national interest ought to be very difficult but also on the further premise that no such interest should be deemed permanent. The processes of authorization and appropriation and the requirements for election and reelection of presidents and members of Congress mean that definitions of national interest come under more or less constant review. And this is review not only of the interests themselves but of the policies and procedures adopted to pursue those interests. The political system is designed to reflect the changing concerns and values of a variegated and changing population. It would not have surprised James Madison to see Congress and the country condemn in the 1970s covert actions carried out in the 1950s and 1960s. They had changed their minds.

The United States can only rarely have the "coherent policy" that Roy describes as a precondition for effective covert action. And the coherent policy of one period may not be that of another.

Second, the government functioning under the Constitution has evolved in ways that make extremely difficult any coordinated action, even regarding commonly accepted national interests. The only exceptions have been during periods of real emergency. This is partly because the Constitution provided for shared powers, with the result that each executive agency and each congressional committee tends to be a representative body, with its own distinctive constituencies. Except in genuine emergencies, no one can force these units to act in concert; they must be moved by persuasion, not by command. Consider in our context the fact that the bureaucracy with the weakest domestic base—the Foreign Service—has been able consistently to complicate the provision of effective cover for officers of the clandestine service working out of embassies.

The difficulty of achieving coordinated action is also due to post-1789 developments not then foreseen. The Framers had expected a government of gentlemen, in the eighteenth-century sense. These gentlemen might duel; they would not necessarily be polite to one another; they could even be uncouth. But holders of office at the national level were expected to be leaders of, not panderers to, the constituencies from which they came. The Framers envisioned a republic ruled by lawgivers. The United States became instead a democracy ruled by popularity-seekers. The result was a government that, until the twentieth century, functioned usually as either pork barrel or a tub for tub-thumping.

In the twentieth century, "gentlemen" returned in large numbers to public office. Very few, however, arrived as holders of elective office. They came into appointive posts, especially after the national security establishment mushroomed. They thought—as Roy does—that government ought to have coherent policies tailored to well-understood national interests. As a rule, they found themselves in actuality functioning as brokers adjusting relations among sluggish career bureaucracies, congressional committees, executive budgeteers, electorally preoccupied presidents, and lobbyists for special interests, harassed meanwhile by a growing and increasingly diligent Washington press corps.

To the extent that the U.S. government achieves coordination such as Roy desires, it does so outside of Washington—at overseas missions. But this further inhibits coordination in support of coherent national policy because each mission has its own idiosyncratic conception of interests and policies. Each chief of mission views his or her country as among the United States's most vital concerns. The result, to borrow a phrase from Harold Nicolson, is a sense of "riot in a parrot house."

The final criterion—sustained covertness—is made extraordinarily difficult by the same factors that impair coherence and coordination. Covertness cannot be maintained once there is serious questioning of the interest it is supposed to serve. It was possible in Afghanistan but not in Central America. And covertness cannot be maintained once the consensus shifts. When "doing in" communism in South Vietnam ceased to be an agreed-upon national interest, the Phoenix Program ceased to be a heroic undertaking, properly kept under cover. Instead, it became the subject of exposés.

This is not intended as a brief against any covert action. The point is that no covert action should be prepared or undertaken without clear recognition of the extent to which it must be circumscribed. Unless there is again the sense of real emergency predominant during World War II and the first two decades of the Cold War, Roy's three criteria will never be met. Three other criteria should be substituted.

• Is there clear public and congressional consensus about the national interest to be served? Would Ronald Dellums and Newt Gingrich agree on it? How about Mary McGrory and Robert Novak? If there is doubt about the answers, no covert action should be organized, no matter how important the interest may seem to officials in the executive branch.

• Is the projected covert action bureaucratically feasible? Do the planners know exactly who will do what, and when? Are they sure that no other office, division, bureau, agency, committee, or unit will stick a screwdriver under a cam just to serve some unrelated end? *Really* sure?

• Are the authorizing parties in the executive and in Congress prepared to live with the consequences when (not "if") covertness is lost? The consensus about interest may fade. Someone, at some time, may stick in that screwdriver. Some reporter, some lawyer, or some scholar will eventually insist on making the matter public. If that will hurt too much, the covert action is not worth it.

Does this leave room for any covert action? I believe the answer is "yes"—but not much room. The interests that are now sufficiently matters of consensus to warrant covert operations may be no more than two—limiting the spread of weapons of mass destruction and aborting acts of terrorism. Almost every American probably would agree to covert operations to cripple another country's clandestine nuclear or chemical or biological weapons programs. All but a few would approve covert operations that frustrated the blowing up of a passenger plane or the gunning down of an Olympic team. Oversight arrangements are adequate to ensure that such covert operations do not stray into just destroying an industrial competitor's laboratories or just helping out the police forces of a repressive government.

Countering the narcotics trade might make the list but probably should not. The extent of real consensus is not as clear, the objective is too ill-defined, and the scope for unpardonable error is too wide.

My conclusions are not apt to be applauded by those who think that almost all criticism of covert operations is mushy McGovernism that ought to be ignored. Neither, however, would they be applauded by those who think it best to undertake no covert operations at all. In a period of deep cuts in all national security programs, moreover, they may seem quixotic, because I urge that we develop a more substantial capability for covert action than the one we now possess. (I gather that we could not have taken out Saddam Hussein's nuclear facilities by covert action even if we had good early intelligence about them.) I also urge that this capability be used only if the three stated conditions are met: public consensus on the interest being served, clear feasibility, and tolerance for disclosure. This is a recommendation, in other words, for spending a great deal for a covert action capability rarely to be used.

PART III:

POLICIES AND POLICYMAKERS

13

ECONOMIC ESPIONAGE

Randall M. Fort

ince the demise of the Soviet Union, the headlines on the issue of
economic espionage have been tantalizing: "Security Agency Debates New Role: Economic Spying"; "Should the CIA Start Spying for
Corporate America?"; "Some Urge CIA to Go Further in Gathering
Economic Intelligence"; and "Next for the CIA: Business Spying?"[1]
These headlines reflect the considerable debate that has occurred on
the issue of whether the U.S. Intelligence Community should provide
direct intelligence support to the U.S. private sector.

The genesis for much of this debate has been concern over the
alleged decline in U.S. economic competitiveness and the need to prevent it. Ostensibly, conducting economic espionage against foreign
trade and business competitors to support the U.S. private sector
would "help" U.S. competitiveness. In addition, with the end of the
Cold War, U.S. intelligence must refocus its efforts and resources, and
it has been suggested that supporting economic competitiveness could
be defined as a new intelligence requirement. Although it may sound
like a good idea, it is wrong, for reasons of practicality, utility, legality,
and morality. Asking the U.S. Intelligence Community to conduct economic espionage on behalf of U.S. companies would most decidedly be
a bad idea.

There is considerable misunderstanding about the issue, much of
which stems from a confusion over terminology. *Economic espionage,
industrial espionage, commercial spying*, and other such terms may or
may not refer to the same thing, but are frequently used interchange-
ably. In this chapter the term *economic espionage* will be used, defined
as the clandestine acquisition of economic, financial, trade, and/or proprietary information by an official intelligence service using intelligence sources and methods. Further, the key issue under consideration

---

This paper was first presented on April 8, 1993.

is not whether such intelligence should be collected, but rather whether it should be provided by the U.S. Intelligence Community to the private sector.

What Is Economic Intelligence?

An additional point of confusion arises from a misunderstanding of the appropriate role of economic intelligence compared with that of other intelligence functions. As a first principle: There is a historic and legitimate role for economic intelligence in support of government policymaking. Although economic policy has become a more visible, priority issue recently, it has been an important area of intelligence collection and analysis for many years.

The Intelligence Community (IC) has traditionally been active in three key areas: First, the IC has provided support to government officials as they make economic policy. This support has included analysis of bilateral and multilateral economic negotiations; identification of economic trends and understanding the intentions of economic competitors; integration of vast amounts of disparate data to present a complete picture of the economic and political factors affecting international stability; and helping policymakers understand the "rules of the economic game" as it is played by others (e.g., to monitor foreign subsidies, lobbying, bribes, and import restraints). The Treasury Department, U.S. Trade Representative, State Department, National Security Council, and Commerce Department have all benefited considerably over the years from such support.

Second, the IC has monitored trends overseas in technology that could affect U.S. national security. The U.S. government must be aware of foreign developments in computers, semiconductors, telecommunications, and the like, which might affect U.S. military capabilities or national security interests.

The third area of IC responsibility is economic counterintelligence, that is, the identification and neutralization of foreign intelligence services spying on U.S. citizens or companies and stealing information and/or technology for use within their own countries. With recent revelations of spying by the French and Israeli intelligence services against U.S. companies, the issue of foreign intelligence collection against U.S. economic interests has seized attention. It is not, however, a new issue.

Remember the KGB?

Throughout the Cold War, economic information was a major target for the Soviet KGB and the Warsaw Pact. In fact, the KGB dedicated significant resources to the collection of economic information—Line X from the old KGB organization chart was responsible for acquiring scientific and technical information. Additionally, the massive Soviet signal intelligence (SIGINT) site at Lourdes, Cuba, gave them unique and in-depth access to a wide spectrum of U.S. commercial communications. Although the Soviets were interested principally in technology or information relevant to building or countering weapons systems, this was not always the case. For example, in the early 1970s, the Soviets used communications intercepts to negotiate very favorable terms with U.S. companies on large wheat purchases.

Because economic information was one of the things the Cold War adversaries of the United States were trying to steal, it was also one of the things that U.S. counterintelligence (CI) services were organized to try to protect. For example, for twenty years the FBI has operated a program called Developing Espionage and Counterintelligence Awareness (DECA), which provides briefings and information to U.S. companies, particularly defense contractors, about hostile intelligence threats and activities. In the post–Cold War world, defending against foreign intelligence threats, whether against U.S. military secrets or proprietary economic data, remains a legitimate national security interest.

Current Intelligence Support to the Private Sector

Support for U.S. business has been and remains an important policy priority for the U.S. government. In December 1991, then-Deputy Secretary of State Lawrence Eagleburger stated, "U.S. competitiveness in the global economy must become one of the pillars of U.S. foreign policy and of our projection of strength and influence."[2] More recently, Secretary of State Warren Christopher declared in a speech in March 1993 that one of the first pillars of foreign policy is that it serve the economic needs of the United States.[3] As the government makes policy in support of U.S. competitiveness, it will be supported in part with information and analysis provided by the Intelligence Community. U.S.

businesses are the indirect beneficiaries of that intelligence support because the policies are being made on the private sector's behalf.

The Intelligence Community is not, therefore, new to the issue of economic intelligence, either the collection of such information for official government requirements or the prevention of such collection by foreign intelligence services. Further, economic issues are and will remain a foreign policy priority and therefore will be the focus of considerable activity by the Intelligence Community in order to provide support to U.S. government officials.

A New Threat?

What is new is the suggestion by some that intelligence resources should be used in an entirely different way, to provide direct support to the U.S. private sector. This idea is sometimes justified by an attempt to define the various economic challenges as new "national security threats" worthy of treatment by traditional national security tools, such as intelligence support. One of the leading proponents of this view has been former Director of Central Intelligence (DCI) Stansfield Turner. Admiral Turner stated:

> The preeminent threat to U.S. national security now lies in the economic sphere. . . . We must, then, redefine "national security" by assigning economic strength greater prominence. . . . If economic strength should now be recognized as a vital component of national security, parallel with military power, why should America be concerned about stealing and employing economic secrets?[4]

"America should be concerned" because such an effort directly on behalf of the private sector would do little to improve U.S. economic competitiveness and would quite likely cause great harm to other important equities. Before looking at the costs and benefits of such a program, however, it is important to address the notion that economic competitiveness should be redefined as a national security threat.

The U.S. economy has suffered from a number of economic problems and dislocations in recent years. Many of them, however, are of our own making. The immense and all but uncontrollable budget deficit, with its impact on interest rates, availability of investment capital, and so forth is 100 percent "Made in the USA." Low savings rates, onerous regulations, and tax burdens are contributing "nonforeign" factors. Some of the United States' economic problems are the result of pressures from and actions by foreign countries, but those factors vary widely, from unfair trading practices to simply building better, cheaper products.

Regardless of the provenance of these problems, it is pernicious to define them as "threats," especially "national security threats." They are more correctly labeled economic "challenges"—obstacles that can be overcome if we follow sound economic, financial, trading, diplomatic, and business policies and practices. A "threat" is appropriately defined as something that can cause demonstrable physical harm; a national security threat is, therefore, something that can cause tangible, physical harm or destruction to the United States. For example, the existence of tens of thousands of Soviet nuclear weapons posed a considerable "threat" to U.S. national security. Thought of in another way, carrying out a "threat" implies a zero-sum game at best—one side winning means the other side would have to lose. In the worst-case national security threat scenario—a nuclear war—no participant could expect to win much.

Economics Is Not War

Economic competition, however, is not a zero-sum game. There are winners and losers, certainly, but the gains and losses transcend national boundaries. If Honda of Japan makes an excellent car and sells a large number of them in the United States, then Honda is a winner and the U.S. car companies that lost those sales are losers. But the interactions are more complicated. For one thing, American consumers who buy those excellent cars of a type and quality not produced in the United States are clear winners. American auto parts companies that sell to Honda are winners, and American companies that produce and broadcast Honda advertisements are also winners. Further, increased market share for Honda, among other reasons, led to their building production plants in the United States, which is clearly to the economic advantage of the American workers employed in those plants, not to mention the increased tax revenues available to the local jurisdictions hosting such plants. Americans who have invested in Honda have been winners, and even American car companies are better off ultimately because they have had to become more efficient and productive to meet the foreign car challenge posed by Honda and other foreign car makers.

The list of winners and losers from even the limited example of imports of Honda automobiles goes on and on, but suffice it to say that in economics, competition is not a black-and-white, zero-sum game.

"America" does not "lose" when faced with foreign economic competition. That competition poses challenges to various sectors of the U.S. economy, challenges that must be overcome certainly, but these are not threats to national existence.

Undertaking a program of providing direct intelligence support to the U.S. private sector would be both a significant departure from past practice and a major operational challenge. Therefore, it should be incumbent upon those who advocate such an effort to describe how it would be accomplished. Rather than making their case, however, proponents usually sidestep or ignore this critical point. Indeed, Admiral Turner blithely stated, "There are problems galore, but these are for the Commerce Department to handle on a case-by-case basis."[5] There are certainly "problems galore," but they are beyond the ability of the Commerce Department or any other government agency to resolve.

Practical Concerns

The first significant problem is the matter of practicality. Attempting to define a workable program to share intelligence with the private sector immediately raises a host of practical problems, both in how to implement a program as well as the consequences of doing so. One of the first questions to address is how a program would be set up and operated. There is, for example, the issue of defining the beneficiary. What sectors of the economy and what companies would be targeted for assistance, because the IC could not help them all? Who would make those choices? Would all companies within a particular sector receive assistance, or just some? Again, who would choose and on what basis—size, profitability, or market share? The U.S. government, which wasted billions of taxpayers' dollars trying to support the development of synthetic fuels in the 1970s, would need to create a mechanism to decide which sectors and companies would be supported.

The fairness and wisdom of the selection process notwithstanding, intelligence support would ultimately come to be recognized as just another subsidy and, as such, would be subject to the same vagaries of politics as any other subsidy. Anyone who is confident that the government could make wise and farsighted determinations about which sectors or companies to assist should look no further than the April 6, 1993, issue of the *Washington Post*. An article entitled "Hair That Defies Cutting" describes the continued existence, after thirty-nine years, of a $180-million-per-year program to subsidize the growth of mohair wool. Strategic necessity, economic efficiency, and other such logical measures are clearly not relevant in government (political) decision making about who or what is to receive government support and assistance. There is no reason to be confident that decisions about which companies to provide with intelligence support would be made with any more wisdom than has been shown in the mohair support program. Companies with the biggest political clout—not the greatest strategic need—would likely demand and receive the greatest support.

Who Is "Us"?

Before devising a support process, however, there is an even more fundamental question: Exactly what defines a U.S. company? The Commerce Department defines a U.S. company as any enterprise with a majority of stockholders and assets in the United States. But, in the present era of multinational corporations and voluminous international trade and investment flows, the question of nationality is becoming ever more blurred. Would overseas subsidiaries of U.S. companies be assisted? What about U.S. subsidiaries of foreign companies? Should an "American" company be provided intelligence if it would use that information to win a contract to make a product in an overseas factory, if it were in competition with a "foreign" company that, should it win the contract, would make their product in a factory located in the United States? What about "American" companies working in cooperation, via joint venture, technology sharing, or other arrangements, with foreign firms? How are those interests separated in order to share intelligence with only the American entity? These questions are not mere abstractions; they are very real issues that must be sorted out and addressed in any intelligence support program. The following concrete example is illustrative: In February 1993, six major companies—AT&T; Motorola, Inc.; Apple Inc.; Sony Corp.; Matsushita Industrial Electric Co.; and Philips NV—announced an alliance to develop new portable communication devices. The first three are U.S.-based corporations; the last three are foreign-based. How could only the U.S. companies be helped without at least indirectly helping the foreign companies? And wouldn't helping those foreign companies hurt other U.S. companies that will surely enter the market for such devices?

These questions about what is "American" and what is "foreign" are growing more complicated and are a consequence of an increasingly economically integrated world. Secretary of Labor Robert Reich studied these issues of national corporate identity and national economic interests closely during his tenure as a professor at the Kennedy School of Government at Harvard University. Reich published two compelling articles in the *Harvard Business Review* that describe the complex and fragmented nature of today's global economic environment. In the first, he noted that:

> Today, the competitiveness of American-owned corporations is no longer the same as American competitiveness. Indeed, American ownership of the corporation is profoundly less relevant to America's economic future than the skills, training, and knowledge commanded by American workers—*workers who are increasingly employed within the United States by foreign-owned corporations*. So who is us? The answer is, the American work force, the American people, but not particularly the American corporation.[6]

The issues of corporate identity promise to become more, not less, complicated as the world economy continues with its rapid pace of integration. Those changes will affect a host of government policies (such as corporate taxation) besides making a new initiative like economic espionage problematic. While determining the identity and national allegiance of corporations will become more difficult, Reich offers a straightforward answer to the question: Who is us? (and therefore who or what is worthy of government support). It is "the American work force, the American people." Under those circumstances, it would be inappropriate for the U.S. government to provide support to entities with uncertain identities if doing so would cause injury to other, clearly identifiable American interests (e.g., the American citizens who work for foreign companies).

WHAT KINDS OF INTELLIGENCE?

Assuming one could resolve the issue of "who" to support, other vexing practical problems would remain. What kinds of information should be shared with the private sector? Should companies be given tactical data about specific projects or contracts for which they are competing, or broad, strategic estimates about economic prospects in particular countries or regions? Considerations of what kinds of intelligence data should be shared strike at the heart of one of the canons of the Intelligence Community—protection of intelligence sources and methods.

Maintaining the security of sources and methods, while preparing the intelligence for purposes for which the entire collection and analysis system was not designed, would be a daunting task. The information of greatest use, especially for specific contracts or projects, might well be among the most sensitive and highly classified. Any "scrubbing" process to remove those aspects that might reveal the source could also remove or obscure the details that made the report useful in the first place. The IC would face a continuing conundrum: if the intelligence to be shared were too vague, it would be useless; but if it were too specific, then it would threaten the security of sensitive sources and methods.

The sources and methods issue may strike some nonintelligence professionals as abstract bureaucratic pettiness, but to the professional, the issue is seminal, in some cases literally a matter of life and death. As the professional intelligence officer knows well, the technical collection systems that produce much of this nation's intelligence have cost tens of billions of taxpayer dollars and tens of millions of man hours to design, build, operate, and maintain; a single unauthorized disclosure of information derived from one of those sources can diminish if not destroy its effectiveness. In the area of human intelligence collection, the stakes are even higher. If information supplied by a human agent is compromised, his or her safety and security are jeopardized. In many cases, the agents risk losing their lives.

Besides security, intelligence professionals must also be concerned about the productivity of their sources of information. Would current and future sources of information want to provide secrets to the U.S. government if those sources thought the information was only going to advance an American company's bottom line? Clandestine collection of information would not be the only affected area. Department of State diplomatic reporting and Defense attaché reporting could also suffer if a perception were to grow overseas that anything told to the U.S. government was to be used by U.S. companies. To the degree intelligence sources are harmed or dry up because of this, government intelligence consumers will have less intelligence available to draw upon.

These are the realities of the intelligence business, and they cannot be ignored if intelligence products are to be shared and used outside of established security controls. Once again, real-world situations would raise complications for a support program. How would the security of shared intelligence be enforced and maintained? For example, what if an American corporate officer were the recipient of intelligence information about a foreign contract, and then left the U.S. company to work for a foreign competitor? Would he or she be bound by whatever secrecy agreement had been signed, or by their fiduciary responsibility to their new employer? In this era of corporate shake-ups and massive personnel turnover, concerns about protecting the intelligence that would be shared are very real.

COSTS AND DRAWBACKS

Just as there are practical problems of implementation, there would also be practical consequences to an economic espionage program, and many of them would affect the U.S. government. First, the Intelligence Community is not currently organized to produce and disseminate classified information to the private sector. Undertaking such an effort would, therefore, require a new commitment of personnel and resources. In a period of declining intelligence budgets, the resources for a private sector program would most likely be allocated at the expense of government policymakers, who are the only economic intelligence consumers at present. Therefore, policymakers need to ask themselves if the gain to U.S. companies would be worth the possible loss of their own intelligence support.

A second issue for the government to consider is the occasions, sometimes frequent, when the intelligence available on a particular issue is uncertain. Policymakers do the best they can in such instances, but complications could easily arise if that same uncertain information were to be shared with the private sector. The private sector consumers might decide that the intelligence contradicted policy decisions, or at least cast doubt on the viability of the policy. For example, the government might be trying to encourage private U.S. investment in a country or region, but if intelligence analysis shared with the private sector indicated that the economic prospects for that area were poor, then the U.S. companies might well choose not to invest. Government officials would end up arguing about the accuracy of intelligence reporting and estimates not just among themselves, but also with the private sector groups they were trying to influence.

A final concern for the government about an economic espionage program would be its serious and deleterious impacts on U.S. foreign policy. Although the United States is the only remaining superpower, its influence is increasingly dependent on its ability to create and maintain coalitions of different countries to support a particular policy or achieve desired objectives. The core of many of those coalitions is the group of countries that constituted the old Western alliance. Those are also the countries that the United States most frequently competes against economically. To make those countries and their companies the target of economic espionage activity on behalf of the U.S. private sector would undermine the trust and confidence that have served as the historic basis for the existing political alliance, and it would cripple diplomatic efforts to build the coalitions necessary to achieve important foreign policy goals. Granted, the world is changing and the old alliance structure is not as vital as it once was. But the consequences should be thoroughly considered before the United States undertakes actions that could rend the existing relationships and complicate the handling of a host of issues, such as coordinating aid by the G-7 to Russia and confronting Serbian aggression in Bosnia.

Is It Useful?

After practicality, a second major category of problems relates to the issue of utility. The usefulness of intelligence to the private sector has been assumed, but that assumption has not been proven or effectively tested. Certainly the IC produces prodigious volumes of economic and financial information, but that intelligence is produced in response to the needs and requirements articulated by government consumers, not the private sector. There is no doubt that some incidental data now being collected would be of use to a business consumer. But it would take a significant retooling of the intelligence requirements on economic issues and the processing of that intelligence to ensure the routine, timely delivery of relevant information.

Throughout the debate on this issue, has anyone listened to what the private sector has to say? Or asked them if they want or need such information? Interestingly, there has been mostly silence—not one chief executive officer or other senior official of an American corporation has gone on record advocating or supporting such a program. In fact, what little reporting there is suggests that businesses are at best dubious about the idea. In a March 1993 *Washington Post* article, local executives worried that intelligence sharing "could give an unfair advantage to big companies," and "would run the risk of 'spoiling relationships with other countries who would become suspicious of how level the information playing field is.' "[7] *Time* notes that "many U.S. executives fear that suspected CIA involvement in their business could scare off customers and suppliers overseas. They're also afraid that American companies themselves may eventually fall under the spy agency's watchful eye."[8]

Do business executives think that the IC has anything useful to offer? Apparently not. As one senior executive from a major U.S.

corporation said, "If a company needs the CIA to tell them what's going on in their area of business, then they're already in Chapter 11 [bankruptcy]."[9] If sharing intelligence with the private sector is such a great idea, then why is there no demand for such support from the intended recipients? Certainly the private sector is not shy about asking for government assistance in any number of other areas, such as import restraints, foreign market access, or tax breaks. If intelligence support for business had any utility at all, the private sector would have spoken up by now.

Legality

Would a program to provide intelligence support to the private sector be legal? As with most legal questions, the answer is "it depends." A significant number of hurdles can be identified that would have to be surmounted if an economic espionage program were to be legal. First, are the existing legal authorities sufficient to justify and allow collecting and disseminating intelligence to a nongovernment consumer? Various enabling statutes and executive orders would need to be reviewed and possibly modified to permit a private sector support effort. Second, intelligence collected under such a program would likely include trade secrets, and the Trade Secrets Act might need changing to allow such information to be disseminated without criminal liability. Third, wire fraud statutes might also need amending if it is decided that collection of intelligence through fraud or deceit (tactics used frequently in clandestine collection) for passing to the private sector violated that statute. Fourth, the Communication Act and the Foreign Intelligence Surveillance Act might require amendments to allow dissemination of certain kinds of intelligence. Fifth, there would be a substantial risk of extensive civil litigation against the U.S. government in both U.S. and foreign courts: management and shareholders of companies not selected to receive intelligence could sue; individuals injured by products resulting from the intelligence could sue; and companies or individuals whose trade secrets or intellectual property were taken without compensation could sue.

In addition, legal protection now afforded intelligence sources and methods would be weakened, as would the government's ability to defeat legal discovery and Freedom of Information requests if those requests related to information that was disseminated under a support program. Additionally, treaties of trade, commerce, friendship, and navigation currently in force might be breached, and intellectual property rights treaties and agreements might be affected. Clearly such a program would be inconsistent with the long-standing U.S. policy of "national treatment" for foreign investment; that is, foreign investment should be treated the same as domestic investment—if the IC is not spying on domestic companies, then it should not spy on foreign companies.

These legal concerns are largely speculative because there has been no litigation involving economic espionage that would offer a record for more certain legal analysis. Traditionally the courts have shown great deference to the requirements of national security. But it remains to be seen if the courts would view intelligence support to the private sector as a bona fide national security issue worthy of special legal forbearance. Threats to corporate profits are not the same as threats to the nation's existence, and the traditional balancing of secrecy (among other intelligence equities) against other legal rights might well experience a shift in the legal fulcrum to the disadvantage of intelligence interests.

The list of legal problems, while not exhaustive, is indicative of the many pitfalls inherent in any effort to assist the private sector. Given all of the obvious legal impediments (and likely many more not so obvious problems), it is hard to understand how anyone would seriously advocate such an idea. In the recent past, Congress launched a major investigation of a fantasy called the "October Surprise" from the 1980 presidential election campaign, where there was no serious evidence of a real violation of the law. Who would be so bold (or obtuse) to launch an effort that would almost certainly violate constitutional amendments, statutes, executive orders, international treaties, and open exposure to civil liabilities? Intelligence officers asked to manage such a program should heed this warning: Today's good idea is grist for tomorrow's congressional inquisition.

Morality

Do the ends justify the means? This philosophical question should be applied to the subject of economic espionage. If economic competitiveness is really a national security priority, then national security tools could reasonably be applied to effect a desired outcome. The legitimate requirements of national security have traditionally allowed for extraordinary measures to be undertaken. For example, the United States conducts espionage abroad, activity that invariably violates the laws of the countries where it occurs. Moreover, when espionage is conducted by foreign powers in the United States, it is considered a crime. But the United States justifies its own espionage activities because they serve the defense of the nation's security.

This chapter has presented the argument that economic competitiveness is not a true national security issue, and so is not worthy of application of extraordinary national security measures such as intelligence support. Those who argue that competitiveness is a national security issue, however, must explain what other steps should be taken besides providing direct intelligence support to the private sector. Given all the difficulties in structuring an economic espionage program (as previously described), are there not some ideas that would be more timely and effective? For example, why not change the law that prohibits bribery of foreign officials to enable U.S. companies to win overseas contracts? Or why not change the antitrust laws to allow combinations of more powerful U.S. companies that could better compete with foreign companies? If this is indeed a genuine national security threat, then the United States should be willing to consider other such extraordinary steps. Such sentiment is not now in evidence, however, either in Congress or among the general public.

Much attention has been given to the actions of other countries using their intelligence services to spy on U.S. companies for the benefit of their domestic business. The French, according to numerous press reports, have aggressively used the resources of their intelligence services to spy on and steal information from foreign businessmen. (Pierre Marion, former head of the French external intelligence service, DGSE, bragged in his memoirs about French efforts to spy on foreign companies during his tenure.) IBM and Texas Instruments were among the U.S. companies victimized. Peter Schweizer's recent book, *Friendly Spies*, describes economic intelligence collection activities by the Israelis, Germans, Japanese, and South Koreans, as well as by the French. American proponents of economic espionage make frequent reference to these incidents in an attempt to justify a U.S. program to do the same thing. These examples are noteworthy, however, not because they are admirable but because they are reprehensible. It is instructive to remember the old saying, "Two wrongs do not make a right." There are many examples of behavior by foreign countries that Americans find objectionable. The appropriate course of action, however, is to convince the country through diplomatic or other pressures to change or modify its behavior, not to emulate it. The actions of other countries do not justify the United States doing the same thing.

In any event, countries inclined to conduct economic espionage on behalf of local businesses will face growing complications. The "blurring" of companies' national identities is happening not just in the United States, but in the rest of the world as well. The economic integration occurring in Europe as a result of the EC-92 initiatives, for example, makes intelligence support by European countries for domestic companies increasingly problematic. Even France may find itself confused about who the customer for its intelligence support should be. The new conservative government has mentioned selling many of the state-run companies (which have received much of the intelligence support) to the private sector. As those companies inevitably become more "European" and less "French," the French government will find it more difficult to target the intelligence to support specific French interests.

"What Is Sauce for the Goose Is Sauce for the Gander"

The remarkable fact is not that some governments have engaged in economic espionage, but rather that there has been relatively little of it reported and acknowledged. Given the number of intelligence services around the world, and the importance of economic issues, one would expect to have seen a great deal more of such activity. Although there may be no formal treaties, the traditional Western allies (with the exception of the French) are reluctant to conduct espionage against one another. A U.S. economic espionage program, however, would drastically change that equation. If foreign governments thought that the United States was spying on competitors and aggressively supporting U.S. companies, it would release whatever restraints that now exist and permit them to do the same. Thus, American businessmen abroad would potentially become subject to a wide range of pressures and harassments, including entrapment, robbery, and blackmail. Because the United States would be engaging in similar activity, the United States would have no moral standing to protest the treatment of its citizens. In addition, it is quite possible that many countries would be better at economic espionage than the United States (if only because the U.S. legal protection for the individual would preclude the more heavy-handed pressures), negating the value of the U.S. program. There is relatively little such activity now. Should the United States be the one to start an "intelligence war" supporting domestic businesses?

Who Will Spy?

It is not certain that intelligence professionals want to be engaged in an economic espionage program. Former DCI Robert Gates stated, "Some years ago, one of our clandestine service officers overseas said to me: 'You know, I'm prepared to give my life for my country, but not for a company.' That case officer was absolutely right."[10] Intelligence officers sign up to serve their country and defend its security. Can they be convinced that (in some cases) risking their lives—or at the very least their career success—for a company is the same as for their country? It remains an open question whether the intelligence services would extend their best efforts to support such a program, but is it worth the gamble? There is also the risk of corruption, less by individual intelligence officers participating in a program than by the intelligence agencies participating in a program. Those institutions would likely become targets of the intense business lobbying that occurs whenever the economic stakes are high, and there could be temptations to make biased decisions about allocation of resources and effort.

"Fraught with Difficulties"

Then-DCI James Woolsey raised eyebrows and expectations during his Senate confirmation hearing when he described economic espionage as "the hottest current topic in intelligence policy." Subsequent news stories indicate that he has reached some unenthusiastic conclusions about such an effort. One year later, he was quoted as stating that such a program would be "fraught with legal and foreign policy difficulties."[11] Woolsey's disapproving tone is not surprising. Anyone who gets past the rhetoric about economic competitiveness and closely examines the nuts and bolts of how an economic espionage program is supposed to work cannot fail to reach the same negative conclusions.

Sound management practice (and common sense) dictates that major new initiatives should be preceded by some form of cost/benefit analysis. In the case of conducting economic espionage in support of the U.S. private sector, the costs—practical, legal, and moral—as outlined previously are very high. There would undoubtedly be additional costs that would surface only upon implementation of such a plan. On the other hand, the benefits of such a program are at best uncertain and quite likely nonexistent. There are many policies and programs the U.S. government can pursue that will improve the competitiveness of U.S. companies; conducting economic espionage to provide direct support to U.S. businesses should not be one of them.

14

FIGHTING PROLIFERATION

Henry Sokolski

Prior to Operation Desert Storm, U.S. policy toward strategic weapons technology proliferation was to delay or prevent it through nonproliferation. Export controls, customs interdictions, end-use checks, diplomatic demarches, nonproliferation pledges, regional arms control talks, and safeguarding sensitive nuclear activities constituted the West's approach to the problem. Desert Storm changed all that. Scud missiles were targeted and intercepted. Coalition forces were inoculated against possible Iraqi use of biological weapons. Iraq's missile, nuclear, chemical, and biological weapons facilities were bombed. Finally, these and related facilities were ferreted out and dismantled as part of the UN's cease-fire plan. In short, with Desert Storm the United States and its allies moved beyond preventing proliferation to fighting it quite literally.

This change from nonproliferation to fighting proliferation is fundamental. Indeed, the U.S. government has yet to comprehend fully what this more combative, proliferated world requires.[1] What follows is an examination of what these new requirements will be. In particular, it will consider how fighting versus merely attempting to prevent proliferation will require policymakers and intelligence officials to work much more closely with one another, not only on the development of new intelligence collection and analysis requirements, but also on the very definition of proliferation and the United States' strategy to combat it.

Instead of pursuing nonproliferation efforts as most governments have—by reacting (often belatedly) to a nation's efforts to acquire a strategic weapons capability—fighting proliferation requires devising a strategy that works backwards from a possible future in which one hypothesizes that these weapons are already employed and might be used against the United States or one of its allies. Such assessments

---

This paper was first presented on May 13, 1993.

will need to spell out the specific military operational implications of these threats so that policymakers can determine the level of attention each deserves and develop strategies to delay, stop, and, if necessary, neutralize them militarily.

All of this assumes that the Intelligence Community and policymakers agree on what proliferation is. It also assumes that they have a way to develop relevant threat scenarios that neither requires policymakers to make intelligence determinations nor forces intelligence officers to arbitrate everyday policy disputes. Finally, it assumes that the U.S. government understands and can meet the new intelligence collection requirements that this approach to proliferation will require.

What Is Proliferation?

Despite (or perhaps because of) the current interest in proliferation issues, determining what proliferation is has itself become a topic of debate. In the past, the situation was simpler; the only proliferation to be concerned about was that related to nuclear weapons. As a result, the definition of proliferation was simple: the spread of unsafeguarded nuclear technology to smaller nations.

Because the security implications of additional nations possessing nuclear capabilities were so unacceptable, and because the technical thresholds that smaller nations needed to attain to build nuclear weapons was so high, U.S. policy was exclusively one of prevention. The prospect of waging war against a nation that had recently acquired nuclear capability was not given serious consideration. Instead, the focus was on the near-term efforts of nonproliferation: preventing certain nations from getting the wherewithal to obtain nuclear weapons. That premise no longer holds.

Government officials now speak not only about the need to prevent nations from achieving nuclear capability, but also about the need to counter the spread of a wide variety of weapons technologies. In recent years, public officials (including those in intelligence) have argued that there is a need to be concerned about the spread of (1) weapons of mass destruction (nuclear, biological, and chemical [NBC] munitions); (2) weapons of mass destruction and the means for their delivery; (3) weapons of mass destruction and the missiles needed to deliver them; (4) special weapons; (5) advanced weapons; (6) advanced conventional weapons; (7) destabilizing numbers and types of advanced conventional weapons; (8) conventional weapons; and (9) weapons of proliferation concern.[2]

THE CONFUSION OF CURRENT VIEWS

The Intelligence Community's role in fighting proliferation is difficult to pinpoint, especially if the list is as vague as that above. In particular, it is not clear what the government's desire to counter proliferation means. The verb *counter* means oppose, offset, or nullify. The question is: In what way—with military countermeasures, counterattacks, counteroffensives, or counterintelligence? The images of the 1981 Israeli air strike against Osirak comes to mind, although the opportunities for repeating such a mission are much reduced.[3] *Counter*, however, just as easily could apply to opposing dangerous proliferation activities through the kind of diplomacy, safeguard inspections, disarmament procedures, export controls, and sanctions that are already in place.[4]

Although the term *counterproliferation* may be useful, it is no substitute for clear thinking about what the problem is. This is especially evident when one considers whose proliferation should be countered. A popular view, particularly among many conservatives, is that the United States should simply focus on its enemies, which was both necessary and possible during the Cold War. Today, however, there are few, if any, clear-cut adversaries. There are nations on the U.S. government's terrorist lists but the United States and its allies still talk and trade with these nations. Also, does the United States care only about nations that have not yet acquired strategic weapons systems of their own? What about the People's Republic of China's (PRC's) efforts to significantly upgrade its existing strategic forces with technology from the West and Russia? What of the republics of the former Soviet Union keeping and upgrading the systems the Soviets left behind? These developments deserve attention, but are they included in the list?

There is also confusion about which weapons technologies are of concern. Many people believe it is necessary to limit proliferation of only apocalyptic weaponry and related technologies. If proliferation can no longer be limited to nuclear weapons, they argue, it would be best to confine proliferation concerns to weapons of mass destruction.

This approach, however, ignores the very real concern that weapons delivery vehicles present. But, if delivery vehicles are included, the scope of the phrase *means of delivery* becomes a problem. Two sorts of solutions have been offered. The first is to limit concerns about delivery systems to missiles and related technology as controlled under the Missile Technology Control Regime (MTCR). The second is to argue that planes as well as missiles should be included. This, in turn, has encouraged an even broader approach: Any weapon that can inflict military harm against the United States or its friends should be included.

Neither approach is sound. To widen proliferation's focus to cover anything of military concern is to trivialize it. Not just strategic systems, but tanks and planes become proliferation worries. Strategic systems, however, are very different from tanks and planes. Nuclear weapons can be covertly acquired and used in small numbers to produce shocking strategic results against the United States or its allies. In contrast, it takes years of acquisition and overt training with thousands of tanks or planes to pose a significant military threat to U.S. forces or U.S.-led coalitions, and, even then, effective defenses against such weapons are available.[5]

A broad definition of *proliferation* would have to include not only the weapons but also the related technology. Making all of these items of proliferation concern would stretch existing export control, customs, and intelligence collection and analysis efforts beyond its capabilities. For these reasons many in the U.S. Intelligence Community prefer to limit their attention to weapons of mass destruction.

Focusing on what has traditionally been of concern, however, runs the risk of ignoring new threats that are likely to emerge. After all, since 1945, what is of proliferation concern has itself changed several times, evolving from a worry about the Soviet Union obtaining nuclear weapons to the current concern regarding smaller nations obtaining nuclear, chemical, and biological munitions, as well as long-range missiles. And there is every reason to believe that new worries are on the way. Certainly, congressional interest in the military implications of satellite services (imagery, navigation, and communications) being sold to developing nations suggests as much. So too does Congress's recent enactment of a law imposing sanctions against nations that sell destabilizing types and numbers of advanced conventional weapons to Iran or Iraq.[6] The U.S. Navy is also concerned about Iran's acquisition of conventional submarines, which will be difficult to find in the Persian Gulf and, if properly armed, could threaten U.S. and allied fleets. In short, the list of concerns is expanding and is likely to include high-leverage technologies and weapons systems that could enable smaller nations to threaten war-winning or victory-denying results against the United States or its friends without resorting to weapons of mass destruction.[7]

Toward a Prescriptive Definition

Defining *proliferation* is difficult, but the intelligence and policy communities should make the effort. In fact, they have no choice; in 1992, Congress tasked the executive branch to identify what "types and numbers of advanced conventional weapons" are "destabilizing."[8] There are two schools of thought on how best to do this. The first is simply to compile new lists of weapons technologies that should be monitored or controlled. This approach is familiar and has the short-term advantage of being simple and direct. The difficulty comes in the long term: As already noted, compiling lists of what might be of concern tends to attenuate the government's already limited ability to maintain a constructive focus.

This legitimate concern with overreach was, in part, what prompted consideration of a second, more prescriptive approach. This approach was first presented before the Senate Select Committee on Intelligence in 1990 by then-Assistant Secretary of Defense Henry S. Rowen.[9] Instead of trying to describe what is of proliferation concern by listing specific weapons and related technologies, criteria were established prescribing what was worth worrying about and why. Three criteria were suggested. A weapon or weapon-related technology was of proliferation concern if (1) it enabled another nation to inflict high-leverage strategic harm against the United States or its friends; (2) the United States lacked effective defenses against this capability; and (3) its mere acquisition could change other nations' perceptions as to who was the leading power in a given region.

High leverage should not be confused with high or advanced technology. Relatively low-technology, nonnuclear submarines in the Persian Gulf, for example, could sink one of the U.S. Navy's capital ships, preclude the navy from identifying the perpetrator, and make the political demands to quit the area nearly irresistible. Advanced jet fighters, on the other hand, might incorporate high technology but are low leverage because it would take hundreds of them to secure local air superiority against U.S. or allied forces. Even then, U.S. air defenses would prove effective against organized air attacks.

The word *strategic harm* also requires definition. During the Cold War this meant global nuclear conflict with the Warsaw Pact. Today, however, wars are more likely to be like Operation Desert Storm than like what was portrayed in the movies *The Day After* and *Red Storm*

Rising. As a result, what constitutes victory-denying harm differs. During the Cold War, it was critical, for example, to U.S. security to keep Soviet nuclear submarines from gaining passage into open seas. Today, however, U.S. and coalition forces could potentially be defeated by an inability to find, identify, and destroy conventional submarines laying mines in the Persian Gulf.

Finally, the adequacy of one's defenses can only be determined in relation to what one is defending against. Certainly, in the 1960s at the height of the Cold War conflict, missile defenses against the Soviets did not seem necessary to most U.S. officials because they believed that any Soviet missile strike against the United States or its allies would prompt a massive U.S. nuclear response. This, they reasoned, would deter such attacks. In Operation Desert Storm, however, nonnuclear missile strikes were made against coalition forces and Israel that threatened coalition cohesion. In this case, even limited missile defenses were understood to be critical.

A key difficulty in achieving the type of military threat assessment called for by Henry Rowen is that it requires intelligence and policy officials to cooperate. Working with the policy community on threat assessments (which include the adequacy of U.S. defenses), however, is something the Intelligence Community has long considered sensitive, if not taboo. The Intelligence Community fears that working on such assessments will inevitably drag it into policy disputes, and that policymakers will make determinations about intelligence data that they have no business making.

The advantage of this prescriptive approach is that it encourages the kind of communication between intelligence and policy officials necessary to anticipate and execute effective diplomatic, commercial, or military operations against proliferation. This interaction is also critical to developing more than merely reactionary or episodic covert action programs and counterintelligence operations against proliferation. Instead of merely following up tips and heading off particularly dangerous shipments on an ad hoc basis, intelligence operatives could be told what proliferation developments deserve special attention and orchestrate a variety of clandestine efforts in advance. These might include leaking damaging information about projects to the foreign press, introducing faulty software and hardware into programs, and encouraging others to take steps to sabotage them.

If the United States were to pursue this approach, the Intelligence Community, starting with the intelligence components of the military services, would have to focus on the potential military threats proliferation developments might pose. The military commands and service staffs, meanwhile, would have to share their views on what they believe high-leverage and strategic weapon systems might be in key scenarios and indicate where their defense preparations might be inadequate. The policy community, finally, would have to work with the military to prioritize the various likely threats and develop strategies in coordination with the military and Intelligence Community to contain, reverse, or combat them.

Rethinking Policy and Intelligence

In addition to working together more closely, fighting proliferation will require the intelligence and policy communities to think about proliferation problems differently. At a minimum, it will require these communities to reconsider their traditional Cold War relationship. At the height of the Cold War this relationship was routinized. The United States knew who the adversary was—the Warsaw Pact; the fear was war. Intelligence was tasked to collect and analyze what the Eastern bloc tried to keep secret: its war plans, capabilities, and true foreign policy objectives.

Such clarity about the adversary's identity and the urgency associated with global war generated a serious effort to learn all that could be learned about existing Warsaw Pact military capabilities, especially its order of battle. This technical aspect of intelligence, in turn, made it relatively easy to establish a division of labor between the intelligence and policy communities. Intelligence collected secrets that the military needed to help bound the uncertainties associated with war, and policy did all it could to reduce the likelihood of war.

As one recent discussion on intelligence noted, what is most required from the Intelligence Community is secret information in support of military operations:

> [a] former senior official suggested that the touchstone for the Intelligence Community should be its concentration on secrets. He contrasted a "secret" with an "uncertainty," which could be studied, and a "mystery," which is unknowable. A secret, he said, is a valued piece of information that gives its possessor an advantage and would give another who acquired the secret an advantage. The government might want to ponder uncertainties and mysteries, but it should reserve the intelligence service for the pursuit of secrets.[10]

This makes sense, but fighting proliferation makes certain adjustments necessary.

First, as noted before, the United States' adversaries are far less apparent than they were during the Cold War. The United States must plan for a security environment in which there may well be a shifting set of allies and adversaries. Moreover, even if the United States had perfect clarity about who its future enemies might be, this would not exhaust the parties the United States would be interested in monitoring for proliferation purposes. For instance, the United States is concerned about what North Korea is doing. But precisely because the United States is worried about having to go to war in Korea and having to cope with nuclear, biological, or chemical weapons and long-range missiles, it is also keenly interested in what South Korea is doing to acquire or use such weapons itself. One of the last things the United States wants is to be drawn into a war with (or by) a friend and then have its joint defense plans undermined by this ally's unilateral employment of illicit strategic weaponry.

Also, the United States is interested in stemming the proliferation of strategic weaponry in general. Given the broad uncertainties of the United States' future security interests and the uncertainty of who its friends and competitors will be, a prudent expenditure of effort today in curtailing proliferation can pay big dividends in the future. Thus, the proliferation activities of a nation such as Indonesia, which at present is neither a formal ally nor an adversary, are still of interest to the U.S. government if, with a modicum of effort, the United States can persuade that country to forgo the acquisition of strategic weapons.

What fighting proliferation requires, then, is something more than what became routine in the Cold War. It requires not just the collection of secrets from known adversaries, but military threat assessments that consider current and possible future threats along with analyses that will enable the government to slow or prevent proliferation in a much more entrepreneurial fashion.

This kind of forward-looking assessment will require intelligence and policy officials to examine a wide set of uncertainties about the future and use a variety of analytic methods to build likely proliferation scenarios. Instead of merely trying to determine which countries have which weapons capabilities, policy and intelligence officials will need to determine how these capabilities might be employed against the United States or its allies, spell out what the military operational implications of these employments would be in the most probable war settings, and pinpoint what military vulnerabilities these employments are most likely to create.

Suggested Hierarchy for Policy and Intelligence

Working together on such assessments will not be easy for the policy and intelligence communities. This is understandable. Collecting and analyzing secrets—information others are trying to conceal from us to prevent us or our friends from taking appropriate action—is what intelligence officials are most comfortable with. Policymakers, on the other hand, are generally at ease developing policy justifications—arguments supporting or opposing positions or actions the government might take.

If the intelligence and policy communities are to focus on the uncertainties that fighting proliferation requires, a new paradigm governing their relationship needs to be established. A model for such a relationship is the operations research and gaming activities that the U.S. military has performed for years in order to anticipate what it will need to meet military contingencies. The following discussion borrows from that experience. It is a suggested hierarchy of policy and intelligence reasoning that would encourage the kind of analysis and operations research that a true fight against proliferation would require.

This hierarchy consists of four kinds of knowledge: secrets, uncertainties, excursions, and policy justifications. Secrets are information others are trying to conceal to prevent a significant U.S. or allied response. This information is collected and analyzed by the Intelligence Community for policymakers. Secrets tend to be straightforward. An example of a secret in the proliferation field might be information as to whether or not the PRC has transferred M-Family ballistic missiles or missile technology to Pakistan in contravention of the guidelines of the Missile Technology Control Regime. This is information that the PRC and Pakistan would want to keep from the United States because such a transfer could trigger trade sanctions and would be diplomatically embarrassing.

Uncertainties are less clear. They can only be known imperfectly because they concern possible future technical, economic, political, or military developments (i.e., educated guesses about the future). A proliferation-related example of an uncertainty might be projections about when Pakistan would be able to produce and operate M-Family ballistic missile systems on its own. Knowledge of such uncertainties in the Pakistani case would be most useful to policymakers because it would indicate to them how much time there might be to head off or prepare for such activities.

Intelligence estimates should highlight uncertainties, but rarely do. Instead of analyzing what the government does and does not know, the variety of futures that might happen, their probabilities, and the independent variables or determinants of each likely future, intelligence estimates have tended to be fixed, oracular "determinations" that simply reflect the consensus of the moment (i.e., what most intelligence analysts agree is the best single guess of what the truth may be). Generally left unaddressed are the gaps in the government's knowledge, which admittedly can be embarrassing. This may be why these estimates are sometimes treated as sensitive secrets rather than as the speculative analyses that they often are.

Excursions take uncertainties one step further. They involve the use of information and uncertainty analysis (i.e., projections) to divine the likely relation or possible operational implications of known or possible developments. Operations research, scenario building, and gaming all fit under this heading. A proliferation-related example might be to game or use operations research techniques to determine the military implications of Pakistan employing M-Family ballistic missiles against Indian forces. This information would be useful to understand just how serious a problem this technology's spread might be and allow the United States and its allies to prepare militarily for the consequences.

Finally, there are political judgments, which are opinions or conclusions about what positions or actions the government should take toward particular developments. These judgments are based on arguments that reflect the best information and analysis of the situation, its possible implications, and full consideration of the ramifications of whatever action or position is decided upon. An example here would be the government's current judgment that M-Family missile proliferation to Pakistan jeopardizes continued peace in Southwest Asia and should, therefore, be opposed.

As noted before, the hierarchy of policy reasoning and the hierarchy of intelligence certitude are opposites. Where policy officials are most comfortable with developing and arguing over policy justifications, the Intelligence Community is most at home collecting and analyzing secrets. As for uncertainties and excursions, neither enjoy much favor in either community because they seem either too complex or technical for busy policymakers or too close in their implications to policy-making for intelligence officers.

Because it was less necessary during the Cold War to have policy and intelligence officials cooperate in doing uncertainty analyses and excursions, the division between policy and intelligence was relatively clear and generally worked. With proliferation, however, such a marked division of labor becomes dysfunctional. Where policy officials are eager to use intelligence to issue demarches to U.S. allies about specific exports, imports, or other activities, intelligence agencies are naturally worried about jeopardizing sources and methods. Also, knowing the military implications of specific proliferation developments is critical to policymakers if they are to gauge the importance of particular developments and to develop appropriate responses. Yet, military intelligence is uncomfortable discussing possible U.S. force vulnerabilities. Finally, policymakers need to know what the full range of technical, political, and military outcomes are possible for a particular proliferation development. Intelligence analysts, on the other hand, are typically leery of making any but the most conservative projections for fear of being accused of being wrong in the future.

Each of these dysfunctions has caused friction between the intelligence and policy communities and is part of the reason why the DCI created the Nonproliferation Center. Designed to coordinate all of the government's intelligence efforts related to proliferation and to serve as a single point of contact within the community that policymakers can turn to, the center has successfully improved relations between policy and intelligence officials working on proliferation. Such liaison work, however, is no substitute for rethinking the policy and intelligence suppositions that are the cause of the friction between these groups.

Certainly, officials who are fighting proliferation need to stop thinking of their goal as simply one of buying time, a static objective; instead, they need to view their efforts as a campaign, which is dynamic. Progress in this struggle would not be measured in terms of how many nations have signed agreements like the Nuclear Nonproliferation Treaty but by how well an agreed strategy to prevent, delay, and combat proliferation has been implemented.

Once policy and intelligence officials begin to think of efforts against proliferation as a kind of warfare, it will be more natural for them to become interested in delving into the uncertainties and excursions normally associated with military planning. In fact, in wartime, intelligence officials' cooperation with policymakers is expected (e.g., the OSS in World War II). Operations research, gaming, and predictive analysis would all be needed in fighting proliferation in order to identify technical, political, and economic opportunities to slow or prevent proliferation, and to disinform and sabotage proliferators' efforts. They would also be needed to identify future proliferation-induced military vulnerabilities both of U.S. forces (and of U.S. allies) and of potential adversaries, and what might be done to mitigate them.

New Intelligence Requirements

STRATEGY AND DEFINITION

The DCI's Non-Proliferation Center has rightly focused on developing an intelligence strategy to tackle the issue of proliferation. However, development of a basic strategy document has been under way for several years. In part, this is because the security environment is changing and an intelligence strategy, like any strategy, must continually take account of those changes. Yet the center's development of a strategy has been and will continue to be hindered by the absence of a coherent, prescriptive definition of proliferation.

The Intelligence Community cannot be expected to develop a definition on its own, but it should work on defining proliferation for two very practical reasons. The first is that the Intelligence Community retains an expertise in proliferation that should not be ignored due to an overly fastidious concern about the line between policy and intelligence. Thus, the Intelligence Community often generates (and rightly so) reports on proliferation matters absent specific requests from policymakers. These reports are intended to alert policy officials to issues and trends that policy has not addressed and presume a definition of what proliferation is. The expertise exhibited in these reports should be used to fashion a realistic and coherent definition of proliferation.

A second, more practical reason for the Intelligence Community to help define proliferation is that without a sound definition, intelligence officials and agencies will be hard-pressed to do their job or measure their performance. How much of a failing would it be, for example, if U.S. intelligence failed to anticipate a country's development of night-vision goggles as compared to failing to anticipate its development of unmanned air vehicles that could penetrate U.S. air defenses? Knowing which is more important is only possible with a prescriptive definition that identifies what is of greater concern and why.

One way to develop this definition would be for the Intelligence Community to work with those in the military who are most interested in proliferation problems, particularly those on the command staffs charged with actually having to worry about fighting a war in their region. This has the immediate advantage of engaging those most likely to be affected by weapons proliferation, and whose views are critical to giving descriptive details to any prescriptive definition once it is in place. Once a working definition has been developed, the other policy elements within the departments of State and Defense can be incorporated. With a prescriptive definition in hand, both the policy and intelligence communities could establish a procedure for gauging proliferation threats, prioritizing them, and establishing an overall strategy of diplomatic, economic, and military activities and goals for fighting proliferation.

COLLECTION

Proliferation-related intelligence collection has tended to be technocentric. Tremendous amounts of attention are focused on imagery and its interpretation, as well as on the collection of signals intelligence. There is also a heavy emphasis on technical matters in the way proliferation issues are handled and discussed. Generally, there is far more time spent on the question of whether a particular nation has a particular capability and the specific technical facts associated with its acquisition than on what such acquisition might mean economically, politically, or militarily.

To some extent, this is unavoidable: Someone tracking nuclear weapons and missile acquisitions or developments will go to rocket scientists and nuclear engineers to make sense of things. Yet relying too heavily on these experts and focusing exclusively on technical issues come at the cost of collecting the kinds of political and economic information about another nation that is needed by the United States to develop policies to help curtail or prevent proliferation in the first place. Proliferation is driven by political, economic, and strategic considerations; countering it often requires intelligence that reaches beyond the details of the weapons programs themselves.

In this regard, what might help most would be a greater understanding, in policy and intelligence circles, of "opportunity analysis."[11] One proponent of this type of analysis wrote that we need much more of the "kind of analysis [that] illuminates for the policymaker opportunities for advancing U.S. objectives and interests through diplomacy, military and economic moves, cultural activities, and other political action."[12] This requires that the intelligence collected point to "opportunities and vulnerabilities the United States can exploit to advance a policy as well as to the dangers that could undermine a policy."[13] It is important, for example, to know the technical details of Argentina's Condor II missile program but no more important than knowing which elements within that country's military are secretly opposed to the missile's development. The former is useful to know if the effort to stem the missile's proliferation fails, while the latter is critical to diplomatic and covert maneuvering to end the program altogether. Both kinds of information are secret, yet only one is especially relevant to policymakers looking for opportunities to defeat proliferation.

To support policymakers, intelligence collectors (and analysts) must pay more attention than they have in the past to making sure they have as much unclassified material as possible on the matters about which they are collecting classified materials. This may not seem a task worthy of agencies known primarily for their work with secrets, but frequently the government cannot make a demarche or inform allies of developments that require their assistance unless the information can be used in an unclassified forum.

Finally, more must be done to collect information relevant to war. How and why other nations might use the strategic weapons systems they are developing or acquiring is at least as important as specifics about the weapons themselves. What kinds of exploitable problems might the employment of these capabilities produce within the military and political leadership? What efforts are smaller nations making to hide development or employment of strategic capabilities from U.S. intelligence collectors? Are U.S. and allied efforts succeeding in forcing them to change their acquisition or employment plans? How are proliferating nations reacting to efforts to stop or hinder their programs? What sectors of those governments or their populations are opposed to acquiring strategic systems? To what extent are these doubts related to U.S. or allied actions aimed against these programs?

If intelligence officers are collecting the answers to these questions, it should be reflected not only by changes in U.S. strategy against targeted proliferators, but by changes in U.S. collection requirements as well. Indeed, if collection requirements stay the same, it is a sign that the Intelligence Community is not collecting what it should, or that the policy community is failing to implement an effective strategy.

ANALYTIC REQUIREMENTS

The effort to fight proliferation will require more than just new targets for collection; intelligence analysis will also have to change. In particular, to support policymakers looking for opportunities to disrupt, slow, or stop a proliferation program of another country there will be an increased need for analysis that lays out the uncertainties and variables connected with a particular program. This is true not only in the technical arena (e.g., what engineering bottlenecks remain for country X to complete project Y; and what are the range of possibilities for country X to master them?) but also in the political and economic arenas.

Recently nuclear and missile programs in Argentina, Brazil, South Africa, and Taiwan have been either terminated or suspended because of political considerations or economic factors. The United States and its allies could have done more to reinforce some of these forces earlier had there been more collection and analysis on what the various domestic constituencies for and against these programs were.

Taiwan's 1991 decision not to develop a space-launch vehicle is an example. After considerable internal debate, Taiwan decided to focus its development efforts on satellite technology rather than on rocketry. Knowing who supported what, for what reasons, and what political and economic costs they were willing to pay to pursue their aims was critical for policymakers wanting to move Taiwan along the more benign path of satellite development.

Beyond this, it would also be helpful to have analyses of how each of these countries could better meet the peaceful goals they claimed they were pursuing by investing in these projects (civilian nuclear and space-launch vehicles, large mainframe supercomputers, etc.).[14] Also, counterintelligence analysis must be done of how proliferators are likely to hide their activities or how they plan to get around weaknesses in existing safeguard and inspection regimens and how they plan to avoid intelligence collection efforts. Such analysis goes beyond uncertainty analysis into the realm of excursions. This work need not be done by intelligence analysts alone; it can be contracted out. In any case, it is work that should be jointly managed by intelligence and policy officials who have a clear grasp of the facts and know what kind of analysis is needed.

This requirement for gaming, economic analysis, and operations research is even clearer in the case of developing military threat analyses. Here the involvement of the intelligence agencies, particularly those of the military services, is imperative. Without their involvement, no threat assessment, no matter how correct, is likely to alter defense requirements in the areas of weapons acquisition and development, or service training or doctrine. Again, this does not come naturally. As one Defense Intelligence Agency (DIA) analyst explained, "We don't do excursions, they are too hypothetical." When analysts in the defense intelligence services attempt to do such work, moreover, it is often heavily edited and reduced to banality out of concern that it might upset one of the military services. The military services have a large stake invested in their five-year spending plans; they do not need or want any second-guessing, implicit or otherwise, generated by intelligence officials. Unfortunately, such a perspective can be self-defeating.

One way to change this is to sponsor threat assessments by analysts from outside the government and arrange for the military commands or service staffs to participate in their production. The money is likely to be there: As currently planned, the policy arm of the Department of Defense will spend millions on proliferation studies, and the Energy Department and the CIA will spend orders of magnitude more.

Given this spending, it is important that a concerted effort be made to focus and manage the government's study efforts. The National Intelligence Council or the Intelligence Community Management Staff can play a useful role in ensuring that this money is used to develop the right kinds of analyses. These organizations have a solid bureaucratic interest in doing so because the studies should have a direct impact on intelligence collection requirements. At a minimum, some effort is needed to keep track of what is being done by the government as a whole. Absent such monitoring, it will be nearly impossible to match analysis of proliferation to the government's nonproliferation strategy.

Conclusion

If the U.S. government wants to do more than just react to the proliferation of strategic weapons capabilities, the role of intelligence in this fight must change along with that of policy. If the United States is to anticipate strategic weapons proliferation developments; slow or reverse them through diplomatic, political, or economic appeals; or develop military options for coping with their employment, the government will have to commit itself to a long-term strategy of competition not unlike what it did during the Cold War.[15] The heart of such a strategy is to match U.S. strengths against an adversary's weaknesses in an effort to force the adversary into less threatening areas of competition.

Instead of engaging in one major competition with the Soviets, the United States will engage in and manage a more complex and varied number of competitions against a large number of suppliers and acquiring nations. As with the earlier competition with the Soviets, the government will need to anticipate each of these entities' reactions to U.S. moves to combat proliferating actions and be able to maintain relative advantage in defeating or mitigating these moves. Yet, as with the Soviets, the end game is the same: The government's goal is to contain the threat until each proliferating government and its motives to proliferate are defeated and give way to new, more peaceful regimes.

For example, Iran, despite severe economic difficulties, continues to pursue costly nuclear programs and conventional military systems in an effort to dominate the Persian Gulf region. Although the United States must worry about the military implications of Iran's acquiring these weapons and about neutralizing them militarily should they be employed, a competitive strategy might also attempt to check Iran's proliferation activities by pressuring Iran in areas where it is especially vulnerable and where the United States holds key advantages. Specifically, in conjunction with allies, the United States could appreciably decrease Iranian access to Western credits and high technology if Iran continues to pursue programs dangerous to U.S. and allied interests in the region. This would economically and politically increase the cost to Iran of pursuing proliferation activities. A second element in a competitive strategy might be to put Iran on the defensive militarily by regularly demonstrating the decisive nature of U.S. and allied air superiority in the region and the potential cost to Iran of ignoring its air defenses. A concerted effort to bring this point home to Iran's leadership by a vigorous enforcement of UN resolutions against Iraq might result in the Iranian government spending its limited resources in a more benign area (air defense) rather than in some other more dangerous one (nuclear).[16]

Thus, developing and implementing such a competitive strategy will require several changes in the way intelligence and policy officials currently address proliferation problems. First, it will require that they at least agree on a prescriptive definition of what it is they are fighting. Second, it will require that they reconsider the basic relationship between the policy and intelligence realms that currently makes fighting proliferation so difficult, if not impossible. It is impractical for policy and intelligence officials to continue to avoid cooperating on the kinds of operations research and uncertainty analyses needed to gauge and give priority to the potential proliferation threats the nation faces. To ensure a meaningful level of success in this area, the role of the military, both the service staffs and the commands, relative to that of the current actors in proliferation-related policy and intelligence, will need to expand.

Developing such a strategy against proliferation will be difficult and will take years, but the United States must put forth the effort if it intends to avoid another experience like that of the war with Iraq.

15

THE FUTURE OF DEFENSE INTELLIGENCE

Walter Jajko

The U.S. national security community is in transformation. Defense intelligence,[1] as a constituent component of this community, will partake in the transformation. To understand the possibilities for the transformation of defense intelligence, it is necessary to consider those factors that place primary parameters on the possibilities for the transformation of defense intelligence because, in so doing, these factors will shape the character and the capability of defense intelligence. Some of these factors are external to defense intelligence and uncontrollable; others are internal to defense intelligence and controllable. Some are transcendental; others are mundane. Some are familiar and taken for granted; others are unfamiliar and only surmised. Several of these factors, although disparate and not all-inclusive, have been specifically selected for discussion because of their intrinsic importance and extended effect. Among them are defense strategy, force structure, roles and missions, organization, programming, and institutional culture. HUMINT (intelligence collected from human sources) has been selected as a discipline illustrative of several of these factors.

Revolution

A transcendent cause of the transformation is the simultaneous revolutions in politics, technology, and economics that the world is experiencing. These revolutions will transform war, its methods, and its conditions. The transformations will delimit what, how, and why intelligence must learn and understand. Intelligence, in short, is facing a new epoch. How U.S. intelligence reacts to these revolutions may determine how U.S. power fares in this epoch.

This paper was first presented on March 4, 1993.

Regional Strategy, Forward Presence

Politically, the twentieth century, the period 1914 to 1991, is finished, ending with the unprecedented military (but not attendant political and economic) domination of the entire globe by one country, the United States. This circumstance, coupled to the system of collective security, caused the Bush administration to conclude that the United States had secured safety through "strategic depth."[2] The assumption of strategic depth is based on the existence of alliances, foremost the North Atlantic Treaty Organization (NATO). However, in recent years, the United States has been forced to accept an emergent independent European security identity, although its institutions are still incomplete and ineffective. This emergence erodes the viability of NATO, the institution that legitimizes U.S. political interference in Europe in return for military security. Eventual unification indicates the end of U.S. involvement in Europe.

Whether NATO survives, and with new purpose and in new form, the premise for U.S. intelligence involvement is fundamentally changed. Furthermore, the physical foundation for U.S. influence in Europe has been undercut. Germany in reunification has regained its independence. Because military intelligence forces for theater commands are forward-based, the removal of most U.S. fighting forces in Europe reduces military intelligence resources. The bases for much of the military intelligence operations in Europe, the Soviet successor states, North Africa, the Middle East, and Southwest Asia are lost as U.S. combat forces vacate them. Except for the defense attaché offices, the Department of Defense (DoD) must rely on resources not under its control. Eventually, the political, economic, and security changes among the United States' European allies will change their attitudes of acceptance of U.S. intelligence operations.

The last administration's assumption of "strategic depth" was intended to permit the United States to provide for its security at less cost, less engagement, and less risk. The administration concluded that less effort and more time could be applied to the world's disorder, notwithstanding its volume, consequences, and violence, managing with far fewer forces than were used to deter war with the Soviet Union. To safeguard U.S. security in these circumstances, the administration articulated a Regional Defense Strategy that is intended to prevent the reemergence of a global threat and the success of a regional challenge. The strategy is dependent on the forward presence of U.S. forces to deter or counter any such threat. Similarly, much of the defense intelligence capability to support the Regional Defense Strategy is forward-based. In fact, bases and access are indispensable to this strategy, yet the strategy is meant to facilitate the withdrawal of forces from forward bases. Pre-positioning of equipment, periodic deployments of forces, occasional exercises with friendly forces, and commercial access to facilities do not provide the necessary sustained access for forces, much less intelligence, that only basing can provide. Forward-basing is critical when crises occur with little or no warning. In fact, the reduction in the forward presence of U.S. forces will preclude military intelligence from obtaining the information that can be learned only on the scene, thus limiting the comprehensive knowledge of changes in the military capabilities of adversaries.

RECONSTITUTION

In order to reduce resources, the Regional Defense Strategy will rely on reconstitution to reply to a resurgent global threat or an emergent regional alliance. Reconstitution assumes adequate warning to provide the time to generate new military forces and to regenerate old military forces from reserves. The infrastructure that allows the ability to form forces in the future includes not only manpower, industry, and technology, but also intelligence. The reconstitution of intelligence itself is problematic. Expanding an existing capability is possible; creating a new capability from sample systems and unskilled recruits is doubtful, even with the duration dispensed by strategic depth. Moreover, it has not yet been discovered which core intelligence competencies in what parts of the intelligence cycle need to be and can be reconstituted, and which must be preserved in service. It is questionable whether investments can develop and maintain the variety of skills needed in intelligence, particularly language and culture skills, in a part-time posture (e.g., in the Reserve Components). A study of potential significance is under way in the DoD to ascertain these possibilities. However, even if these determinations can be made, it is doubtful that the investments necessary to develop new skills and sustain old skills will be available to reconstitute intelligence forces. The conclusion can be drawn that, if a resurgent or emergent threat appears globally or regionally, the United States will go to war with its extant intelligence apparatus alone.

Drug War

The Department of Defense, in fulfillment of its high-priority national security mission of detecting and tracking the production and trafficking of drugs, has applied significant specialized operational and intelligence forces to combat the drug dealers in their own countries in Latin America through support for the host governments. DoD views this military support as a form of low-intensity conflict. Although there has been success in stopping some shipments of supplies, the conditions that support this new commerce have not been corrected. Special operations and intelligence operations, alone, cannot stop narcotics traffic when it is inextricably intertwined with insurgencies, anachronistic economies, irrelevant governments, and the absence of civil societies—in short, the need for nation building.

The base for U.S. intervention, and military intelligence, in South America —not only for counterdrug operations—has been Panama. With the virtual withdrawal of U.S. forces from the isthmus at the end of this century, maintaining the counterdrug war will be difficult. Military operations, including most intelligence operations, south of the border will have to be staged from the continental United States. Nevertheless, for the foreseeable future, intelligence support to counterdrug operations will continue to increase in quantity and cost (as it has, by some 500 percent in five years), notwithstanding the decline in intelligence resources. Absent the dramatic decline of the demand for drugs in the United States, military support and intelligence operations will probably continue to increase.

Roles and Missions

There is considerable discussion about the roles and missions of the armed forces, much of it driven by the desire to downsize and to dispense with duplication. The discussion establishes emphatically that the criterion for cutting the armed forces will not be the traditional hierarchy of objectives, interests, threats, requirements, and strategies. Although intelligence plays a role in determining the missions and tasks of the armed forces by defining threats, the roles and functions of the armed forces will delimit the role of intelligence. The importance of the discussion to intelligence is that the decision on roles and missions will determine the requirement for the capacity of intelligence, and the capacity of intelligence can compromise the ability to execute roles and missions, and functions and tasks.

BASE FORCE

Contemporaneous with, but apparently analytically unconnected to, the discussion of roles and missions has been the discussion of the Base Force. Obviously, the Base Force should be the end point, not the starting point, for a discussion of roles and missions. The Base Force is the minimum size and shape of the armed forces—some based abroad, some based at home—that will be needed to implement the Regional Defense Strategy: namely, to maintain strategic nuclear deterrence and to meet the uncertainties of protecting U.S. national interests in several regions considered critical to U.S. security. These regions include Europe, the Middle East, Southwest Asia, and East Asia. U.S.-based forces capable of rapid response in unexpected contingencies are crucial to the concept of the Base Force, and intelligence is one of the essential supporting services to the Base Force. The size of the Base Force has already been reduced once by the new administration; a further reduction should not be unexpected. The size of the Base Force will shape the size of intelligence. Force structure and posture are as important to intelligence as they are to the fighting forces because they determine the responsiveness of intelligence. The reductions in the Base Force will require earlier and more informative warning intelligence to reconstitute combat capabilities.

Intelligence and War Fighting

The penalty for an intelligence failure in DoD may be defeat on the battlefield. Therefore, the most critical role of defense intelligence is support to war fighting.[3] Planning for and fighting wars are the most important responsibilities of the regional commanders in chief. Yet, notwithstanding the fact that the emphasis of the application of the intelligence effort is at the theater echelon, the intelligence staffs of the combatant commands are manned at low levels, especially after their recent consolidation. The combatant commands rely on intelligence augmentation in case of a crisis. Most of intelligence is located in Washington; therefore, most intelligence support comes from Washington. Although intelligence support is essential to the war-fighting mission, the Washington intelligence organizations do not practice war; they seldom participate as entities in exercises.

The services and the unified and specified combatant commands have unique intelligence requirements for the support of military operations. Despite long-standing agreements for support to military operations, the Central Intelligence Agency (CIA) had not filled these requirements. Since the war against Iraq, there has been much ado about the CIA's support to military operations. During a half-century of a Cold War, in which U.S. survival was threatened, and several hot wars, in which survival was not threatened, the CIA had not accepted its responsibility for support to military operations, which is fast becoming one of its primary missions.

To provide support to DoD, the director of Central Intelligence (DCI) established the office of the associate deputy director of operations for military affairs (ADDO/MA) within the agency. This office was the outgrowth of a temporary assignment of a senior CIA Directorate for Operations (DO) officer to the Joint Chiefs of Staff (JCS) during the war against Iraq. The ADDO/MA is the point of contact for ensuring that the CIA provides intelligence and operational support to military plans and operations. He is also the contact for reverse support from DoD to the agency. In these capacities, he works closely with the J-2 and J-3 of the JCS. In the future, as the United States deals with regional conflicts on their own terms rather than solely in a bipolar context, the CIA's ability to support contingency operations will be essential. The ADDO/MA, who is a serving general officer, has also been assigned the twin duties to educate the Directorate of Operations (DO) on DoD's military requirements and to disabuse the theater commanders of some of their operational expectations. Each institution's understanding of the other, beyond its own cultural confines, must be expanded by the ADDO/MA—probably his most difficult and worthwhile task. The ADDO/MA has the potential to become a pivotal player in the DoD-CIA relationship.

Intelligence and Policy

Defense intelligence supports the formulation of national security policies, the conception of military strategy, the construction of force development, the planning and conduct of military operations, the acquisition of military systems, and the development of countermeasures. Defense intelligence also provides DoD with the expected services that other intelligence organizations provide, for example, warning, current, and estimative intelligence. However, much of intelligence is engaged in supporting policy-making—although, in the past, not systematically. Historically, policymakers have preferred to be their own intelligence analysts, to reach their own interpretations of meaning, significance, implication, and consequence. Therefore, intelligence support to Defense policy-making has been a demand system, neither anticipatory nor initiatory, depending on the inclination of the action officer or policymaker. As policy without intelligence is thoughtless, so intelligence without policy is purposeless; the challenge has been to tie the two together.

The Office of the Undersecretary (Policy) has continuing requirements for analytical intelligence support to the formulation and execution of Defense policy and the formulation of Defense input to national security policy. Until recently, there has not been an organizational connection or procedure that institutionalized systematic intelligence support to policy-making, particularly to the Office of the Undersecretary (Policy). In the last administration, several supplementary steps were taken to solve this problem. The assistant secretary of defense for command, control, communications and intelligence, ASD (C³I), was the cochairman of the Defense Intelligence Policy Council—a committee created specifically to solve the problem of intelligence support to policy-making; he, thereby, personally ascertained the intelligence needs, at a generalized level, of the senior policy officials in DoD. The director of the Defense Intelligence Agency (DIA) merged the Director's Staff Group, which provides direct, personal support to under and assistant secretaries, with the Defense Intelligence Officers into a new Policy Support Directorate. The head of this new directorate was invited to the undersecretary (policy) staff meetings, or at least to those during which sensitive subjects were not discussed. Of course, it sometimes was the case that it was these subjects that, because of their sensitivity, required special intelligence support. The new directorate has emphasized close collaboration between the DIA representatives and the regional and functional deputy assistant secretaries working on their immediate issues. This support is not a mere administrative task but a sophisticated assignment that requires a shrewd knowledge of policy-making, an insightful translation of policy problems to intelligence analyses, and a skillful shaping of intelligence responses for policy positions. It is too early to tell if the new organization will fulfill its twin intent of establishing a permanent procedure that institutionalizes systematic intelligence support to policy-making and performs effectively. However, experience indicates that procedures are dependent on personalities in providing intelligence to policy.

This administration's reorganization of the Office of the Secretary of Defense, particularly the Office of the Undersecretary for Policy into six new assistant secretaries, presents a peculiar problem for intelligence support to policy. Two of the new offices will be charged with functions novel to DoD, namely, peacekeeping, the promotion of democracy and human rights, domestic defense industry conversion, and environmental security. Some of this reorganization matches the novel requirements established in National Security Directive-67, which deals chiefly with economics and ecology. However, the intelligence elements in Defense do not have the experience and resources relevant either to the reorganization or the requirements. Given this administration's deemphasis of "old thinking" in Defense, the expansion of DoD's mission into new functions, the contraction of overseas military basing, and a reemphasis on recourse to rapid deployment joint task forces in contingencies, the definition of what constitutes defense intelligence is likely to change considerably. In fact, much of the intelligence that may be needed in Defense may indeed match the new requirements set forth in National Security Directive-67. And the organizations providing intelligence for Defense increasingly may not be those in defense intelligence.

Reorganization

The organization of DoD intelligence is mandated by several DoD directives, internal regulations having the nature of institutional charters. One such directive prescribes the authority and responsibility of the ASD (C^3I). The Office of the ASD (C^3I) is a small part of the Office of the Secretary of Defense (OSD)—a large, multifunctional staff organization. The ASD, like the rest of OSD, exists to ensure civilian control of the military. Civilian control over the military is exercised through approval authority, derived from the National Command Authorities, the Defense secretary's authority over the department, and budgetary power. Because OSD performs staff, not line, functions, the ASD (C^3I) does not have operational direction of any intelligence activity in DoD. He is charged with *controlling* defense intelligence; he does not *command* defense intelligence.

The most notable fact about defense intelligence during the last dozen years is the lobbying inside and outside defense intelligence for its reorganization. Four reorganizations have taken place, and a fifth is under way.[4] Reorganizations should not be undertaken frivolously or frequently because they cannot be repeated or repaired easily and their unsettling effects impair capability and performance. A major result of the reorganizations has been turmoil. In fact, defense intelligence has been in turmoil since 1990, and the turmoil will continue until at least Fiscal Year 1995 or 1997, when the Base Force is supposed to be completed. When the Base Force is completed, defense intelligence, as a support function, should conform to its mission, organization, structure, posture, and strategy.

Despite all the lobbying for reorganization, there is little satisfaction with the organization of defense intelligence, either within or outside the organization. The last reorganization was the most advertised and ambitious; it was also much compromised. The arcane arguments advanced, attacked, and abjured over the reorganization, reduction, and, ostensibly, reform of defense intelligence were beside the point. Indeed, they were beside the purpose of the reorganization. The latest rearrangement of organizational architecture emphasized reduction in redundancies rather than reform. Its predecessors demonstrated that reform is relevant, but often incidental and sometimes accidental to reorganization.

The reduction wrought by the reorganization affected two components, the DIA and the intelligence staffs of the services' component commands in the unified combatant commands. Beginning in 1991, the DIA has undergone the most basic change since it was organized in 1961. The number of directorates reporting to the director has been reduced from eight to four. Manpower in the DIA is to be reduced by 17 percent. Whether the reduction in personnel and the simplification of organization are relevant to performance is unknown. In the services, the theater component commands' intelligence staffs were reduced, but not eliminated, through consolidation. The consolidation allowed the ASD (C^3I) to create Joint Intelligence Centers at each of the combatant commands. The consolidation should improve the theater commanders' (CINCs) capabilities to conduct combat operations, but this is not certain yet. The consolidation of the several headquarters intelligence staffs in a theater meant that the service that dominated operations, because of the primary warfare environment in the theater, now dominates intelligence. Surprisingly, the OSD intelligence staff was increased substantially. Therefore, the purpose of the reorganization could be perceived to be not only reduction through consolidation at the field level but control through centralization at the headquarters level. Historically, the effect—though not the intention—of these reorganizations in the OSD has been to distance intelligence from policy and from policy-making.

The last reorganization was directed by the ASD (C^3I) Plan for Restructuring Intelligence. A major opportunity, one that might not recur for decades, presented itself. A war had been fought, and the performance of intelligence in that war had been severely criticized. The defense and intelligence budgets were being reduced. The Defense Management Review had recommended major changes in the management of DoD. The DCI had directed the reorganization of the CIA and the Intelligence Community. The roles and missions of the armed forces were to be examined for change. A strategic epoch had ended. Unfortunately, the opportunity was not exploited. The plan was compromised on two levels. At one level, several of the principal provisions of the plan were not realized. Some were withdrawn even before the plan was approved; others were vitiated after the plan was approved. At another, more important level, the plan was compromised because its principal provisions were decided before first-order questions were asked, much less answered. Answers to the first-order questions could have resulted in a significantly different reorganization. The first-order questions that should have been answered concerned changed and unchanged threats, long-term and short-term national interests, the nature of warfare, and the missions, functions, and tasks of the armed forces. The answers then should have been examined for their effects on the mission of defense intelligence. How best to organize defense intelligence to meet this mission should have been derived from this examination.

The last reorganization is remarkable for the number of issues that it addressed but did not answer—issues that were popular among intelligence personnel and for or against which they had lobbied long and hard. The biggest change that did not occur, despite much lobbying for it, was the separation of Command, Control, and Communications from Intelligence in OSD. The ASD (C^3I), who is the principal staff assistant to the secretary of defense for all of these functions, for counterintelligence and security countermeasures, and for mapping, charting, and geodesy, also has control of continuity of operations, all of the department's computers, Corporate Information Management, and Defense Information. C^3I is now really "C^6I^2M." The ASD has staff oversight responsibility for the Defense Information Systems Agency and the Defense Mapping Agency and some ambiguous, indirect influence through varying authority or means over the DIA, the four military services' intelligence elements; intelligence elements assigned to the ten unified combatant commands; the Central Imagery Office; the services' and combatant commands' reconnaissance operations; the National Reconnaissance Office; and the National Security Agency and the services' cryptologic elements—a truly impressive span of control for one man. Parenthetically, this wide span of control of intelligence organizations illustrates the fact that most of the intelligence community is in DoD. Including all "INT's" (HUMINT, SIGINT, IMINT, MASINT), DoD has the most people, the most money, even excluding the Tactical Intelligence and Related Activities (TIARA), the most equipment, most of the collection and processing, and the control of the high-technology disciplines of IMINT (imagery intelligence), SIGINT (signals intelligence), and MASINT (measurement and signatures intelligence). DoD also is a major HUMINT operator.

Organizational assignment is important because it can shape the understanding of the mission and the method of its execution. Whether or not C^3 and I belong in one organization because of an unbreakable bond or unspoken reason has not been explained. Apparently, there is an assumption that systems inextricably interlink C^3 and I, notwithstanding their different missions. In itself, C^3I is an artifice. C^3I is constructed from architectures of artifacts. The architectures fit together functions by their means, not their ends. The means of command and control and intelligence may be similar, but their ends are dissimilar, as are their purposes. If equipment is only a labor-saving device, information systems are a tool to produce productivity. If the measure of effectiveness in intelligence is wisdom, not just more and faster information, then the union with C^3 has not improved I.

In the meantime, C^3 overly influences intelligence with technical and programmatic considerations that intrinsically should not have an influence on it. This influence has the deplorable effect of viewing I as a mere continuation of C^3, rather than as a unique service of common concern to the entire department, independent in its own right. The important issue of whether C^3 and I each can better serve the department separately has been obscured by (1) an argument with Congress whether the secretary has the sole right to organize his department and whether Congress will establish another assistant secretary and (2) a disagreement within Defense whether the assistant secretary should report directly to the secretary or through an undersecretary. The union of I to C^3 means that not only is I poorly conceived, but the assistant secretary cannot devote the full attention to I that is needed. This distraction is compounded by the fact that the union of C^3 and I takes place only in the person of the assistant secretary; there is no organizational junction below him.

Programming

The ASD participates in the Defense Planning and Resources Board, the board of directors of the Planning, Programming, and Budgeting System. It is through this participation that the ASD links the National Foreign Intelligence Program (NFIP) to the six-year Future Years Defense Program (FYDP), and provides direction to the TIARA. The NFIP is a consolidated expression of the best judgments, within prudent financial constraints, of the defense secretary and the DCI as to how to satisfy the intelligence needs of the executive. The FYDP is the defense secretary's consolidation, also within financial constraints, of the services' Program Objective Memoranda (POMs). The services' POMs are the most detailed, stylized, important, peculiarly American, and quintessential expressions of the best military advice provided by the JCS to the commander in chief. The TIARA is not a single program, but a collection of elements found in several major force programs of the DoD budget and includes, for example, most of the large, worldwide joint airborne reconnaissance program. The importance of the board function cannot be overstated because it allows the ASD, by means of programmatic and fiscal guidance, to influence the capabilities of national intelligence systems to support military operations and to develop tactical intelligence capabilities for the direct support of war fighting. Moreover, recently, the ASD (C^{3}I) and the DCI have formulated a method for tying together related major activities in the NFIP and TIARA, which should improve planning and programming.

PLANNING

Principally to improve programming, but potentially useful to planning, the ASD has directed the development of a Defense Intelligence Planning Guidance. This is an instrument long overdue for introduction. Herbert E. Meyer, former vice chairman of the DCI's National Intelligence Council, noted that intelligence is the other half of strategic planning; the reverse is also true. Defense intelligence, indeed the DoD, has long lacked and sorely needed effective, institutionalized, and enforceable strategic planning. International events, the reduction of resources, the reliance on reconstitution, and the requirements resulting from the responses to National Security Review-29 make the present an ideal time to begin the strategic planning of defense intelligence and the participation of intelligence in the strategic planning of Defense. A strategic planning capability in defense intelligence could establish and validate requirements for the development of intelligence capabilities for all parts of the intelligence cycle, for the FYDP, and for the life cycle of weapons systems. The planning of intelligence capabilities to support the latter may become more important as the armed forces become more dependent on prototypes and reconstitution.

GENERAL DEFENSE INTELLIGENCE PROGRAM

The reorganization of defense intelligence has given the DIA director programmatic control over the General Defense Intelligence Program (GDIP), the part of the NFIP that finances intelligence elements in support of the fighting forces—the single most consequential instrument of policy-making in defense intelligence. The GDIP is no longer a compilation of the services' separate submissions. Instead, it is now developed by element managers and is constructed on a functional, rather than organizational, basis. This means that the DIA director, through control of the GDIP, can evaluate and improve the effectiveness of defense intelligence using the total intelligence capabilities of DoD. However, the reorganization created an anomaly: Although control of the GDIP has been assigned to the DIA director by law, the ASD (C^3I) maintains the Intelligence Program Support Group, which develops the GDIP—ironically, using DIA "borrowed" manpower positions.

The Intelligence Program Support Group, potentially, is an important instrument for the ASD (C^3I) and the DIA director. The group provides the critical capability for program analysis, evaluation, and integration across all the disciplines and systems of defense intelligence and even from the GDIP into the NFIP. It has the wherewithal to develop choices, trade-offs, changes, allocations, and cancellations among subordinate programs. What the ASD (C^3I) lacks is the means to follow up on his selections: He lacks an office to evaluate budget execution, establish performance measures, and review mission progress in order to enforce the achievement of long-range goals—provided that those goals are known and accepted.

HUMINT

Perhaps the most significant part of the reorganization of DIA is the restructuring of DoD HUMINT. This restructuring is based on empowering the DIA director for the first time with the authority to exercise direct operational tasking of field collection units and centralized control of all DoD HUMINT resources. The DIA director now exercises HUMINT Operational Tasking Authority (HOTA) over the services' HUMINT collection units, similar to the NSA director's SIGINT Operational Tasking Authority over the community's SIGINT collection units. HOTA permits the director to prioritize and to levy requirements directly on all field collection elements at the lowest echelon, conditioned only on capability, although the military services still must agree to the tasking of their HUMINT resources. This could eliminate echelon layering, processing delays, and jurisdictional conflicts, and expedite and improve DoD HUMINT support to military operations.

These changes in authority over tasking and programming mean that, for the first time, the DIA director has the authority, and not just the responsibility, to truly be the DoD HUMINT manager, and, therefore, for the first time, the possibility exists of creating an integrated Defense HUMINT system in place of the current coordinated service system—if the reorganization works according to plan. The economical, unified effort is yet to be effected.

It is important to remember that, except for DIA, the DoD intelligence elements are organizations belonging to the services and are established by law. Furthermore, all of the military personnel and many of the civilian personnel in defense intelligence belong to the services. The services' intelligence elements cover all "INT's," not just HUMINT. The service intelligence elements are the U.S. Army Intelligence and Security Command, the U.S. Naval Intelligence Command, and the U.S. Air Force Intelligence Command. Understanding these affiliations is critical to understanding these organizations, what they do, why they do it, how they do it, and how well they do it. The army dominates DoD HUMINT, certainly in sheer numbers, and conducts the full panoply of HUMINT operations. The air force's HUMINT element, which conducts primarily overt HUMINT operations to collect scientific and technical information, is small and will become smaller. The navy's HUMINT capabilities are minuscule and marginal.

The service secretaries, by law, are the heads of components having intelligence elements. The military departments, under Title 10, retain the legal responsibility for raising, training, and equipping intelligence forces. The services, of course, will continue to develop their own HUMINT collection requirements to support their forces, weapons, doctrines, tactics, and training. However, the new DoD intelligence organizational scheme requires the military departments to maintain organic HUMINT capabilities to support the central system—not just to service their own needs—and the force structure to support the unified commands' contingencies. Moreover, DIA's tasking of the services' elements and DIA's own HUMINT operations should be directed increasingly to support of the combatant commands.

As part of the reorganization of U.S. intelligence, the DCI has established the National HUMINT Requirements Tasking Center. The DCI has designated the CIA's deputy director for operations as the national HUMINT manager. DoD is included in the new National HUMINT Requirements Tasking Center. Under the DCI's reorganization, the CIA/DDO can task national HUMINT collection requirements on the DoD through the DIA director. National and military requirements are not necessarily always mutually exclusive. However, there is the possibility that this tasking could exhaust DoD's available resources, preempting fulfillment of collection requirements in support of military operations. This fulfillment is cited as the primary justification for the reorganization of HUMINT.

Our Culture

Defense intelligence, even after the latest reorganization, will continue to labor from several anomalous, fundamental peculiarities. It is important to remember that the DIA director is the chairman's intelligence officer, but a flag officer heads a separate J-2 directorate in the JCS that is staffed by DIA. This division does not make, in practice, for clear delineation of functions. The director gives intelligence guidance through the JCS to the unified and specified (U&S) combatant commands.[5] He must ensure that DoD intelligence is responsive to the U&S commands' war-fighting requirements. To fulfill this assurance, the DIA director includes intelligence support in theater operational plans and establishes intelligence architectures. Yet, the challenge to "jointness" from the services is constant and endless. Some of this resistance is a residue from the services' statutory independence. The services still have large headquarters intelligence staffs, although they are not combatant components and since 1968 have lost their operational responsibilities, which had been written into law. In an age of joint and combined warfare, the services' headquarters intelligence staffs are performing some redundant tasks, which should be performed in DIA. The laws need to be amended so that the service intelligence staffs are reduced in functions and manning.

In addition, the national role of DIA should be improved and increased so that it achieves parity with the CIA. The credibility of

DIA with the president should be established so that it is to its director, not the DCI, that the president turns automatically for military intelligence, which historically has not been the case. Sole responsibility for military intelligence, in practice, should rest with DIA. This responsibility should include control of National Intelligence Estimates on military topics. It is amazing that successive DIA directors have not been mortified that the CIA's national intelligence officer for strategic Forces, who annually produced the National Intelligence Estimate on Soviet strategic forces—an intelligence document that for decades shaped the force structure and budget of the services—was usually a visiting scholar from a think tank.

Defense intelligence is, of course, military intelligence. Nevertheless, the office of the ASD consists mostly of civilians, and DIA and the services are increasingly composed of civilians. In fact, there is a trend of increasing civilianization of the military intelligence elements with attendant attrition of military operational expertise. This trend is the result of the military departments reducing their intelligence forces, purportedly in proportion to their combat forces. Cuts in fighting forces make for fewer available uniformed intelligence officers. The trend toward civilianization poses the risk of developing military intelligence organizations whose intelligence officers cannot understand the military uses of intelligence and the military significance of information. The ethos of DIA and the service intelligence elements must not be civilianized to the extent that the agency becomes insentient of the needs of the fighting forces.

As for counterintelligence (CI), such operations in Defense have not had the extensive and intensive policy management from either DIA or OSD that has been accorded to positive intelligence. The peculiar organizational placement of CI is one of the reasons why policy directions to intelligence and counterintelligence are not comparable in comprehensiveness. DIA, in the recent reorganization, has reduced its management oversight even further by resubordinating its counterintelligence staff, which was a purely advisory special staff, to its analytical organization. In the services, counterintelligence is organized by them to suit themselves. The army has organized all of its counterintelligence and intelligence functions in the single Intelligence and Security Command. The air force originally established all of its counterintelligence functions in the Office of Special Investigations, modeled on the FBI, and combined them with its criminal investigation functions under the inspector general, not the assistant chief of staff for intelligence. The navy recently reorganized its counterintelligence. Navy counterintelligence is merged with criminal investigation functions in the Naval Criminal Investigative Service, which reports to the undersecretary of the Navy, but receives technical counterintelligence guidance from an assistant to the director of Naval Intelligence. The current placement of the services' counterintelligence organizations inhibits the development of joint, long-range, strategic counterintelligence capabilities and operations. Furthermore, the placement has hampered the fusion of intelligence (a fetish in DoD for years), which should include the effective integration of intelligence and counterintelligence.

OTHER CULTURES

The capability of intelligence is grounded on the profound knowledge of the culture of the states with whom intelligence is concerned. Profound understanding of a culture is based on the knowledge of the language and history of the people. Understanding the culture is the basis for understanding motivations and expectations and discovering intentions. DIA and the services fund language and area training. The attention to language and culture training varies with the component. Generally, in the services, language and area training receive short shrift in the competition for funds with weapons and equipment—notwithstanding much lip service to the contrary, and they are likely to receive shorter shrift in the smaller defense budgets. One result of this negligence is the paucity of military intelligence personnel trained and trained well in languages, particularly exotic languages. Consequently, the U.S. understanding of adversaries is not always adequate. As a result, deficiencies are decried in all intelligence and counterintelligence, from collection to production, from requirements to analyses, in warning, current, estimative, and scientific intelligence. As crises occur in exotic locales, U.S. policymakers and war fighters will be, at least, disadvantaged by the lack of language skills and country knowledge among intelligence personnel.

The absence of the training can affect the capabilities of intelligence in other ways: HUMINT officers are unable to undertake long-term immersion in and penetration of targets, their way of life, their thinking, and their decision making; counterintelligence officers are unable to mount sustained strategic attacks against hostile intelligence services. This lack of specialized training renders the understanding of foreign targets nugatory. A consequential result of this defect for intelligence is the mirror imaging of other societies. The defect also compromises the validity of intelligence support to long-range planning and to the development of strategy. Most important, the insufficiency of training imposes constraints on the ability of intelligence to support war fighting. The chief function of intelligence in war fighting is to enable the commander to understand the decision making of an enemy commander in less time than it takes the enemy commander to arrive at his decision. Such understanding is much more than the mere mechanical processing of information faster than the enemy's processing. To gain such insightful understanding requires profound cultural knowledge. The 1992 Intelligence Authorization Act legislated a national security educational foundation and fund in DoD to provide precisely this kind of training for students who express the desire to make a career in intelligence. Not all of these students would qualify for or pursue a career in intelligence, and the foundation might be more effective in training personnel already in intelligence. Whether there will be sufficient funding for this establishment to support future intelligence requirements, including reconstitution capabilities, remains to be seen.

Exhortation

Sustaining an adequate intelligence capability will be problematic. Reconstituting an effective intelligence capability is a difficult and possibly unachievable exercise. Nevertheless, as U.S. military superiority dissipates, the need for superior intelligence will increase so that, if necessary, the United States can act more quickly and more effectively. Defense intelligence will be expected to compensate for fewer fighting forces and cope with more missions. Novel planning, resources, capabilities, readiness, and performance will be required—and expected. Although the national backing for an intelligence capability second to none has dropped dangerously, the Intelligence Community must ensure that it does not drop irrevocably.

16

REFORMING INTELLIGENCE: A MARKET APPROACH

Henry S. Rowen

The current period of radical change in U.S. security strategy, including its intelligence component, presents an opportunity to fundamentally rethink how intelligence work is carried out. The dissolution of the Soviet Union, and the resulting decrease in funding, means that security challenges will be quite different from those of the past. There was also the opportunity to learn from the combat experience of the Persian Gulf War. Subsequently, there have been substantial organizational changes in the intelligence system in the past several years and others have been proposed. Still, have the changes that have been made and those that are proposed adequate? In particular, the system now may be too "supply-side" oriented and too centralized, and more attention should be given to the "demand side" of intelligence and to decentralization.

Concerning the huge changes in the national security environment there are three points. First, although major threats to U.S. security have receded for the near term, they will reemerge. As in the past, they will include weapons of mass destruction able to be delivered against U.S. territory from other countries, in addition to those already possessing such weapons. Dealing with these new threats, and dealing with the less catastrophic ones that will be more common, will require better intelligence on more parts of the world than in the past. Second, for strategic intelligence the United States will need to rely less on remote methods of sensing in hard-to-access areas, notably the former Soviet Union, and more on open sources, HUMINT, and local intelligence-gathering methods. Third, the needs for tactical intelligence in conflicts are undiminished and there is much room for improvement in them.

This paper was first presented on June 10, 1993.

According to press accounts, the Clinton administration wants to cut intelligence spending less than military spending overall. This makes sense during a period when much of the world is undergoing extraordinary changes and the likelihood of serious conflict involving U.S. forces in the near future is low. Even so, the trajectory of the defense budget until the year 2000 suggests that the intelligence budget is not likely to escape substantial cuts.

What Is the Problem?

The core problem is that the U.S. information systems are not as well organized to serve users in the field, especially in local crises and wars, as they should and can be. They perform much better on slower-moving topics and in serving national leaders. The recent Persian Gulf War revealed deficiencies that have appeared in other contexts as well.

The Market for Intelligence

Consider the concept of a "market" for intelligence.[1] That is the demand for information about the external environment by many users with diverse needs inside and (to some extent) outside the government. There are varied sources of supply depending on the subject. There are several propositions about this market:

• A familiar one is that data and information are not identical. The former is essential for the latter but there need to be intervening parameters: contexts, questions, and hypotheses are required to turn data into information. This nonequivalence has important implications. In particular, if the ties between collectors or analysts, and users of intelligence are remote, the data supplied may not be as informative to users as is sometimes assumed. The looseness of such ties, while perhaps inevitable in light of the fact that collection systems are often oriented to serving high-level Washington officials, has been a contributing factor to some U.S. intelligence failures.

• Many of the U.S. information needs, a higher proportion than in the past, will be about particular local situations. These will vary greatly in character and many of these local crises will be hard to predict. For example, U.S. intelligence did not predict before June 1950 that Korea would become a significant theater of war, nor did it anticipate before summer 1990 that the northern Persian Gulf would be one.

• Data have some of the properties of public goods; if I share some with you I still have some (although their worth to me might have changed). This property has led to a ramified system for the dissemination of intelligence data to many recipients. But what is being shared is not always "information" because different recipients often have different problems. Consider photographic intelligence of a nuclear facility in Iraq. A DIA or CIA analyst might be interested in what can be learned about the state of the country's nuclear program, whereas an air commander might be interested in where to target bombs. These are very different information needs.

• The existing intelligence system is very top-down. This is true not only of large dollar investment decisions, where centralization of decisions is warranted, but also of the allocation of existing collection, processing, and production assets. A diverse set of users, through various bureaucratic channels, send their intelligence "needs" up the chain. These needs are then aggregated and weighed, resulting in taskings to collectors. Those officials up the chain of command, who ultimately determine the tasking, often know less than those below and, in any case, have their own legitimate and competing interests. The process often works poorly.

• The diversity of users is enormous. Consider a representative set of intelligence users:

   – A battalion commander who wants to look over the hill.

   – An air commander who needs rapid bomb-damage assessment in order to give tasking orders for the next attack.

   – An electronics warfare officer who needs to know exactly what enemy radar frequencies to jam.

   – A theater commander in chief (CINC) who needs to know shifts in the disposition of opposing forces theater-wide.

   – An army doctrine developer who must consider the array of opposing weapons technologies, doctrines, and tactics that army forces might encounter.

   – A weapons designer who must make assumptions about the technical characteristics of expected opposing weapons.

   – A trade negotiator trying to assess the other side's likely moves.

   – A CIA or DIA analyst endeavoring to determine the enemy's order of battle.

– A CINC, the chairman of the Joint Chiefs of Staff, secretary of defense, DCI, or the president considering the evidence on another government's intentions.

The information needs of this set of users vary widely in type, timeliness, and detail and it is unlikely that those at the top of the system can understand them adequately.

• There are often large economies of scale in collecting data. This is most obviously true with space-based imagery and SIGINT, and least true with HUMINT. These economies of scale are associated with large, front-end investments and system operating costs that are relatively lower than they might otherwise be if each customer acquired his own system for collecting data. In effect, the large initial investments create options for obtaining data on a host of topics at subsequently lower marginal cost. These economies of scale are technologically determined and the structure of much of the U.S. system is technologically driven. This is understandable given the remarkable advances in sensing and communications technology, but it has caused the Intelligence Community to neglect the user aspect of the system in some respects.

• There is some competition in supply of data but not as much as might be imagined. Often competition inside government is held to be wasteful duplication. But consider two examples from the Persian Gulf War. Although the air force and army had neglected remotely piloted vehicles for tactical reconnaissance, the Marines had not, and they demonstrated their utility. The navy had neglected air-delivered precision weapons but the air force had not. Fortunately the system permitted such independent decisions to be made by subordinate organizations.

The Analogy of Large, Multinational Firms

There are similarities between the information needs of the U.S. national security establishment today and the information needs of large multinational corporations. It is often said that such corporations need "a global strategy and a local touch." This means that some parameters of the business need to be decided at the top, including much of technology development, investment strategy, money and tax management, and assessment of political risks among countries. Other parameters can best be addressed locally, such as marketing, tailoring products to local tastes, dealing with local regulations, compensation formulas, and so forth.

The data sources for these corporations need to conform to this dual concept. Too much centralization can cause firms to miss crucial aspects of local scenes and too much decentralization can risk making global errors. Today, many large firms, such as IBM, GM, and DEC, are finding it necessary to become less vertically integrated and to get closer to customers in order to survive. One aspect of these changes is the role of corporate information systems that tie the company together while permitting ample scope for accepting inputs from many sources and distributed data processing.

Multinational corporations typically allow dispersed subordinate units a good deal of autonomy in data gathering on their environments, within certain guidelines, while the top levels decide both how much local data need to be fed to the center and how much of what the center collects for its own needs should go to the field. Implicit in this structure is a mix of what Robert Nesbit calls data "push" versus "pull," where "push" has to do with supply and "pull" with demand.[2] Top management of companies "pull" data from subordinate units for their purposes and "push" data to them that they have reason to believe would be useful—perhaps because field managers have expressed a demand or "pull" for them. Clearly both types are needed; getting the interaction right between them is the key to having an effective information system on the external environment.

In companies, as in the U.S. security establishment, this "push-pull" process is typically handled internally through administrative methods, not by one department "purchasing" data from another. However, data are bought on the market as well as acquired through business contacts, benchmarking, reverse engineering, the press, and so on. Because field units usually generate revenues (i.e., they are profit centers), they have money at their disposal for acquiring data without approval of the center except for large expenditures.

Although there is much in common between the data needs of corporations and government, the needs are not identical. There is no equivalent in the firm to the importance of decisions that presidents sometimes face and that strongly affect the demand for data at the top of the government. Nor is there a parallel to the government's very large capital investment in collection systems. In addition, the government has structured its data acquisition and dissemination needs very differently. Specifically, people in the field are given little authority and money with which to collect data for their needs. There is only a weak counterpart to business unit autonomy within the U.S. national security structure as it is now constituted.

Architectures

Nesbit usefully distinguishes "data" from "information" architectures based on the existence of editors between sources and users. ("Editing" is a flexible concept. There are hardly any types of data that are or should be transmitted directly as sensed. "Editing" here refers to a high degree of selection and discretion in the choice of data to be transmitted and to the formats used.) This editing parameter can also be mapped against the data "push-pull" process discussed above. An editor is not appropriate or needed where the data at issue (1) are simple, (2) come from only a few sources, (3) are of wide interest, as with threat warnings, and (4) concern issues where timeliness is critical. A missile launch detection system is a classic example of a data "push" process in a (relatively) unedited system.

In contrast, an editor is appropriate when (1) the data sources are numerous, (2) there is a processing need, (3) there are many, diverse users, and (4) delays are tolerable. There are many examples of architectures, or rather publications, with editors: the *National Intelligence Daily*, the DIA counterpart to it, specialized DIA and CIA publications, and so on. These publications may or may not match user needs well. The fact that the jobs of the people producing them do not rest on a fee-for-service basis suggests the possibility that some of these might serve the tastes of the producers at least as much as the needs of the users.

"Pull" architectures are those in which users must transmit messages in order to obtain data from repositories. They can do so directly from accessible databases or through higher levels in the chain of command. Such "pull" systems are appropriate when user needs are special and it is costly to hold the data locally. The task of "pulling" data through a hierarchical command structure is difficult, and so works well only for those near the top of the hierarchy, or for urgent needs.

Clearly, the proportion of data needs that should be met through "push" versus "pull" architectures and with editors intervening or not varies greatly with circumstances. Nesbit estimates that a very high proportion of requests for data are "pulled" through the command and control hierarchy. If so, it might be an improvement to shift more user demands to a "pull" system independent of the command structure by accessing directly from databases or from edited sources. There might also be a good case for disseminating more information in a "push" mode, analogous to CNN or Reuters, but it is not obvious how many of these "pushed" data publications would be useful without some better method of ascertaining user demands.

Some collection activities are compatible with a degree of decentralization: some HUMINT, some tactical reconnaissance, and some SIGINT. Moreover, a basic trend in electronics is for things to come in smaller packages. This is illustrated in cellular communications, small satellites for communications, and some other functions. An "intelligence market" perspective suggests that unless there are strong economies of scale reasons, the choice of collectors should be biased toward smaller ones that lend themselves to closer integration with users. There are, of course, physical constraints on these possibilities (e.g., the physics of "optics" and orbital mechanics), but even here collectors may have the option of putting sensors in nonspace vehicles.

Two examples of the potential for decentralization are:

• The greater use of remotely piloted vehicles (RPVs), if the marketplace offers them at a low enough cost. The Persian Gulf War revealed important limitations in tactical reconnaissance, access to satellite imagery, and accurate and timely battle-damage data. The sources of these failures are complex but it is relevant that the principal war fighters, the regional CINCs, are relatively weak players in the resource allocation process.

• If higher resolution products than those currently produced by SPOT, France's space-based imagery system, become available, for instance, from Russia, there could be widespread government user demand. (Exploiting the buying power of the U.S. government suggests consolidating such purchases).

Why We Are Organized as We Are

First, for about forty years the United States focused on one overriding intelligence target: the Soviet Union and various members of the Soviet empire. Moreover, many U.S. resources were directed against Soviet nuclear forces and its conventional forces threatening Western Europe. These targets not only absorbed many U.S. intelligence resources, but also reinforced the top-down character of the system. In other words, the U.S. government believed that it knew in great detail what the main problems were, and the problem was collecting data on them. The crises and wars during the Cold War, however, occurred elsewhere: Korea, Vietnam, Cuba, and the Eastern Mediterranean, and the intelligence system adapted to these events although not always with great success.

Second, although much is in flux now, some things *are* known. There is some continuity in policy issues, in regional situations, in military forces, and in technology. For example, there will be continuing interest in countries that have the capacity to do significant damage to the United States (i.e., those with weapons of mass destruction). Similarly, the United States will continue to focus on regions where it has commitments, notably Europe, Northeast Asia, the Middle East, and the Caribbean/Central American areas. There will also be continuing interest in technical developments that might become a threat to the United States or affect its future military operations. In short, those at the top need to set global priorities, because no one else can. (This is the intelligence equivalent of the multinational corporation's need for a centrally determined global strategy.)

Third, most of the intelligence budget is spent on collection and most collection activities have been driven by the fact that important collectors come in large and costly lumps: big satellites, major SIGINT facilities, photointerpretation facilities, and so on. Moreover, the proper exploitation of such collectors generally involves a high degree of technical know-how, which is costly to develop and maintain, and cannot be widely available throughout the community of users. For many of these functions, the costs of operation and distribution of data are modest relative to the initial capital investment. There are also advantages in training and logistics for having common systems, procedures, and standards that might be lost in a more decentralized system. In this system, collectors have a considerable degree of autonomy, especially on technical matters.

Fourth, there is competition among analysts, which is essential. The users are so numerous and diverse that the system cannot be rigidly hierarchical. In addition, the Intelligence Community has recognized through hard experience the value of multiple sources of data and competing opinions. More should be done to promote such diversity on both the supply and the demand sides, and to organize U.S. intelligence accordingly.

Fifth, the theory of the existing budgeting system is that the military departments and defense agencies receive appropriated funds and supply trained units, beans, bullets, and intelligence data to the operators who, with minor exceptions, do not have any funds. The military departments have become progressively less important in the making of policy, while the chairman of the JCS and the regional CINCs have gained authority, and funds are still appropriated to the departments and to such data-supplying organizations as the National Reconnaissance Office (NRO) and the National Security Agency (NSA). The CINCs have never had budget authority; they are planners and war fighters, and they fight with the forces that others supply them. They can state requirements, but they depend on the services and Defense Department to meet them. The services and the department have their own missions and interests, however, and although the CINCs are consulted on programs, the effectiveness of their advice varies.

Sixth, in normal times (i.e., other than during crises and wars that affect the United States directly) strategic intelligence needs dominate, and the main consumers are in Washington. That is also where the main technical and budget decisions are made and it is therefore natural that strategic intelligence needs have heavy, indeed dominant weight in the choices made. The dominance of strategic intelligence on the former Soviet Union, especially its nuclear forces and its compliance with arms agreements, contributed to the neglect of tactical intelligence. Those government officials involved in making major technical and budget decisions are likely to be those most interested in strategic intelligence and less interested in tactical intelligence.

The Need to Empower Users

As mentioned above, there are many categories of users with diverse interests, and several ways of empowering them should be considered. One step would be to strengthen the hand of users in the requirement generation and budget allocation process by forming strong user organizations and having them represented at various levels. Walter Jajko observed that the General Defense Intelligence Program (GDIP) is no longer a compilation of service sub-missions but is now developed by element managers and is constructed on a functional rather than an organizational basis.[3] That is a step in the right direction. In the theaters, component command's intelligence staffs have been reduced through consolidation, and Joint Intelligence Centers (JICs) have been created. These changes form the basis for strengthening the position of users.

As an experiment, the government might try using "vouchers" or the equivalent of "green stamps" to elicit users' data preferences. These would be allocated based on some theory of who, inside and outside of

Washington, needs to be given more power over intelligence products. The recipients would then "spend" them as they saw fit.

Going further, the present system might be amended by requiring and permitting those with a need for intelligence to pay for some products. Because of the properties of data and the scale economies described above, they would be required to pay only for the marginal costs of processing and producing some kinds of finished intelligence.[4] Such a system would elicit from users their real priorities for data and would be a powerful signal and incentive to producers on what is wanted. This does not mean that all intelligence products should be paid for. Clearly this would not apply to warning information, nor to broad area surveillance. But it might be appropriate for certain kinds of "pull" data. Such an innovation would not pose much of a problem for those already receiving appropriated funds (e.g., the services), but it would be a problem for the regional CINCs who do not have funds, and who might find that the system burdens them with tasks that distract from their diplomatic, war-preparation, and war-fighting missions. Still, this change might be implemented via the familiar method of "industrial funding." This is how many transportation services are funded; users reimburse the airlift and sealift commands for services rendered. In this case, users would be allocated funds to pay intelligence agencies for certain categories of data.

Game playing is to be expected in such a system, as it is in the current "requirements" system. Users might have a disincentive to reveal the true value to them of intelligence data by stating what they would be willing to pay for it. Users would believe, often correctly, that the intelligence data would be provided anyway, bought largely by others or freely provided in a time of crisis. Moreover, much collection is technology driven, and the many thousands of users cannot be expected to know what is possible nor to understand the value of types of information that they have not had before. Nonetheless, their pattern of "expenditures" would probably tell managers at the top more than they now know about the demand for intelligence.

Finally, one way to bridge the gap between some collectors and some users is for the intermediate analytic function to take on more of a "brokering" role between them. This happens now to some extent through various committees that task the collectors, although it might be made stronger. Among the users, including the DIA, the assistant secretary of defense for command control, communications and intelligence (C^{3}I), the CIA, and the Intelligence Community Management Staff, there is scope for aggregating users' demands and making trade-offs among them and among alternative collection technologies. The aim would be to determine which functions could best be decentralized and which served by central "utilities."

This approach argues against czars in general. This is especially true for analysis, which must, on important topics, be performed by independent, competing staffs. Such competition is compatible with having central analytic staffs (such as the National Intelligence Council) pull together all-source materials and to interact with policymakers as long as the rules of the game assure the presentation of alternative views and so long as other, independent materials (both analytic and raw) are distributed to policy personnel.

17

INTELLIGENCE AND LAW ENFORCEMENT

L. Britt Snider

In September 1992 Congress enacted new legislation to set forth missions and functions for the Intelligence Community. One of the responsibilities of the director of Central Intelligence (DCI), as head of the Central Intelligence Agency (CIA), was to "collect intelligence through human sources and other appropriate means, *except that the Agency shall have no police, subpoena, or law enforcement powers or internal security functions*" [emphasis added]. This latter phrase was a verbatim reenactment of the proviso contained in subsection 403 (d)(3) of the National Security Act of 1947 as originally adopted.

When Congress considered new organizational legislation for intelligence in 1992, the Bush administration urged that the language of the law enforcement proviso not be changed. While no one was certain precisely what it meant, or what its effects had been, the proviso had been on the books so long that no one was precisely sure what Congress might be changing if the wording were changed. Therefore, the old language was left intact.

Coincidentally, this decision was made about six weeks before the Senate Select Committee on Intelligence began its investigation of the Banco Nazionale del Lavoro case—the BNL case—an investigation that took about four months and resulted in a 130-page unclassified staff report that was published in February 1993.

Had the BNL investigation happened before the legislation was enacted, the committee might not have been so eager to avoid the issue. For the BNL investigation demonstrated that there is a great deal of confusion on both sides of the divide between intelligence and law enforcement and, to some degree, the statutory formulation contributes to the confusion.

BNL demonstrated much more than confusion over the statutory proviso. The case brought to the surface numerous practical problems

---

This paper was first presented on June 21, 1993.

in the day-to-day coordination of these activities that need to be addressed. These have, in fact, been the subject of a year-long inquiry commissioned in April 1993 by the attorney general and the DCI. The interagency task force that conducted this review is expected to issue a public report on its findings by the end of 1994.

Rather than examining the shortcomings of the coordination process, however, this chapter will trace the development of the policy that governs the relationship between intelligence and law enforcement generally, and what its impact has been at the operational level. Then, I will consider whether the rules should be changed; and, if so, how they should be changed.

The National Security Act of 1947

The sum total of congressional direction on the subject is contained in the language used to begin the chapter: the law enforcement proviso from the National Security Act of 1947, which survived the 1992 revision of the law. It says only that the CIA shall have no "police, subpoena, or law enforcement powers or internal security functions." The legislative history of this provision is not especially illuminating. Essentially, in 1947, there appear to have been three predominant concerns:

- Congress clearly wanted the focus of the newly created CIA to be foreign and not domestic. The dividing line between the two domains was seen as quite clear: law enforcement was "domestic," intelligence was "foreign."

- Congress was also concerned, in the wake of World War II, that it not create a "Gestapo-like" organization. Although the legislative history is not clear on this point, the formulation that appears in the proviso denying the CIA "police, subpoena, or law enforcement powers" largely reflected a desire that the CIA not be able to arrest, detain, interrogate, or otherwise compel information from U.S. citizens against their will.

- Finally, there was a concern, in creating the CIA, that Congress not encroach upon the jurisdiction of the Federal Bureau of Investigation (FBI). "Internal security functions" were the FBI's responsibility, and Congress sought to make it clear that the FBI and not the CIA would remain responsible for monitoring the activities of foreign intelligence services or "subversive elements" within the United States.

Beyond this, however, the legislative history said very little about how the fledgling CIA, or intelligence agencies in general, were expected to relate to law enforcement.

Not until the mid-1970s was more light shed on the issue in public documents, in the reports of the Rockefeller Commission and Church Committee. Both found it necessary to interpret the law enforcement proviso as part of their respective analyses of the CIA's domestic collection activities in the 1960s and early 1970s.

The Rockefeller Commission did not construe the statute as prohibiting the CIA from sharing foreign intelligence information with law enforcement agencies. Similarly, the commission did not find it inappropriate for intelligence agencies to share with law enforcement information pertaining to criminal activity that had been collected incidental to its intelligence mission. Indeed, the commission viewed it as an affirmative duty on the part of intelligence agencies to pass along such information to law enforcement.

The Church Committee acknowledged that the law permitted the CIA to operate domestically to the extent of seeking foreign intelligence from U.S. citizens who had traveled abroad. But it concluded that the law did not permit the CIA to collect information on domestic political groups in order to determine whether there were foreign connections to these groups. The Rockefeller Commission had addressed the same point and found that this sort of collection was appropriate, but concluded that the CIA collection had far exceeded what was necessary to ascertain foreign involvement. The commission also noted three instances where the CIA had collected information on "strictly domestic matters" and found this to have exceeded the CIA's statutory charter.

Finally, the Rockefeller Commission recognized that the CIA might legitimately provide technical assistance and expertise to law enforcement agencies so long as the agency did not "actively participate" in the activities of these agencies.

Executive Order Limitations

In February 1976, after the Rockefeller Commission had reported and while the Church Committee was still investigating, the first executive order on intelligence (EO 11905) was issued by President Gerald Ford. This order, which applied to all intelligence agencies—not just the CIA—reflected several of the conclusions of the Rockefeller Commission:

• It provided that nothing in the order prohibited the dissemination to law enforcement agencies of "incidentally gathered information indicating involvement in activities which may be in violation of law."

• It prohibited intelligence agencies from participating in or funding any law enforcement activity within the United States, but excluded from this general prohibition cooperation between law enforcement and intelligence for the purpose of protecting the personnel and facilities of intelligence agencies, to prevent espionage or "other criminal activity related to foreign intelligence or counterintelligence."

These elements of the Ford order were largely repeated by President Carter's order (EO 12036) issued in January 1978. The wording of the provision in the Ford order saying it was permissible for intelligence agencies to disseminate "incidentally gathered information" to law enforcement was dropped by the Carter order. The updated language provided that nothing prohibited the dissemination to law enforcement of information "which indicates involvement in activities that may violate federal, state, local, or foreign laws," whether it was incidentally gathered or not.

In 1981 came the Executive Order (EO 12333), which remains in effect today. The Reagan order was deliberately drafted to be more positive than the Carter order in this respect. Gone was the prohibitory language where assistance to law enforcement was concerned. The effect of the Reagan order was to authorize the Intelligence Community to render whatever assistance it wished to law enforcement that was not precluded by law (presumably referring to the law enforcement proviso in the National Security Act). At the same time, the Reagan order returned to the concept of "incidentally acquired information" as used in the earlier Ford order, requiring intelligence agencies to adopt procedures to provide for the dissemination of "incidentally obtained information that may indicate involvement in activities that may violate federal, state, local or foreign laws."

This is essentially where the policy remains today. To summarize, the CIA is precluded by law from having "police or law enforcement powers" or "internal security functions," but the executive order does not elaborate on what the law means. It does require the CIA, as well as other intelligence agencies, to adopt procedures providing for the dissemination of information to law enforcement—that they acquire information incidental to their collection operations if the intelligence agencies determine the information may indicate possible violations of U.S. or foreign laws.

While the executive order requires intelligence agencies to have procedures governing dissemination to law enforcement, it does not necessarily require such dissemination. In addition, the executive order does
not contain any language expressly prohibiting intelligence agencies
from deliberately (as opposed to incidentally) collecting information
for law enforcement purposes. Indeed, the order specifically includes,
within the mission of intelligence agencies, collection of information
that could be directly relevant to U.S. law enforcement authorities in
two categories: information on international narcotics trafficking and
international terrorism. Beyond these, there is no express authorization to collect information for law enforcement purposes, and the
absence of such express authorization might be interpreted to suggest
an intent to preclude such collection.

Interpreting Existing Policy

Given the ambiguity in both the statutory proviso and executive order,
it is not surprising that the Senate Intelligence Committee in the
course of its BNL investigation found considerable confusion at the
operational level in terms of precisely what existing policy permits and
what it does not. While there was a general perception on both sides
that the CIA is prevented "by law" from engaging in law enforcement
activities, there were widely disparate views on how this translates into
practice.

As far as intelligence operatives are concerned, practical considerations tend to dominate. While few of those interviewed could explain
precisely what existing law or the executive order allowed, there is an
instinctive recognition that using intelligence assets to collect law
enforcement information could lead to their disclosure in court and,
thus, is something to be avoided, if at all possible. There was some
awareness that there are ways to protect classified information in court
(e.g., the Classified Information Procedures Act), but how and whether
this could be counted on is far too murky for most to risk a valuable
asset. Most also sense they are somehow precluded from deliberately
collecting information for law enforcement purposes, although opinion
varied in terms of whether this policy applies overseas as well as within
the United States. It is generally perceived that if intelligence agencies
come across something useful to law enforcement incidental to their
foreign intelligence activities, it could be shared in appropriate circumstances, but most see this as a matter of case-by-case determination.

Understanding of applicable policy is no more consistent among law enforcement officials. Some think the CIA is precluded from domestic operations, but not from collecting information overseas that relates to criminal investigations in the United States. Others see no reason why law enforcement should not get whatever information the intelligence agencies have. Still others see intelligence agencies as more to be avoided than cultivated—as more trouble than they are worth.

In fact, the "historical separation" that has characterized the relationship between law enforcement and intelligence probably owes more to the operational concerns of each side, to their difference of purpose, and, indeed, to the difference in their cultures, than it does to applicable law and policy. This is not to say that law and policy necessarily lead to a different result, but rather that the ambiguities in law and policy have left it largely to the working level to determine the contours of the relationship between the two disciplines in the context of particular circumstances.

Leaving relations between law enforcement and the Intelligence Community ambiguous and subject to ad hoc determinations in the field inevitably fosters inconsistent results and may or may not serve broader U.S. interests. Clearer guidance is needed.

What the Approach Should Be

If a case is made for clarifying applicable law and policy, what should the approach be? Should a policy to reinforce and maintain the de facto separation between the two disciplines be adopted, or a policy that permits or requires greater interaction?

I believe the latter approach would be better. While the historical reasons for keeping law enforcement and intelligence separate have not changed, the U.S. interests in bringing them into closer harmony have grown. While the need to protect intelligence sources and methods from disclosure will require a great deal of thought if this approach is taken, it is no longer necessary, or even desirable, to continue to maintain the "Chinese wall" between the two disciplines. There are essentially two reasons for this conclusion.

First, crime in the United States is becoming more international in character. The old notion that "crime is domestic, and intelligence is foreign" is growing increasingly obsolete. As the extent of foreign ownership in U.S. business increases, as the number of foreigners doing business in the United States continues to grow, as international communications make it possible to shift funds in and out of the United States in a matter of seconds, and as U.S. business, itself, becomes more international, criminal enterprises within the United States increasingly have a foreign element. This occurred in the BNL case. Was the parent bank in Italy aware of or involved in the fraudulent activities of its Atlanta branch? This occurred in the BCCI investigations. Did BCCI officials deliberately deceive the likes of Messrs. Clifford and Altman in terms of their control of First American? This occurred in the prosecution involving a Florida company owned by Carlos Cardoen, the Chilean arms manufacturer, for violating U.S. export control laws. Foreign entities and individuals are increasingly being targeted for criminal investigation within the United States. These entities and individuals may also be of interest to foreign intelligence agencies of the U.S. government, which may be uniquely positioned to obtain information of law enforcement value.

Second, international crime is having a growing and an increasingly adverse effect on U.S. security. In August 1993, the National Strategy Information Center published a report that documented many of these activities and their effects on U.S. security. *Newsweek* magazine also had a lengthy cover story on the same topic.[1] More recently, the director of the FBI spoke out publicly on the effect of organized crime activities in Russia and their potential impact on U.S. security.

Of particular concern are the narcotics activities carried out by these criminal groups, which have had huge costs to the United States in terms of the criminal justice and health care systems as well as the toll they take on what may otherwise be useful, productive lives. But what about groups outside the United States who smuggle aliens into the United States, or who extort money from ethnic groups in the United States, or perpetrate large-scale fraud in the United States? This is not speculation, as the *Newsweek* article demonstrated. It has happened and continues to happen. What about organized crime activity in countries like Russia or Italy that debilitates the governments concerned and works against what the United States is attempting to do bilaterally? What are the costs here? And, finally, is it unthinkable that organized crime might attempt to obtain a nuclear, biological, or chemical weapon, or the components of such weapons from a former communist state that is hard up for cash?

The Intelligence Community is focused on things foreign: foreign governments, foreign entities, and foreign individuals. It has capabilities to collect information abroad that are not available to law enforcement authorities within the United States and cannot be provided through cooperative law enforcement arrangements or by international law enforcement organizations like Interpol. To forswear use of these capabilities to deal with problems of significant importance to U.S. interests is not prudent.

On the other side are those who argue that using these capabilities for a law enforcement purpose makes little practical sense. Such capabilities are often expensive and time-consuming to develop and maintain (e.g., a technical collection system that has cost billions of dollars to develop and field, or a reliable human source with access to critical intelligence). These assets might provide important information to the United States for long periods of time, which would easily outweigh their benefit in a particular criminal case. Because secrecy is jeopardized by employing these assets in support of a criminal investigation and prosecution, employment for law enforcement purposes should be avoided. In any case, the opponents would say, intelligence agencies can never be as conversant with the facts of a particular criminal investigation as the investigators themselves and, as a practical matter, can contribute relatively little of importance to prosecutors.

One can concede the validity of these points in most circumstances and still reject the absolutist "either/or" position. One can envision circumstances, for example, where a human source might be a provider of marginally used intelligence, but holds the key to conviction in a significant prosecution in the United States. One could envision cases where a technical collection capability might be employed in a way that was not intrusive and could be used to develop "lead" information for investigative purposes, which need not become evidence in a criminal trial. There might also be cases where the analytical capabilities of the Intelligence Community could provide valuable insights to criminal investigators, for example, in providing leads to similar conduct carried out by a particular foreign national or entity that is the subject of the investigation.

Even if one were to take the view that separation should be maintained "at all costs," where would the line be drawn if the subject of a U.S. criminal prosecution also happened to be someone of significant foreign intelligence interest? General Noriega? Carlos Cardoen? Which interest should predominate? Should intelligence gathering cease while the criminal case is ongoing? If not, should intelligence refrain from collecting information that might be useful to the prosecution? Even the absolutist must have qualms about maintaining purity in these circumstances.

In sum, while the use of intelligence capabilities for law enforcement purposes needs to be carefully weighed against the consequences of possible disclosure, to determine a priori that the interest of the

United States will always lie in keeping intelligence assets away from problems that have serious repercussions for its security and well-being seems neither practical nor appropriate.

What the Rules Should Be

If one concludes that it is desirable to foster greater interaction between intelligence and law enforcement, what rules should govern this relationship and what might such interaction properly consist of? This question is addressed below from the standpoint of the Intelligence Community's three functional areas: collection, analysis, and other types of assistance, overt and covert.

COLLECTION

The most obvious, and yet most problematic, form of interaction would be using intelligence collection capabilities to collect information for law enforcement purposes.

Within the United States, a prohibition on intelligence agencies deliberately collecting information for law enforcement purposes should be maintained in law and, indeed, should include intelligence agencies in addition to the CIA. Intelligence agencies should be permitted, if not required, however, to acquire and disseminate information for law enforcement purposes that is gathered in the United States incidental to their foreign intelligence activities (e.g., by interviewing foreign individuals within the United States for foreign intelligence purposes). If follow-up within the United States is required, it should be accomplished by appropriate law enforcement authorities, not intelligence.

Outside the United States, intelligence agencies should be given wider berth. Although collection for a law enforcement purpose that involves a "U.S. person" should be subject to the same standards that apply to criminal investigations within the United States, the law should expressly authorize intelligence agencies to collect information outside the United States regarding a foreign person or entity for a law enforcement purpose if the attorney general and the DCI, or their representatives, have authorized such collection as consistent with the overall interests of the United States. Where such collection is undertaken by intelligence agencies, the attorney general should be directed to take such measures as may be lawful and appropriate at each stage of the criminal justice process to preclude the public disclosure of any intelligence sources and methods that might be employed.

Requiring such collaboration would presumably ensure that the important competing interests involved would be sorted out within the context of the particular facts involved. Requiring a decision "at the top" would presumably result in greater consistency and uniformity in terms of the decisions that are ultimately reached. Finally, committing the attorney general at the outset to the protection of the intelligence sources and methods employed would presumably require consideration of how information is collected and, subsequently, how it is used by criminal justice agencies.

New bureaucratic mechanisms to accomplish these functions in a timely fashion would be needed because none currently exists. New procedures would also be required at both intelligence and law enforcement agencies (including U.S. attorneys' offices) to facilitate the initiation and handling of such requests, again, because none currently exists.

Yes, this framework would require some effort to build, and expertise and commitment to make it work. Some would undoubtedly argue that the value added by intelligence would be so marginal that it would not justify the effort, but this will remain unknown unless it is tried.

ANALYSIS

Law enforcement agencies routinely receive intelligence reports and estimates relevant to law enforcement concerns, particularly in the areas of counternarcotics and counterterrorism. There is relatively little communication taking place, however, between the law enforcement and analytical communities in terms of requesting intelligence analysis—either in terms of analyzing broad topics (e.g., the nature and extent of international organized crime) or to meet the needs of a particular prosecution.

In the latter case, while law enforcement is often concerned with whether persons proposed for indictment have had relationships with the Intelligence Community and, therefore, may complicate the prosecution, there is rarely consideration of what the Intelligence Community might do to support a criminal investigation or prosecution, even where it involves foreign entities or individuals. To be sure, specific analytical support to individual cases would raise the same types of concerns as collection (i.e., increase the risk of disclosure of intelligence sources and methods) and could complicate the criminal justice process if the analysis proved at odds with the prosecution's case. (The BNL case provides an excellent example of this phenomenon.) But it also appears that intelligence analysts may well be able to provide analysis that might suggest new avenues to criminal investigators or provide evidence of past conduct of foreign entities or individuals not available through other sources.

Less problematic would be analysis of broader topics of particular law enforcement interest: How does the system for smuggling Chinese aliens into the United States operate? What is the likelihood that international organized crime would be able to obtain plutonium from a country that is dismantling its nuclear weapons, and sell it to a rogue state? What countries are engaging in economic espionage within the United States or against U.S.-owned firms overseas? Where and how are narcotics traffickers laundering their money? Are other countries able to circumvent U.S. trade controls by getting their goods into the United States through a third country?

This kind of analysis is currently done by the Intelligence Community, but to a relatively small degree and typically on its own initiative rather than at the request of law enforcement agencies. In part, this is because of the confusion over precisely what intelligence agencies can and should do to support law enforcement activities.

As with collection, the policy with respect to analysis in support of law enforcement needs to be clarified. Analysis of broad topics relevant to law enforcement should be specifically authorized, and mechanisms established to ensure that such analyses address the most pressing law enforcement concerns. With regard to analysis in support of particular criminal investigations, while the value of such analysis and potential involvement in the prosecution must be carefully weighed, such support ought to be routinely considered in significant criminal investigations with foreign targets. At present, such support is minimal and largely a function of the investigator or prosecutor's familiarity with the capabilities of intelligence agencies. The interests here seem too substantial to continue in this ad hoc manner. It should be made clear that intelligence has a role in analyzing criminal activities abroad that directly affect U.S. interests. Mechanisms are also needed to systematically consider intelligence support in major cases involving foreign elements.

Other Forms of Assistance to Law Enforcement

There are other possible forms of intelligence assistance to law enforcement—some controversial, some benign. Among the controversial possibilities is covert action. Should the CIA undertake covert operations to disrupt major criminal enterprises overseas if they are having a significant adverse effect on the United States? For example, should the CIA attempt to covertly disrupt the operations of international narcotics traffickers who are planning to introduce drugs into the United States? Should it attempt to disrupt the activities of international smuggling rings that are trying to get illegal aliens or prohibited goods into the country? If intelligence agencies themselves should not engage in such activities, should they be authorized to provide money, equipment, or technical assistance—covertly or overtly—to other governments to have them disrupt such activities before they can affect the United States?

Whether such activities could be undertaken consistent with existing law and policy is not the issue. Rather, should applicable law and policy permit such activities in appropriate circumstances? The government has not thought through its approach in this regard. Clearly there has been more U.S. involvement (covert and otherwise) in the areas of international narcotics and terrorism, where the United States has often provided assistance to other governments to help them cope with, and disrupt, the activities of narcotics traffickers and terrorists. But beyond these two areas, the application of covert measures to disrupt international criminal enterprises affecting the United States has received relatively little consideration.

Finally, there is the issue of providing surveillance equipment or expert personnel to assist domestic law enforcement agencies—whether or not the targets are foreign entities or individuals. Under the existing executive order, intelligence agencies are permitted to provide "specialized equipment, technical knowledge, or the assistance of expert personnel" to federal law enforcement agencies and, "when lives are endangered," to state and local law enforcement agencies. Of all the forms of possible assistance to law enforcement, this type of assistance, which involves the use of intelligence personnel and collection assets within the United States, appears to be the most developed, regulated, and coordinated. Intelligence personnel assigned to such duties typically do not participate in the operational aspects of a criminal investigation (e.g., surveillances, arrests, interrogations), but rather assist with the operation of technical equipment, translations, and other tasks where specialized skills are required. Use of specialized surveillance equipment is carefully assessed for legal implications (e.g., does its use require a search warrant?) as well as the likelihood of its being publicly disclosed in a judicial proceeding.

Law Enforcement Assistance to Intelligence?

This chapter has thus far focused upon what intelligence might do to assist law enforcement. Is there any area in which the reverse might make sense? Sharing information that relates to a particular criminal activity would seem to hold little potential. On one hand, law enforcement authorities are typically proscribed by law, grand jury secrecy rules, or applicable policy from providing the details of criminal investigations to non–law enforcement agencies. Moreover, investigations of particular crimes are likely to have little value in terms of the interests of intelligence agencies.

On the other hand, sharing information collected by law enforcement agencies at a "macro" level merits further consideration. Information that comes to federal law enforcement agencies through their foreign counterparts, or through Interpol, concerning criminal activities abroad that directly affect the United States might be one area of possible sharing. Various types of statistical information maintained by law enforcement agencies (e.g., information on immigration flows into the United States, or the types and quantities of imports to the United States, or information regarding foreign investment in U.S. business) might also be useful information to intelligence agencies. To some extent, such information may be available already, but intelligence agencies are unaware of it. In other cases, it may not be currently available but could be made so with little effort or expense. It is an area that merits further exploration.

Conclusion

The time has passed when "crime" could be regarded as domestic, and "intelligence" as foreign. The time has also passed when one was able to think of "international crime" as someone else's problem, not a U.S. problem.

While it will continue to be wise policy in most circumstances to maintain separation between law enforcement and intelligence, the U.S. interest may not always lie in blindly maintaining "separation at all costs." More thought must be given to how these two disciplines might profitably interact to benefit broader U.S. interests. Clearer laws and regulations are needed, as are better bureaucratic mechanisms to provide adequate and timely coordination.

COMMENTS: ELIZABETH RINDSKOPF

Having worked on a joint Department of Justice–Intelligence Community report on the relationship between law enforcement and intelligence during 1993, I know how difficult it is to discuss the issues raised in this chapter. The worlds of law enforcement and intelligence are far apart. They have different roles, different rules, and different cultures, and often they do not speak the same language. These differences make writing about these subjects extremely challenging, but the relationship between law enforcement and intelligence is a timely topic on which more discussion is needed.

Why is the subject of law enforcement and intelligence worthy of extended conversation, discussion, and writing? These are complicated areas of human endeavor, but understanding how the two worlds interact and the impact of their interaction is not simply a matter of deciphering complicated rules and regulations. These two areas are fundamentally distinct; they have different worldviews and missions. As a lawyer—never previously exposed to intelligence—I was surprised when I first joined the NSA Office of General Counsel in 1984 to see the vast, but highly classified, regulatory structure that governed how intelligence was both defined and used. Learning about these classified structures from an outsider's point of view, I recognized some important, even essential, facts that explain why these two communities find comprehending one another so difficult.

To understand these two communities and their differences requires that we return to "first principles." As a lawyer, I look to the U.S. Constitution for guidance—this is where government lawyers in particular like to begin any analysis. In fact, ensuring that their clients operate within the constitutional framework is at the heart of their professional existence. The government lawyer spends his or her time in the search, first, for authority and, second, for its limitations. Because the U.S. government is a government of limited powers, we must ask again and again: Where is governmental action authorized and what limits does the law place upon that authority?

These questions about legal authority and their answers are less common in the intelligence world. Gradually, I came to understand why. Operating primarily outside the United States and beyond the constitutional and legal interests of U.S. citizens, the Intelligence Community evolved with less need for concern about such limits. As mentioned before, in the United States, intelligence must follow all applicable domestic law, but abroad intelligence must support the Constitution. In short, intelligence has grown up not so much *above* the law, as *outside* its normal reach.

The Framers of the Constitution and the courts that have interpreted it appear to have anticipated this difference in the way they allocated various responsibilities to the three branches of the government. The president's role, as it is constitutionally defined, contains several types of authority. In brief, the president serves as commander in chief; is principally responsible for the conduct of the nation's foreign affairs; and, finally, is charged with executing all domestic laws. Each role is different, particularly with regard to the citizenry served. Thus, the president's conduct of foreign affairs has little directly to do with the legal rights of individual citizens. Yet when the president is responsible for executing the laws, the reverse is true; citizens' rights are directly affected. The great differences in these responsibilities over time have produced different roles, rules, and cultures for the agencies charged with executing the president's various authorities.

Historically, foreign and domestic responsibilities remained separate. But today, this has changed, and the president no longer functions in his three roles "one at a time." His responsibilities may overlap in any given situation. An example is the prosecution of Gen. Manuel Noriega, the leader of a foreign nation that the United States ultimately engaged militarily, but also the subject of a domestic law enforcement investigation that ultimately led to a federal criminal prosecution. In such a situation, which of the president's responsibilities takes precedence: the president's role as commander in chief, his role in foreign affairs, or his responsibility to enforce domestic criminal law?

The problem of overlapping areas of responsibility and interest becomes more difficult because the approaches that intelligence and law enforcement take to problem solving are necessarily different. Intelligence looks at the total picture, focusing on broad, strategic fact patterns. In contrast, law enforcement is more tactical in its view of the world: it gathers specific information in support of individual investigations and prosecutions, but is little concerned with the broader picture, if it does not assist the investigation or prosecution of the moment. Thus, the analytic processes employed by these two communities differ as a result. The logic employed by intelligence and law enforcement is akin to the distinction between inductive and deductive reasoning.

To confuse matters more, some of the techniques that both communities employ are essentially the same, but are described differently and operate under different rules. For example, both gather information, and sometimes the means that they employ, although differently described, are essentially the same. An example is the intrusive collection provided for law enforcement by wiretap authority under the Constitution and specific enabling legislation. Similar collection capabilities might also be employed by the Intelligence Community under the label of "signals intelligence," operating outside constitutionally protected areas and pursuant to a far different regulatory framework. Different rules and regulations are employed because different purposes are intended to be served, even though the collection activity itself may appear objectively to be the same.

This overlap in both the means and ends of achieving different missions creates other problems. Sometimes these two communities use the same words to mean different things. It might be said that they have become separated by a common language. Indeed, it is often difficult to have effective discussions between law enforcement and intelligence officials until these language differences are understood. For example, when intelligence analysts speak of "evidence," they do not have in mind the type of "evidence" that lawyers think of when they seek to introduce information in a court of law. Intelligence analysts are including in this term information that may be untested, more akin to rumor than fact—intelligence analysts rely upon a much broader range of information than could be considered factual and admissible in a court of law. But the intelligence analyst is an expert, trained in the art of evaluating such information. And to him or her, it is "evidence." This difference in the use of language was the basis of the confusion that gave rise to the BNL matter where an intelligence analyst spoke about evidence "confirming" a conclusion, failing to recognize the impact that this use of language might have on persons whose training was in the law enforcement world.

Thus, we have a double task today. We must first understand the fundamental differences that exist in the missions, methodologies, and limitations of law enforcement and intelligence. We must then decide how these two great capabilities can work together. To do this, we may need to make important decisions. We must decide which of the differences between intelligence and law enforcement are essential to be maintained if our constitutional democracy is to be preserved and which are not.

Like many in the Intelligence Community, I have long believed that keeping intelligence and law enforcement in their individual, hermetically sealed, and isolated worlds was essential to preserving important constitutional guarantees. Perhaps this view flows from lessons learned during the Watergate period and specifically in the hearings of the

Church and Pike committees during the late 1970s. I have said before that the results of this period, over time, seem to have been reduced to two simple rules: intelligence should not "do law enforcement," and it should not "collect on" U.S. persons. Such simplistic statements are easy for conveying a general message to a large, decentralized, and very busy work force. Yet while these "slogans" may be easy to keep in mind, and certainly convey some general truth, they are far too simplistic to describe in a useful way the real underpinning of the Constitution, law, and regulations as they direct the ways in which intelligence agencies function in the complicated modern world. Learning lessons from events such as BNL and BCCI, the Intelligence Community has been forced to look carefully at its authorities. It must distinguish what is legally required from what is simply convenient or traditional. The Intelligence Community must, of course, take care to ensure that the fundamental principles of the Constitution are maintained; but it must also use its authorities for the purposes they are intended: the protection of U.S. national security.

What makes this review of roles so very important today is the seriousness of the areas of overlapping interest that are emerging. For example, consider the potential overlap between these two communities on a topic such as weapons proliferation. It is appropriate for intelligence agencies to monitor closely the dangerous, illegal weapons trade around the world. Yet some of that activity will also be of interest to domestic U.S. law enforcement agencies as they seek to execute their own responsibilities under a variety of statutes, to investigate, and to prosecute weapons trafficking that violates U.S. law. This is an overlapping area of interest and there is a corresponding need to sort out what the respective roles will be. At least initially, it may be necessary to "hand tool" each of the cases of overlap in order to ensure that the various roles and missions are properly established and executed. If this coordination is not handled correctly, the country may pay a very dear price: criminals of significance to domestic law enforcement may go unapprehended; intelligence methodologies may be used in ways that ignore constitutional protections as law enforcement responsibilities are executed; or for fear of acting at all, critical national security interests may be neglected. There are numerous other examples of such overlap: counternarcotics, counterintelligence, and, more recently, international organized crime with vast political implications for many emerging democracies.

To coordinate the various roles and responsibilities of law enforcement and intelligence, one must keep in mind the difference in the mission that should and must separate these two large communities. The work of intelligence is to gather information for use by policymakers who may choose to employ the intelligence-provided information in support of a variety of initiatives. In response to this intelligence, policymakers may consider taking a traditional diplomatic or military action, or they may, with increasing frequency, elect a law enforcement response. The Intelligence Community understands how to support the military or diplomatic initiative. This has long been its business. Law enforcement initiatives, on the other hand, are new to the Intelligence Community. Moreover, because law enforcement actions ultimately result in court cases under a constitutionally imposed set of rules applied by the court system, they pose new risks. The court system, with its constitutionally defined mission, operates in the open: protection of information will often be inconsistent with justice. This must be kept in mind as we consider how intelligence can be coordinated with law enforcement initiatives. Stated another way, because the Constitution places great value on public trials, in many cases reliance on information produced by intelligence activities is likely to be problematic. The information typically cannot be publicly used in a trial if its source is to be protected. Thus, even when topics are appropriate for foreign intelligence collection, it may not be expedient to pursue them by intelligence means if to do so will lead to a public trial.

The conclusion is simple to state, yet the solution is difficult to achieve: the new post–Cold War world requires constant coordination between law enforcement and intelligence if the contributions of both to U.S. national security are to be maximized. Among agencies trained to preserve the separation of governmental powers, in a way that also prevents their abuse, coordination is the hardest goal to attain. Too often, attempts to coordinate remind me of Pogo: "We have met the enemy and he is us."

COMMENTS: JOHN COLEMAN

There is much with which one can agree in both Britt Snider's chapter and Elizabeth Rindskopf's comments. The remarks that follow, therefore, will not challenge what they have said but, rather, discuss a few of the practical problems that arise in connection with the relationship between the law enforcement and intelligence communities.

First, with respect to incidental data collection, this was part of the cooperation in law enforcement that the law enforcement community received from the military in the past. Previously the law enforcement community could not specifically task the military because of posse comitatus. But the military would tell the community if they happened to see something on a training mission that was of law enforcement interest. Over time, this grew into the law enforcement community asking the Intelligence Community to perform training missions—in effect, working around the system, while still trying to adhere to its rules. Eventually, Congress changed the rules and gave the military the authority to detect and monitor on its own. Once the need to work around the system was eliminated, cooperation started to work much more smoothly and the contribution of the military has been even greater.

With respect to incidental data collection by the Intelligence Community, the relationship with law enforcement has been more complicated. First, intelligence is often difficult to work with; it is uncertain and is somewhat unfocused. The worst part about information generated by the Intelligence Community is that it is not easy to go back and say, "OK, now that you have these great leads, can you get me more?" A key feature of law enforcement is following up on information and leads to obtain further information. It is rare that a lead has enough substance to make it possible to conduct a major investigation based on it alone. An exception might be a lead that is keyed to interdiction: "There are 1,000 kilos of cocaine about to enter the port of Miami on the SS *Michaels.*" You then go out, board the SS *Michaels*, and get your kilos. But such leads are not typical. More likely is information of the following sort: "There is an organization called the XYZ, and they are in charge of something, and they are going to be moving drugs in the direction of the United States." It might be great information, but it needs substantial development.

There is also frustration on the part of law enforcement agencies with some of the procedures followed by the Intelligence Community. For example, if the Drug Enforcement Administration tasks the NSA to collect specific information, current regulations require NSA to report whatever it collects to all the law enforcement agencies. The result is often a "food fight" among the agencies, causing duplication of effort, confusion, and possibly danger to law enforcement officers who might be acting on the information they think they alone have. (To address this problem, the Intelligence Community has been asked to review this procedure. One possible solution might be to "tag" the intelligence so that it is reported back to the agency that originally requested it. Or, if it has to be "broadcast," at least the other agencies will be told that the information request originated with agency X in order to cut down on the confusion at the users' end.)

With respect to the law enforcement community, there is probably a need for a better understanding of the Classified Information Procedures Act (CIPA). There is a technicality in the law that has generated a number of motions where defendants have put in a request to the court for information on all relevant intercepts. Although the government might ultimately be able to file a motion to suppress its own case, in order to avoid having to disclose sensitive and confidential techniques, there is always a minor risk of disclosure. Closing that loophole in CIPA would give the law enforcement community a greater ability to work with classified information.

In addition, the stark division between the disciplines of law enforcement and intelligence has outlived its usefulness. However, law enforcement managers are very reluctant to embrace procedures that are not based solidly in law. The further away from the law one gets, the more likely it is that law enforcement officials are in situations in which they exercise discretion well beyond the normal course of their business. Again, unlike in the Intelligence Community, the finished product of law enforcement will generally end up in a court of law where every step of an investigation is likely to be examined and disclosed.

Regarding covert action, although vital and sometimes necessary, there are potential problems, especially in coordination. In the area of drug enforcement, for example, it is likely that covert action in a foreign environment is directed against and involved with drug shipments to the United States. Eventually, the information developed by the operation will touch directly on a violation of U.S. laws. If that information is not acted upon at the U.S. end, the operation will find itself involved in allowing a serious felony to take place within the United States. There is also the possibility, which has happened in the past, of a law enforcement agency working on the same target but on the other end of the operation. Thus, cooperation, as difficult as it may be, is essential.

In general, the remedy to these and related problems is greater cooperation and understanding. The law enforcement business has grown more sophisticated over the past decade. There was a time when drug law enforcement was two guys and a cloud of smoke. Now there are SIGINT and HUMINT, other sophisticated collection techniques, and esoteric operations such as "reverses," international "stings," money laundering investigations, and the like. Yet precisely because such operations are complicated and sometimes global in character, there exist serious risks if everybody who is involved in these efforts is not adequately informed about the operation and in agreement about how it is to be carried out.

International crime has gained much publicity of late, and rightfully so; crime is occurring on a global scale. It is no longer just drugs and terrorism; there are wide-scale fraud, white-collar crimes, and illicit financial schemes operating globally. As a result, there is room for greater cooperation between law enforcement and the intelligence agencies in some of these areas.

If there is to be greater cooperation, however, one area that needs to be examined is the way in which the Intelligence Community develops liaison relationships with foreign officials. Given responsibilities in these new law enforcement areas, it is natural that intelligence officers in the field will want to develop contacts with the appropriate law enforcement people in those countries. However, those law enforcement people are frequently the same people that the DEA is working with as well. This creates a situation in which separate U.S. agencies are working with the same department, possibly different people within the same department, on related concerns. Conflict, competition, and confusion are the likely results if there is not proper coordination on the U.S. government's part.

Another concern is how the host nation views the U.S. side. In some countries, it does not make a difference; where the DEA and the CIA work side by side, no one really cares if the DEA or the CIA is involved. Other countries, however, can be very sensitive about the presence of the CIA. There is not as much concern about the DEA because the DEA has a single mission that is well understood by the host government. That is not the case with the CIA, and its overt presence can be a problem. In addition, when the CIA and the DEA are involved in a mission within certain countries, this could cause a problem for DEA officers if they are wrongly thought to be interested in more than drugs or, because of their association with agency personnel, misidentified as CIA officers.

The problems raised here should not be taken as a sign that the relationship between the law enforcement and intelligence communities is in terrible shape. The fact is, many of the rules defining the spheres of intelligence and law enforcement were written in an era when concerns were different. It is time to take a new look at these rules. Nevertheless, the overall relationship between the Intelligence Community and law enforcement is excellent, and the relationship between the CIA and the DEA, good. There have been problems, but, generally, when those problems develop, it is because both the communities are moving into new areas and facing new challenges. Part of the problems are a reflection of the dedicated effort of people trying to deal with novel challenges. Progress has been made in relating intelligence and law enforcement, and more will occur in the future.

18

INTELLIGENCE AND THE REVOLUTION IN MILITARY AFFAIRS

James R. FitzSimonds

The Revolution in Military Affairs

P rodigious technological development over the past several decades has led an increasing number of observers to postulate significant changes in the future conduct of warfare. Advanced sensors offer increasing situational awareness of the battle space; information handling systems provide more rapid command cycles, speeding up the pace of war; and stealthy, long-range precision weapons allow discrete destruction of targets. These and other developments may result in a new regimen of warfare in the coming decades: a battle space dominated by new systems, doctrine, and organizations.

Throughout history, the exploitation of evolving technology has resulted in profound changes in the way wars are fought, a development that has been termed a Military Technical Revolution (MTR) or, more recently, a Revolution in Military Affairs (RMA).[1] The definition of an RMA is somewhat subjective; it is a phenomenon that, to date, has been recognized ex post facto. A list of technology-based revolutions that have occurred in the last two centuries would likely include the following:

- The mechanization of land warfare (railroad, machine gun, telegraph, internal combustion engine, etc.)

- The transition from wooden sail to armored steam ships

- Blitzkrieg (combined arms maneuver warfare)

- Strategic bombing

This paper was first presented on November 29, 1994.

- Long-range power projection at sea (aircraft carrier and amphibious warfare)

- Strategic nuclear warfare

The essence of an RMA resides not in the speed of change or force effectiveness relative to military opponents, but rather in the magnitude of change compared with preexisting capabilities.[2] The ability to anticipate and deal with an emerging RMA is vitally important to the future security of the United States for two reasons. First, an RMA presupposes profound military leverage over those who do not adapt to the new regimen of warfare. By not competing successfully in an RMA, the United States faces the prospect of catastrophic defeat on a future battlefield, and possibly the imperilment of its core national interests. The nation's commitment to a strategy of forward engagement may deny the country the time it has previously had to observe and adapt to revolutionary change from a position of geographic isolation. Thus, U.S. peacetime innovations must be successful at the start of the next war, or the U.S. military must be able to adapt very rapidly to profound changes it did not anticipate. Second, an RMA presupposes the obsolescence of military systems, operations, and/or organizations that are currently considered state of the art. With significant force decisions pending—decisions that will define U.S. military capabilities as far as fifty years into the future—the United States does not want an emerging RMA to render this investment obsolete before its time.

There is unquestionably an advantage for the United States in achieving an RMA because it offers significant military leverage against existing and future adversaries. However, this same quality of relative military power makes it vital that a competitor not achieve and exploit an RMA before the United States. Thus the RMA offers two significant challenges for the U.S. Intelligence Community:

- *Achieving a U.S. RMA.* U.S. military leaders are beginning to delineate revolutionary goals for U.S. military capability over the next two decades—advances that center on information management. Operational intelligence will be the key "enabler" for achieving these new concepts.

- *Anticipating the RMA competition.* It is vital for the United States' future national security that it accurately evaluate the threat posed by those future competitors who also have a vision of the emerging RMA. More important, the United States must anticipate those competitors who will seek a different RMA by exploiting technologies in ways that the United States does not yet foresee, and possibly does not understand.

Successfully meeting these challenges suggests major changes in the way that intelligence has been collected, analyzed, and disseminated. Thus, as intelligence itself becomes more vital to future national security, the unfolding RMA may render current U.S. intelligence organizations increasingly irrelevant to that effort.

Intelligence and the Emerging RMA

The emerging military revolution—commonly referred to as "the" RMA or "this RMA"—is generally postulated as centering on two basic elements at the operational level of warfare: precision strikes and information dominance.[3] While the Persian Gulf War offered a glimpse of the military potential of these two elements, most observers have concluded that the achievement of revolutionary military effects using today's technology will require significant innovation in both operational doctrine and organization.[4]

A clear vision of what the RMA will ultimately consist of has not been fully articulated. The uncertain character of the emerging regimen of warfare is evident in the fact that this RMA has, as yet, been accorded no common moniker such as blitzkrieg. Indeed, the true nature of this RMA may not be manifest until it actually unfolds in combat. Nonetheless, operation characteristics of future U.S. forces are being postulated that point toward profound change in the conduct of warfare over the coming decades. These stated criteria clearly indicate the critical importance of information processing and control to this emerging vision of the RMA:

- Gen. Gordon Sullivan sees tomorrow's battlefield information-handling capabilities as allowing real-time observation, continuous orientation, immediate decision making, and action within an hour or less.[5] The C^3I (command, control, communications, and intelligence) loop from decision to action is expected to be compressed by orders of magnitude—increasing the tempo of operations such that U.S. forces will be well within the command cycle of any adversary.

- Adm. William Owens predicts that as early as the year 2005 there will be "a battlefield 200 by 200 miles in which you know almost everything that matters to you."[6] Advanced sensors and information fusion will be expected to provide near-perfect, real-time discrimination between targets and nontargets.

• Lt. Gen. Buster C. Glosson came out of Operation Desert Storm viewing airpower as offering a "war-winning strategy" by threatening "every enemy's leadership, infrastructure, military, and national will on day one of the conflict."[7] Under this strategy, any adversary's nation-state system will be reduced to critical centers of gravity; strategic leverage will then be gained by targeting and destroying those nodes in real time with very precise and very lethal conventional weapons.[8] In its ultimate form, ground operations, if necessary, would be limited to low-level occupation of enemy territory by perhaps nothing more than a gendarme force.

• Gen. Charles Horner articulated a future requirement not only for "accurate, near real-time situational awareness" but also for knowledge of enemy "intentions" to ensure future U.S. success.[9] Thus, U.S. commanders will need to know not only what the enemy is doing, but also what he is going to do.

The qualities of combat that the United States seeks through advanced technology encompass rapid, decisive victory; very low casualties and collateral damage; and strategic results using conventional weaponry. The emerging picture of this future battlefield centers on an integrated system of battlefield assets—a reconnaissance-strike complex—that offers significant, perhaps orders of magnitude, increases in present intelligence collection, processing, and dissemination capabilities. The improvements include:

• Global coverage—broad-area, all-weather, day-night identification of both fixed and mobile targets ashore, at sea, in the air, and in space.

• The ability to distinguish a broad range of targets from nontargets at the strategic, operational, and tactical levels of warfare—thus, discriminating between Scud transporters and tanker trucks, and distinguishing air raid shelters from command bunkers.

• The ability to identify critical targets from all targets—discrete "centers of gravity" whose destruction will paralyze everything from a tank platoon to a national economy.

• Continuous targeting and mission planning in real time (or close to it). This includes accurate battle damage assessment for precision-guided weapons designed specifically to cause pinpoint destruction.

• Real-time linking of targeting information to warheads, including those in flight.

• Continuous and reliable operations against those adversaries who are able to discern and exploit vulnerabilities in U.S. high-technology offensive and defensive systems.

THE DESERT STORM "REVOLUTION"

Despite the "revolutionary advance in military capability" that has been attributed to U.S. forces during Operation Desert Storm, severe deficiencies in information handling were revealed during the war that suggest how far the United States may be from achieving a precision in intelligence to match its precision in weaponry.[10] A congressional study of wartime intelligence support released in 1993 rated U.S. theater intelligence collection as "very good" (albeit with "some major problems"), intelligence analysis as "mixed," and dissemination as "very poor."[11] The common denominator at the theater level was the absence of a unifying intelligence architecture—systems, concepts, and organizations—to integrate fully and employ reconnaissance and strike assets. At the strategic level, the U.S. ability to destroy targets deep within enemy territory with pinpoint accuracy was indeed impressive, yet postwar analysis showed how little the U.S. forces had progressed since World War II in their ability to identify and locate the enemy's critical "centers of gravity."[12]

The scope of the future challenge is highlighted by the fact that 85 percent of the country's existing reconnaissance assets were devoted to Operation Desert Storm support, yet the requirements of that war were minuscule compared with the performance expected in the not-too-distant future. In the context of the Persian Gulf War, the ability of the United States to meet its stated goals for intelligence will truly constitute a "revolutionary" achievement.

ENABLING THIS RMA

The basic sensor, penetration, and aerodynamic technologies required to achieve a revolutionary strike capacity are currently available or available in the near future. Simple demonstrations have been conducted that have linked weapons platforms to single remote sensors in real time. Yet as impressive as some of these capabilities are, they are a far cry from a reconnaissance-strike complex that promises continuous, near-real-time, sensor-to-shooter links between *all* targets and *all* available weapons in a battle space. Indeed, the challenges that remain to implement such a system are daunting.

• *Sensor.* The U.S. military operates a wide range of national, theater, and tactical sensors, all of which provide valuable information, but none of which alone provides consistent "target quality" intelligence (i.e., identification and continuous tracking). The goal of operating "across the full range of threat and conflicts: small to large, conventional to weapons of mass destruction, including information war" will require an increasing number of both platforms and sensors to provide consistent target location and identification.[13] An ambitious program to provide a family of long-dwell, unmanned aerial vehicles with a wide array of sensor packages is envisioned to close significant gaps in current battlefield coverage.[14]

• *Fusion.* The critical element in providing a continuous, consolidated, target-quality intelligence picture to the war fighter—in other words, the synthesis of disparate sensor data into a real-time intelligence picture—is real-time data fusion.[15] This requires not only the interoperability of theater assets in real time, but also a highly automated capability of positively identifying a wide range of targets from masses of disparate data. The volume of information generated by the multiplying family of battlefield platforms and sensors will be orders of magnitude beyond that which has been dealt with in the past: active and passive broad-area coverage of thousands of square kilometers and hundreds to thousands of point targets per day. Data fusion capabilities demonstrated to date are relatively simplistic and highly reliant on time-intensive human analysis. Significant technological breakthroughs in the field of artificial intelligence may be required to attain the level of performance that is sought. In the absence of a technological solution, fusion effectiveness may require entirely different conceptions of "battlefield awareness," in which military goals are attained without the creation of a consolidated picture of the battle space. Where enhanced fusion will allow the separation of targets from nontargets, the identification of those critical targets may require the development of a dynamic, computer-generated model of the enemy's target system—a model that will continuously and automatically reevaluate system vulnerabilities and order strikes on those nodes. Such a model will demand profound increases in our depth of understanding of a multitude of political, military, and economic systems over a wide range of countries.

• *Dissemination.* The real need of the individual war fighter is near-perfect discrimination of actionable *intelligence* from sensor *data*. As U.S.

collection capabilities continue to increase, so must the ability to filter the resulting data down to that exact information that is needed and provide it only *when* and *where* it is needed. Such a "smart push," near-real-time movement of actionable intelligence from sensors to shooters will require near total automation in order to overcome natural limits on human cognition and span out of control.[16] The need for system centralization to enhance speed and fusion will have to be balanced against a need for distributed operations to avoid single-node vulnerabilities.

ENABLING CONCEPTS AND ORGANIZATIONS OF THIS RMA

Assuming that the technological hurdles of generating target-quality intelligence can be overcome, the next issue is how best to exploit it. This challenge may be no less difficult, as it presupposes fundamental changes in the manner in which information is analyzed and distributed to the war fighter. Indeed the molding of stovepipe and noninteroperable systems into a unified reconnaissance architecture implies organization change so profound that it might be termed a "revolution" in intelligence. For example:

• Achievement of significant military leverage through discrete application of force requires a profound depth and breadth of understanding of an adversary's political, military, and economic systems. Critical to this process is the development of accurate measures of effectiveness by which to gauge the effects of military strikes. The capacity for such in-depth analysis of an adversary's systems will itself require a systems approach—a synergistic, multidisciplinary effort that merges traditional stovepipe specialties across military, political, and economic spheres.

• This RMA presupposes target and mission-planning sets that are "locked and loaded" 24 hours a day against all potential adversaries worldwide, or the ability to generate such a global "conventional SIOP" very rapidly. The ability to provide continuously updated targeting and near-real-time mission planning of a global target set may lend itself to increased automation, but will undoubtedly require a tremendous expansion of the human analytical effort. Constrained by limited budgets, these human resources can come only from the large-scale reassignment of intelligence personnel from nonanalytic areas. A great many human functions related to information packaging, presentation, and management—positions that have come to form so large a part of the culture of the Intelligence Community—will disappear.[17]

• Real-time data analysis and movement will require total interoperability of intelligence collection, analysis, storage/retrieval, and reporting functions across all agencies and commands—a goal of standardization that has eluded the Intelligence Community for decades. Activities and products that do not directly support the central architecture will be eliminated.

• Real-time sensor-to-shooter architecture will eliminate the need for intermediate command echelons and associated intelligence staffs. Command positions that do not support the sensor-to-shooter link will be eliminated, very likely along with the traditional distinction between "operations" and "intelligence" specialties. Cryptology, communications, operational deception, and analysis may merge into a unified information structure.

Real-time system responsiveness will drive increasing demands for computer decision making. In its ultimate conceptual form, the reconnaissance-strike complex will become a "virtual" organization—a self-configuring computer-based system where command relationships and hierarchies are largely transparent or superfluous. Individual reconnaissance, surveillance, and strike systems will check themselves into and out of the virtual organization. The complex will itself determine the optimum utilization of each asset—activating, deactivating, assigning, and directing the individual pieces for maximum effect, faster than a human could think or act.[18]

Nonetheless, even the most profound advances in automation will never remove the need for continuous human decision making within the system. Measures of effectiveness will always exhibit a high degree of subjectivity that only humans can effectively gauge. Moreover, only humans can assess risk—an indispensable function in determining when and whether to shoot. Targeting intelligence will never be perfect, and munitions arsenals will always be limited. Only an informed human can make the inherently subjective decision of relative values in the fog of war. A critical question in developing the reconnaissance-strike architecture is how and where the human decision makers must fit into the system.

INFORMATION AS WARFARE

This vision of a future reconnaissance-strike complex that profoundly speeds up the pace and effectiveness of warfare is only an interim step to a conceptual regimen of warfare based upon offensive information operations. Evolving technology may result in a transition from information *in* warfare—information as a supporting function of the traditional attrition/maneuver operations—to information *as* warfare—in which attrition and maneuver become supporting elements of military, political, and economic leverage through information control.[19]

Historic evidence demonstrates that military leverage at any level emanates not from attrition or maneuver per se, but rather from the perceptions of individual decision makers.[20] Thus killing, destruction, and movement have served only as a means to the end of causing the adversary to perceive a future so bleak that his least objectionable option is to accede to one's demands. Only the limited capabilities to conduct offensive information warfare have traditionally forced a recourse to the crude and blunt efforts of physical movement and attrition. Emerging technologies show the prospect of profound improvements in the ability to ensure that the United States receives necessary information, while controlling what the adversary receives. Future information control may provide not only situational awareness, but also a profound degree of information manipulation—to the extent that one might control or destroy the very fabric of an opposing command structure, induce command paralysis, and force an adversary to recognize his defeat.

The idea of information dominance does not necessarily connote a future war without attrition. On the contrary, key enablers in information warfare will likely include the physical destruction of critical C^3I nodes, along with lethal weaponry. In addition, information control must always be backed up by the enemy's belief in one's ability and will to apply real force—and significant demonstrations of that capability may always have to be made in combat. Rather, this end state of information as warfare recognizes the centrality of information to the achievement of victory, and the supremacy of information control of attrition and maneuver in force organization and operations. As the logical evolution from the reconnaissance-strike complex, the Intelligence Community should be positioning itself to best manage the profound operational, organizational, and cultural implications of this future dominance of information in war.

THE ART OF THE POSSIBLE

The ultimate visions of battlefield omniscience, near-instantaneous action, and military leverage through information control may prove unattainable, and indeed may be overtaken by technological developments leading to other, as yet unforeseen, RMAs. Nevertheless, present technologies and systems already offer profound improvement in combat performance to those who can envision and implement the operational and organizational concepts necessary to exploit them. The challenge to participants in this RMA is how best to reorganize with available technologies to do things not just better, but very differently. This likely means that there will be a transition to a new organizational culture in the military services and the Intelligence Community that centers on functions rather than interests. It may well mean a significant change in traditional conceptions of "battlefield," "warrior," and "weaponry." These cultural barriers to change will likely be the hardest to overcome.

Innovation is not inevitably good. Profound change within the military, as in any bureaucracy, must justify both its cost and its institutional disruption. Indeed, without the benchmarks of combat, one risks the possibility that change may be tragically unsuccessful. The most pressing imperative of this RMA is not technological, but rather theoretical—the articulation of an end state of the revolution so compelling as to justify significant institutional disruption to achieve it.[21] To date the Intelligence Community has eschewed a lead role in this issue, allowing the operators and decision makers to establish future intelligence requirements. Given the profound demands that will be levied on intelligence over the coming decades, it is imperative that experts within the Intelligence Community itself begin to address the critical issues posed by revolutionary change. For example:

- What is the character of the end state of this RMA? Where does the United States want to be at the end of this revolution and why? What leverage can be attained and what trade-offs will declining U.S. defense expenditures require?

  - Is the U.S. vision of an RMA executable, or do some of its key attributes, such as increasing the tempo of war, make it ever more problematic for the U.S. deliberative political process?

- What capabilities are truly achievable over the next few decades? What are the measures of effectiveness?

– How transparent must the battle space be for the war fighter? For each incremental increase in targeting information, what additional cost is one willing to incur?

– How near to real time must the command loop be? How fast can it actually become, and what price is one willing to pay for this increased speed?

– Can one consistently identify and gain strategic leverage through discrete "centers of gravity"? In what areas and to what degree of fidelity can one expect to identify these key nodes?[22]

– Is it a credible goal to be able to discern an adversary's "intentions"? If not, to what extent can one expect to know his capabilities and options?

• Will the increasing automation and centralization by the United States provide critical vulnerabilities that its adversaries can exploit? Will these vulnerabilities offset its gains?

• What is the projected state of sensor/fusion/filter technology? Are plans and expectations based on yesterday's state of the art, or tomorrow's? Is the faith in future technology realistic?

• Where must human analysts and decision makers fit into this system? What must they know and how should they be trained?

• What is "information warfare"? What responsibility does the Intelligence Community have for enabling this concept?

• In the absence of a compelling threat, can profound organizational change be implemented from within the Intelligence Community itself to achieve this RMA? Indeed, is the traditional Intelligence Community even relevant to this problem?

Analyzing Future Competitors

More critical for the Intelligence Community than enabling the United States' RMA is its ability to anticipate a military revolution by another power. A competitor may be striving to exploit the same technologies that the United States is, thus neutralizing the leverage over him that the U.S. military seeks, and nullifying its own costly investment. The United States needs to know who is entering this competition and the status of their capabilities relative to its own. More important, another power may seek to achieve a revolution that is entirely different from that which the United States postulates—one that is not anticipated, and possibly not understood. At the very least, such an RMA would present the United States with a long and perhaps costly adaptation to a new regimen of warfare. At worst, the United States could face a capability that truly threatens its vital national interests at home. Anticipating and understanding these emerging RMAs is vital for continued national security and for the development of the nation's long-term strategies to manage military competition.

The ongoing effort to anticipate the characteristics of the next RMA—to predict the heretofore "unpredictable"—is unique in history, and not an easy task. U.S. intelligence organizations as they emerge from the Cold War do not appear well configured to evaluate this type of nonlinear change. Its present analytical focus, for instance, tends to project what kind of advanced tanks a given country will acquire over the next decade or so, while the more critical question is how that adversary will try to redefine ground combat so that tanks are no longer relevant.

Anticipating a future that is dangerous specifically because it is very different from current projections requires a new intellectual approach, new methodologies, and likely major organizational changes in intelligence. Some in the Intelligence Community question whether this is not really an academic exercise rather than an intelligence problem—an exercise dealing with "mysteries" rather than data. The counterargument is that blitzkrieg became an intelligence issue from its moment of inception some twenty years before the Battle of France. If one draws an analogy between the interwar period and the present, Operation Desert Storm may have been a harbinger of profound change in the conduct of warfare that could culminate by the year 2010. Operations other than war notwithstanding, discontinuous change at the high-intensity end of conflict is potentially the most serious threat to U.S. national security in the coming decades.

THE PROCESS OF PEACETIME INNOVATION

One cannot predict with certainty who the adversaries will be over the next twenty to thirty years, but the history of previous RMAs provides some insight into the process that will lead participants in military competition to profound innovation:

- Critical RMA technologies will emerge from civilian sources, and will be exploited for military use through the development of innovative doctrine and organizations within the military itself. Innovative powers will attempt to capitalize on their own, often unique, core competencies to leverage their military strengths against enemy vulnerabilities.

- Adversaries may innovate in many areas as they perceive significant changes in their security environment, but they innovate most profoundly in response to a well-defined threat to their vital national interest—a threat that can be overcome only by instituting significant changes in the way they have previously organized and operated.[23]

- Battlefield failure is not a prerequisite for profound change.[24] On the contrary, most recent RMAs have originated in countries that emerged victorious from the previous war. Even blitzkrieg capitalized on combat operations that had proven largely successful in World War I.

- Severe constraints not only do not inhibit innovations, but seem to be a critical factor in driving it. The most innovative concepts during the interwar years—blitzkrieg, carrier aviation, strategic bombing, and amphibious warfare—arose in a period of international arms limitations and declining budgets. One can argue that the present era of military contraction is more dangerous than the height of the Cold War since it offers greater stimulus for new ideas.

- Military leverage arises from an ability to innovate and exploit change faster than the adversary can adapt to it. Since the leverage is likely to be temporary, innovators have an incentive to initiate military action on their own terms—to preempt—in order to gain maximum advantage from their new force. (Military preemption is an option that the United States has historically conceded to its enemies).

As only combat can determine which peacetime innovations are successful, long periods without war can therefore lead to significant asymmetries in relative force capability—and dramatic demonstrations, like blitzkrieg, of the change that an RMA has ushered in. It has been more than fifty years since the world has experienced high-intensity combat between the leading military powers. The next few decades may therefore be a critical period for the United States, as potential adversaries seek to exploit an ever-increasing number of military options offered by accelerating technological developments.

FUTURE RMAS

The present RMA—that centering on precision strike and information dominance—is clearly only one of many possible outcomes of the revolutionary exploitation of emerging technologies. Unless the cost of precision munitions and sensor-to-shooter architectures drops dramatically in the coming years, the sheer expense of "buying in" to this RMA guarantees that only a small number of countries will be able to compete. Thus, those who seek military leverage will look toward the exploitation of other concepts and other technologies. One can postulate the emergence of revolutionary capability from a number of different developments in the coming decades:

• *Advanced simulations.* Improving simulation technology (perhaps leading to a truly high-fidelity virtual reality) may have revolutionary implications in many areas. Simulations that replicate combat could compress the period for developing radical new doctrine from years to months. Moreover, simulated combat could potentially compress lengthy troop training cycles by orders of magnitude—creating "super" units within months, or weeks.[25] Advanced simulation and modeling technology may also offer rapid and agile capabilities for design and manufacturing—reducing significantly the time from system conception to battlefield deployment.

• *Logistics.* The traditional tail of the "combat tooth" is projected to become increasingly vulnerable to enemy targeting and destruction as the present RMA matures. A battlefield revolution may emerge from innovative methods to eliminate the logistics footprint of powerful attacking forces.

• *Maneuver.* Increasing the tempo of a conventional strike results in a temporal mismatch between target destruction and maneuver unit exploitation (i.e., an RMA may compress months of air campaign to hours of strikes, but ground troops may still require weeks to arrive on scene). Revolutionary leverage may emerge from an ability to rapidly move high-technology ground forces to critical areas.

• *"Spin-on" technologies.* A growing number of civilian technologies ranging from computer networks to global cellular communications have yet to be fully exploited for military use. Such technology "overhang" may offer significant but, as yet, unforeseen military leverage to that competitor best able to conceptualize innovative doctrine and organizations to exploit this potential. MEMS (micro-electromechanical systems) is a specific technology that might offer significant military potential. Mass-produced in the billions for distribution in the battle space, simple MEMS devices could offer capabilities ranging from intrusive sensors to "fire ant" weapons.[26]

• *Information warfare*. The increasing dependence of modern societies on interconnected information databases and information flow may offer critical military and national vulnerabilities and, for an adversary, strategic leverage for minimal investment. The future battlefield may be the interconnected databases of cyberspace, where software engineers are warriors and computer viruses the weapons of choice.

• *Applications of physics*. Various nations continue to invest in advanced technology systems in pursuit of weapons of so-called "new physical principles." From particle beams, to radio-frequency warheads, to infrasonic waves, and nanotechnologies, some will undoubtedly prove of practical military utility if the weaponization expense is justified by a perceived threat.[27]

• *Biotechnology*. Some analysts believe that ongoing efforts to achieve this RMA are mired in an increasingly anachronistic era of "physics-based" warfare that became obsolescent with World War II. Revolutionary military leverage—perhaps the next real RMA—awaits the application of emerging biotechnologies such as bioelectronics to military application.[28]

What is important to remember is that technology is only the starting point for an RMA. The true revolution is achieved after years, and often decades, of doctrinal development, experimentation, and organizational adaption. A technological surprise can never be ruled out, but history tells us that truly profound military innovations experience long gestation periods in which competitors have significant opportunity to observe, evaluate, and adapt.

One also cannot rule out the possibility of a non-technology-based revolution in warfare over the coming decades. Vast changes in the world's social, political, and economic environments following the collapse of the Soviet Union have led some to postulate a revolution in security affairs that may have a profound impact on the future nature of warfare. Comparisons have been drawn to the Napoleonic era, which introduced the national army based upon full mobilization of the state and characterized by a tremendous increase in size and regenerative capability.[29] Although the evidence of such a future in nontechnical revolution is not yet apparent, the implications for U.S. security interests of a profound change in the very nature of warfare make it an issue of continuing concern for the Intelligence Community.

THE EMERGING COMPETITION AND THE FUTURE OF WARFARE

In the near to mid term—perhaps the next ten to fifteen years—there is not likely to be any nation that will be able to compete with the United States as a military peer. In this time frame, the U.S. concern is with the "niche" RMA competitors who are able to leverage only one or a few key areas of technology to the detriment of the United States. In the longer term—perhaps twenty to thirty years—a combination of reduced U.S. military investment and high economic growth rates in other areas of the world may result in the emergence of a major power, or coalition of powers, that is able to challenge the United States across many aspects of warfare—in other words, a "peer" RMA competitor.[30]

Future RMA competitors may not be limited to traditional nation-states, or to the core competencies of nation-states. Technology may be available to nongovernment entities and alliances, or may migrate freely across borders, allowing adversaries to bypass traditional resource or cultural deficiencies while gaining significant military leverage. Additionally, other nations may develop an effective RMA capability simply by exploiting emerging technologies without ever fully articulating or even understanding the overarching RMA concepts. Stealth, integrated strike/defense systems, streamlined command structures, information warfare concepts, and the like all contribute to a potential military revolution. The United States must be cognizant of even its allies developing and transferring RMA-related systems, concepts, and organizations to other nations.

INDICATORS OF COMPETITION

There is probably no single methodology that will serve U.S. needs to identify the next blitzkrieg. The defense and intelligence communities should be pursuing many avenues of analysis until they can better bring the future into focus. But the history of RMAs suggests that one can do more than conjecture about emerging world developments. There are, or should be, empirical indicators offering insight into potential changes in the conduct of warfare. The task is to identify them, analyze them, and exploit them.

Mid-term competition. The force decisions that nations are now making will largely determine what their military capabilities will be over the next ten to twenty years. Thus, the roots of any significant doctrinal and organizational change that might appear by the year 2010 or so should be becoming apparent today. The analytical focus should be on discerning the empirical indicators of how other nations are or might be innovating. Analysts must ask themselves what particular technologies nations are attempting to leverage, and which aspects of present-day warfare—methods, systems, doctrine, platforms—they are attempting to render obsolete. Any focus on technology proliferation alone is too limited. The issue is not just what technologies the adversary has available to him, but how he is able to use those technologies for military advantage. Indeed his technology base may not have to be nearly as good as that of the United States if he is able to fully exploit it to its maximum potential (and which may be easier if he is unconstrained by much of the cultural and bureaucratic "overhead" that impedes the efforts of an established military to change). For any particular competitor, the indicators of ongoing innovation should be fairly well-defined and would likely include:

• A change in focus of military acquisition and systems deployment. In particular, an increased emphasis on systems that the United States might consider nontraditional. The postulated use of new types of systems in war games, simulations, and exercises—along with the assumed obsolescence of current state-of-the-art systems.

• An articulation of innovative operational concepts and organizations in military writings, studies, war games, and so on, including the stipulation of new measures of effectiveness for combat.

• Experimentation with new concepts and organizations, and their subsequent adoption.

• Trends in force quality, readiness, complexity, and realism of operations. A trend toward increased systems integration across all services.

• An active intelligence interest in RMA issues, especially those associated with the U.S. military.

The history of RMAs suggests that the most critical factor to profound innovation is the character of a nation's commissioned officer corps. These are the individuals who will have to adapt to the new technologies and implement the changes. An ability to identify key innovators and to track them and their ideas over the succeeding decades may provide the most significant information about the status of another nation's RMA.

Long-term competition. Competitors who might emerge twenty to thirty years from now may not as yet perceive a security problem that requires an innovative military solution. In other words, there might not yet exist indicators of ongoing innovation within their national security organizations. For this potential long-term competitor, the U.S. focus must be on the *capacity* of a nation to innovate successfully once it decides to do so.

Empirical indicators of such a capacity to innovate are difficult to clearly define. Without being able to identify the characteristics of an emerging RMA, one can only speculate as to what the general prerequisites of a specific revolution might be. Indeed, those prerequisites and indicators are likely to vary among competitors as each attempts to leverage its resources and competencies against unique geostrategic problems. Nevertheless, a better understanding of the core national competencies that any country can draw upon if needed can help better define the scope of the future threat. Indicators of a capacity for competition in the long term might include the following:

• Capacity to develop and exploit new technologies for military application:

    – Specific technology interests

    – Number of scientists, engineers, and technology specialists

    – Long-term R&D investment funding and direction

    – Patent applications and grants

    – Technology information acquisition and exchange

    – Successful innovation in the civilian arena

    – Quality and focus of the national education system

• Capacity for military systems innovation:

    – R&D investment as a percentage of military budget

    – Indigenous design and production achievements

    – Development of dual-use and "spin-on" technologies

    – Relative percentage of traditional and advanced/high-risk military systems

    – Propensity to assume risk in systems design, development, and deployment

- Capacity for doctrinal/organizational innovation:
    - Level and quality of operational-technical writings
    - Orientation of curriculum for military service schools
    - Utilization of war gaming, simulations, and modeling
    - Existence and utilization of internal/external think tanks
    - Analysis of foreign developments
    - Propensity for doctrinal/organizational change
    - Propensity for self-analysis and self-criticism
    - Propensity of individuals to assume risk
    - Discernible reward system for military innovation and individual innovators

More historical analysis of past RMAs would likely provide better insight into the long-term indicators of potential military power, and it might help determine how far in advance one could expect to identify unambiguous indicators of profound change. It also might help to identify any investment thresholds—money, human skills, and access to technology—that might be necessary to create or "buy in" to an RMA. The periods of the interwar years that saw the development of many radical innovations may be particularly instructive. The roots of blitzkrieg can be traced back more than two decades before the Battle of France, yet the growing potential of that innovation was apparent to virtually no one—either within or outside of Germany—until it was demonstrated with catastrophic consequence on the battlefield.

COLLECTION, ANALYSIS, AND DISSEMINATION

The utility of any methodology is dependent upon the quality of information that is collected, the analysis of the data that is generated, and the effective utilization of that information. The nature of an RMA suggests a very different approach by the Intelligence Community to collection, analysis, and dissemination.

- *Collection*. The indicators of mid- and long-term innovation may not lend themselves to the collection assets and techniques most relied upon during the Cold War. For long-term competition in particular, the indicators one is seeking will not become evident to U.S. technical sensors until innovative programs are in place and doctrine adopted. In addition, U.S. technical sensors might not be configured to look at the right things (if the "right" thing turns out to be a nontraditional military area).

The most insightful information for the United States during the interwar years was probably generated by U.S. military attachés abroad—through liaison, observation, and reviewing open literature. Human intelligence collectors—attachés, exchange officers (especially attendees of foreign war colleges), military advisers, and others—well-grounded in the theory of military innovation and the RMA may once again be the country's most valuable source for discerning long-term future capabilities.[31] It is likely through them alone that one will be able to identify and track the von Seeckt and Guderian of the next blitzkrieg.

•*Analysis*. Analysts must use the data collected to elicit critical insights—to gain a full appreciation of an adversary's geostrategic imperatives, his competencies, his cultural attributes, his values, and his resource base—all from *his* perspective. He will innovate most profoundly in response to what he perceives to be a threat to his vital national interests. To understand this innovation, analysts must see the world from an adversary's unique point of view. It is vital that U.S. analysts meld an analysis of his technology with that of his evolving operations and organizations. This is a multidisciplinary issue for which the Intelligence Community does not appear to be well configured.

An RMA "Red Team" approach focusing on specific adversaries (individual countries or alliances) and on specific aspects of future warfare (e.g., information warfare) may offer the deepest insight into the emerging competition. With membership drawn from a broad array of communities and agencies, Red Teams might be able to penetrate the cultural mind-set of the adversary, offering nonlinear but realistic analysis for scenarios and simulations, and challenging opposition play for advanced war games.[32]

•*Dissemination*. It is not enough that insights into the RMA are gained; those insights must reach the right individuals and be exploited for daily decisions relating to procurement, doctrine, operations, and organization. Not only key decision makers at the top, but also those individuals throughout the defense organization who are, or will be, the key innovators for future U.S. forces must have continual access to innovative developments abroad. Because one generally does not know who the critical innovators will be, widespread dissemination of the unfolding vision of future warfare throughout the U.S. military ranks is essential—especially to the broad population of junior officers who will be leading the U.S. military when the next peer competitor arises. New and creative ways of information dissemination and exchange must be explored, especially those avenues made available by emerging technologies, such as distributed war gaming and telecommunications networking.

ASYMMETRIC WARFARE

Despite the urgency of dealing with an emerging RMA, there can be little doubt that the majority of America's future military opponents will approach and fight war in a traditional manner—one that departs very little from their current capabilities and is characterized by their willingness to resort to attrition warfare, insurgency, or even terrorism. Consequently, the bulk of intelligence support in the future will continue to be focused on these very conventional threats.

Additionally, U.S. pursuit of an RMA may make it mandatory to deal increasingly with weapons of mass destruction. What the U.S. military ultimately seeks through the RMA is strategic leverage with advanced conventional weaponry. Unable to compete with the United States in that arena, some future adversaries will no doubt respond with nuclear, biological, and/or chemical weapons. An oft-repeated remark by a retired Indian army chief of staff summarizing the lesson he learned from the Gulf War—"don't fight the Americans without nuclear weapons"—may presage a growing attitude about the need for RMA "deterrence."[33] Indeed the Russian Military Doctrine of 1993 eliminated the traditional Soviet "no first use" pledge, implicitly because of the "nuclear effects" of the U.S. conventional arsenal.[34]

The bottom line is that the U.S. movement toward enhanced conventional capabilities may elicit a reaction that puts even greater emphasis on this nation's ability to deal with the very kinds of warfare that it is seeking to avoid. As such, the Intelligence Community's efforts to deal with these older regimens of warfare may become even more important in the future.

Conclusion

PREPARING FOR A DIFFERENT FUTURE

The challenges to be levied upon the Intelligence Community by emerging military revolutions will be the most significant that it has ever faced. The present national strategy of forward engagement denies this country the advantage it has historically enjoyed of being able to watch high-intensity conflict for several years from the sidelines before becoming actively involved. If the United States is to emerge preeminent in the next war, it must either have the correct innovations in place from the very outset or be able to adapt very rapidly to profound change that it does not now anticipate.

For both enabling the nation's own vision of the RMA and anticipating others', the goal lies less in any formal organizational structure than in an acculturation of the entire Intelligence Community to the need for change, and the unique demands that emerging technologies will present. First, the entire community, from the highest to the lowest levels, must become cognizant of the implications of a future RMA, and begin to articulate visions of a very different regimen of warfare within the next two decades. Without developing a fairly clear idea of what the demands will be, it will be impossible to find and justify the right innovations. Second, the community must conduct an assessment to determine what systems, concepts, and organizations are required to meet the challenges of the new regimen. An RMA presupposes an inability to make existing organizations fit into the demands of the new regime of warfare. Thus, the issue is not whether intelligence must change, but rather, how and when. And because this revolution in intelligence will likely take a generation to achieve, developing a strategy to start that process should become a community priority.

Adapting to the changes dictated by the emerging military revolutions will center on the long-term indoctrination of the Intelligence Community into the challenges posed by such profound innovation. The approach should likely include:

• Participation in, and the sponsoring of, briefings, symposia, and workshops concerned with the implications of the revolution in military affairs. Senior representation at such activities would emphasize the importance of the effort.

• The incorporation of RMA and innovation concepts in formal education—especially initial training—to reach the rising generation within the Intelligence Community who will actually have to implement the profound changes.

• The creation of multidisciplinary working groups to begin breaking through collection and analytical stovepipes.

• The incorporation of nonlinear threat projections into all long-range analyses.

A common excuse offered by those cognizant of the RMA is that the Intelligence Community is organizationally reactive; it cannot take the lead in broad new initiatives until operators and decision makers have levied formal requirements. Yet the very nature of the RMA suggests that such requirements are unlikely to emerge; the obsolescence presupposed by the RMA is in the programmatic or professional interest of very few, while the status quo is in the interest of many. If the Intelligence Community does not take the lead in pursuing the RMA, no one else may.

THE PERMANENT REVOLUTION

Finally, as the preceding analysis of the RMA suggests, there is no "ultimate" end state for U.S. intelligence systems and organizations. Through evolving technology and the competition's own innovative concepts, the United States will be continuously challenged to maintain its competitive edge. The ultimate goal of U.S. intelligence is not a definable product, but rather a process—a capacity for continuous innovation and adaptation to new challenges and possibilities wrought by evolving technologies and international developments. The real measure of success, then, is not how well the Intelligence Community did yesterday, but rather, how well it can anticipate and adapt to revolutionary change in the future.

NOTES

Introduction

1. The Consortium for the Study of Intelligence (CSI) is a project of the National Strategy Information Center, a nonprofit, nonpartisan educational organization. CSI was formed in 1979 by academics from universities and research centers around the United States whose goal was to promote the study of intelligence as an element of democratic statecraft. Among CSI's publications and programs is the eight-volume series on U.S. intelligence requirements for the 1980s and 1990s, edited by CSI Coordinator Roy Godson.

2. During the 102d Congress, Sen. Daniel P. Moynihan (D-NY) introduced "The End of the Cold War Act of 1991" (S. 236). The legislation would have transferred the powers and duties assigned currently to the director of Central Intelligence to the secretary of state, making the secretary the senior government official responsible for coordinating intelligence and managing its gathering.

3. On February 5, 1992, Sen. David Boren (D-OK), chairman of the Senate Select Committee on Intelligence, and Rep. Dave McCurdy (D-OK), chairman of the House Permanent Select Committee on Intelligence, introduced bills (S. 2198 and H.R. 4165, respectively) reorganizing the U.S. Intelligence Community. For background, see also, *Authorizing Appropriations for FY 1991 for the Intelligence Activities of the U.S. Government*, report, U.S. Senate, Select Committee on Intelligence (Rpt. 101-358), pp. 4–5, and *Review of Intelligence Organization*, hearing, U.S. Senate, Select Committee on Intelligence (S.Hrg. 102-91), March 21, 1991. In addition, the *National Defense Authorization Act for FY 1991* (P.L. 101-510) required a 25 percent reduction in defense intelligence manpower, to be taken over a five-year period, and directed a joint review by the secretary of defense and director of Central Intelligence to eliminate redundancies, strengthen joint intelligence functions, and realign priorities to take account of the new security environment. See also, *National Defense Authorization Act for FY 1992 and FY 1993*, report, U.S. Senate, Armed Services Committee (Rpt. 102-113), ["Defense Intelligence Reorganization"], pp. 271–275.

4. For an overview of Gates's reforms, see his testimony in *Joint Hearing: S. 2198 and S. 421 To Reorganize the United States Intelligence Community*, joint hearing (S.Hrg. 102-1052), Senate Select Committee on Intelligence and House Permanent Select Committee on Intelligence, April 1, 1992, pp. 14–19.

5. "Commission on the Roles and Capabilities of the United States Intelligence Community," Title IX of *Intelligence Authorization Act for FY 1995*. See

U.S. House of Representatives, Conference Report (Rpt. 103-753), 103d Cong., 2d sess., pp. 36–41.

6. Address by R. James Woolsey, "National Security and the Future Direction of the Central Intelligence Agency," Center for Strategic and International Studies, Washington, DC, July 18, 1994.

1. What Is Intelligence? Information for Decision Makers

1. Jeffrey T. Richelson, *The U.S. Intelligence Community* (Cambridge, MA: Ballinger, 1985), p. 2. Richelson is quoting from the *Dictionary of U.S. Military Terms for Joint Usage* (Departments of the Navy, Army, Air Force, May 1955).

2. Quoted in Ernest R. May, ed., *Knowing One's Enemies: Intelligence Assessment Before the Two World Wars* (Princeton, NJ: Princeton University Press, 1984), p. 3.

3. Thinking About Reorganization

1. Some useful studies of government reorganizations are: Tyrus G. Fain, ed., *Federal Reorganization* (New York: R. R. Bowker, 1977); George D. Greenberg, "Reorganization Reconsidered: The U.S. Public Health Service," *Public Policy* 23 (Fall 1975); Rufus E. Miles, Jr., "Considerations for a President Bent on Reorganization," *Public Administration Review* 37 (March/April 1977); Frederick C. Mosher, *Governmental Reorganizations* (Indianapolis, IN: Bobbs-Merrill, 1967); Patricia Rachal, *Federal Narcotics Enforcement: Reorganization and Reform* (Boston, MA: Auburn House, 1982); John Tierney, *Postal Reorganization* (Boston, MA: Auburn House, 1981); James Q. Wilson, *The Investigators: Managing FBI and Narcotics Agents* (New York: Basic Books, 1978); James Q. Wilson, *Bureaucracy: What Government Agencies Do and Why They Do It* (New York: Basic Books, 1989), esp. pp. 11–12, 212–213, 218–220, 264–268.

5. Intelligence Reform: Beyond the Ames Case

1. Walter Pincus, "CIA: Ames Betrayed 55 Operations," *Washington Post*, September 24, 1994, p. A1.

2. According to one account, Ames's activities resulted in the death of at least ten CIA and FBI assets, the compromise of perhaps one hundred U.S. and allied intelligence operations, disclosure of scores of undercover and "deep" cover agency officers, and the loss of thousands of pages of top secret documents. U.S. Senate, Select Committee on Intelligence, *An Assessment of the Aldrich H. Ames Espionage Case and Its Implications for U.S. Intelligence*, November 1, 1994, p. 85.

3. This fact alone indicates an inattention to security and counterintelligence considerations. It was not until after problems arose in 1985 that, according to the report of the CIA's inspector general, the Directorate of Operations

established new compartmentation measures. See Senate Select Committee on Intelligence, *An Assessment of the Aldrich H. Ames Espionage Case*, p. 76; "Unclassified Abstract of the CIA Inspector General's Report on the Aldrich H. Ames Case," October 21, 1994, p. 4.

4. Ames began working for the KGB in the spring of 1985, at which time he was Counterintelligence chief for Soviet–East European (SE) operations. A year later he was posted to the U.S. embassy in Rome, where he served until July 1989. Ames then returned to CIA headquarters, where he again worked within SE and, subsequently, on the staffs of the Counterintelligence Center and Counternarcotics Center.

5. This problem was not new to the CIA. As noted by the Senate report (p. 27) on the Ames investigation, in the mid-1980s, PFIAB had issued an assessment of "the CIA's handling of the Howard case [the ex-CIA operations officer who defected to the KGB], which specifically identified serious institutional and attitudinal problems in the CIA's handling of counterintelligence cases. The PFIAB report noted in particular that 'senior CIA officers continued to misread or ignore signs that Howard was a major CI problem.' This myopia was partially ascribed to 'a fundamental inability of anyone in the SE Division to think the unthinkable—that a DO employee could engage in espionage.'"

6. Consider the following: On December 5, 1990, the CIA's Counterintelligence Center (CIC), where Ames was assigned at the time, sent a memo to the Office of Security requesting a reinvestigation of him. The memo listed several suspicious facts: Ames's purchase of a house for $540,000 in cash, its expensive redecoration and renovation, the purchase of a Jaguar for $49,500, and various large bank transactions. The memorandum notes that there is "a degree of urgency" in the request because the CIC had been limiting Ames's access to sensitive information, but it was "quickly running out of things for him to do without granting him greater access."

The degree of urgency may be surmised from the government's "Statement of Facts" submitted in connection with the plea bargain. Just twelve days after the CIC's memo, according to this statement, "Ames obtained valuable intelligence information regarding a KGB officer cooperating with the CIA. Ames prepared a letter . . . advising the KGB of this information. . . ." It is not clear whether Ames obtained this information officially or through corridor gossip.

In either case, the lack of a "CI mentality" is striking. Either the CIC provided Ames access to sensitive information just days after expressing serious concerns about his reliability, or the general atmosphere at Langley was such that this type of information was passed around via corridor gossip regardless of "need to know."

Faced with this kind of record, DCI Woolsey, in a speech designed to rebut Ames-related criticism, resorted to the CIA's all-purpose excuse: James

Jesus Angleton. Despite the fact that Angleton had been sacked almost twenty years earlier, Woolsey claimed that, even in 1994, the CIA's "culture with respect to security and counterintelligence" should be viewed in the light of "a reaction against the highly centralized management of counterintelligence in the 50s, 60s and early 70s." While Woolsey claimed that he wanted to change this culture—the DO, he said, cannot "function as a fraternity, . . . whereby once you are initiated, you're considered a trusted member for life"—he concluded that section of his speech with the hyperbolic warning that "We all at the CIA want to continue to serve in today's Virginia, not in 17th century Salem" (address by R. James Woolsey, Center for Strategic and International Studies, July 18, 1994). It appears that Woolsey's view is shared by many within the CIA's Directorate of Operations. According to the agency's inspector general, the "Angleton Syndrome" has become "to some extent . . . a canard," used by DO officers "to downplay the role of CI in the Agency" ("Unclassified Abstract of the CIA Inspector General's Report," p. 6).

7. "Why Spy?" *New York Times Magazine*, May 22, 1994.

8. In introducing their bills, Sen. David Boren, chairman of the Senate Select Committee on Intelligence, and Rep. Dave McCurdy, chairman of the House Permanent Select Committee on Intelligence, said, "The world has changed, and the Intelligence Community must change with it." Joint press release, February 5, 1992.

9. When the bills were introduced, one Senate staffer was quoted as saying that the Intelligence Community was marked by "structural fragmentation. . . . If the Joint Chiefs needed reform, intelligence needs it twice as badly."

10. Of course, if he rejected hard evidence, he *would* be acting irrationally—a difficulty policymakers often face, however, is in determining whether an intelligence analysis with which they disagree reflects the analyst's possession of evidence of which they are unaware, or represents a differing assessment of the facts as they are known to all.

11. Senator Boren emphasizes the importance of human source intelligence, but redefines it to mean "people who understand public opinion and mass movements in those areas of the world where power has become much more decentralized. We will need more economists and business school graduates who understand commercial competition." "The Intelligence Community: How Crucial?," *Foreign Affairs* 71, no. 3 (Summer 1992): 55–56.

6.   *The Tradecraft of Analysis*

1. One former CIA officer has noted that this system, on more than one occasion, resulted in a product being disseminated to a person who was deceased or who had left his or her position.

2. One of the specified objectives in the studies of potential changes in organization currently being conducted is to facilitate the "flattening" of the review process while maintaining the benefits of management accountability.

3. During March 1994, the DI delivered 647 briefings to policy officials at the deputy assistant secretary level or above; 552 were on demand.

7.   Estimating the Future?

1. See Joseph S. Nye, "What New World Order?" *Foreign Affairs* 70, no. 2 (Spring 1992).

2. Peter Schwartz, *The Art of the Long View* (New York: Doubleday, 1991), p. 8.

8.   The Intelligence Industrial Base

1. "Perry Forges New Shape for Industry," November 15, 1993, p. 52.

2. Following the paper's presentation in December 1993, both the Intelligence Community and Congress began to address the problems and implement some of the recommendations put forward in the original paper.

•The House Permanent Select Committee on Intelligence scheduled a hearing in February 1994 on the future of the intelligence industrial base, at which Kohler was invited to testify. In its report on the Intelligence Authorization Act for Fiscal Year 1995, the committee concluded "that there are significant and vital elements of the intelligence industrial base that may now be at unacceptable risk" and tasked the DCI to study the issue and report back its findings with the FY 1996 intelligence budget submission (U.S. House of Representatives, Permanent Select Committee on Intelligence, 103d Cong., 2d sess., H.Rept. 103-541, pp. 28–29).

•The government agreed in 1994 to allow private companies to attempt to market imaging systems with up to one-meter ground resolution capabilities commercially, including to overseas markets. The Department of Commerce recently issued licenses to two separate business entities permitting them to market and sell their systems to commercial customers.

•Finally, both Congress and the Clinton administration have agreed that a review of the fundamental roles and capabilities of the Intelligence Community is in order (Intelligence Authorization Act for FY 1995, Title IX). A key component of this review should include an examination of how to maintain the intelligence industrial base.

9.   Denial and Deception: The Lessons of Iraq

1. My conclusions are drawn largely from Iraq's nuclear program since 1981; however, I believe these are largely representative of deception and denial activities used in other weapon areas.

2. The extent to which the Israeli attack was assumed to be decisive can be gleaned from a 1982 Congressional Research Service analysis prepared for the Senate Committee on Foreign Relations, Subcommittee on Arms Control, International Operations and Environment:

> Without this reactor as the core for its nuclear research center, Iraq has little to attract scientists and engineers from other Arab countries for study and research there, which would have benefited the cadre of professional and technical personnel that Iraq is trying to develop. Without the reactor, Iraq has no consequential source of plutonium for experimental work to gain firsthand experience with properties of this nuclear material. . . . Iraq's industrial base has little, if any, capability in technologies associated with weapons production, such as electronics, mechanical engineering, chemical engineering, metallurgy, and nuclear engineering. While Iraq apparently has been able to buy uranium concentrates from other suppliers, it appears not to be producing uranium itself. So, at the time of writing, Iraq's potential for attaining nuclear weapons capability within a few years, which was not high to begin with, had faded markedly. . . . By 1990, Iraq could have more nuclear scientists, engineers, and technicians, but no domestic source of highly enriched uranium. . . . It will depend also upon the willingness of other states to provide Iraq with supplies, equipment, and technical assistance, for it appears unlikely that Iraq could become independent of foreign help by 1990. . . . It seems unlikely too that Iraq's own industries will be able to design and build a reprocessing plant, and enrichment plant, or a nuclear power station for many years to come.

Analysis of Six Issues About Nuclear Capabilities of India, Iraq, Libya, and Pakistan, Library of Congress, Congressional Research Service [Washington, DC: Government Printing Office, January 1982], pp. 36–38.

3. Al-Ashimi (Iraq's delegate to the IAEA's general conference in 1981) declared that Iraq "had been one of the first countries to ratify the Treaty on the Non-Proliferation of Nuclear Weapons (NPT), despite the discrimination introduced by that Treaty . . . the Iraqi Government had always given its full support to the Agency's activities with respect to the peaceful uses of nuclear energy and the control of proliferation" (IAEA, 24th regular session, GC (XXIV) OR.220, February 1981).

4. *Analysis of Six Issues About Nuclear Capabilities of India, Iraq, Libya, and Pakistan*, op. cit., pp. 37–39.

5. Each of these nine areas is worthy of a much fuller treatment. I hope that as pending criminal actions are completed and some serious security concerns become less pressing, a fuller treatment of these techniques will be possible.

6. In a case that came to light during the inspections, Iraq ordered preforms for centrifuge endcaps from a Swiss firm, Schmiedemeccanica SA, a metal forging company, and declared that the end use was for automotive part forgings. In 1992 the Swiss decided to drop prosecution after determining that these preforms so closely resembled the end use declared by the Iraqis that the Swiss firm could not be reasonably expected to know otherwise.

7. *Nuclear Fuel*, June 20, 1994, reports that several shipments of preformed tubes for scoops in gas centrifuges from the German metalworking firm, Team GmbH, were shipped to Pakistan after being declared as bodies for ballpoint pens. (pp. 9–11).

10. Angleton's World: Lessons for U.S. Counterintelligence

1. Samuel Halpern and Hayden Peake, "Did Angleton Jail Nosenko?" *International Journal of Intelligence and Counterintelligence* 3:4 (Winter 1989): 451–464.

2. This statement was made prior to the arrest of CIA operations officer Aldrich Ames for espionage. Ames has admitted in court documents to compromising a number of U.S. intelligence assets in the former Soviet Union, including, it is reported, General Polyakov.

3. Robin W. Winks, *Cloak and Gown: Scholars in the Secret War, 1939–1961* (New York: William Morrow, 1987), ch. 6 ("The Theorist"), pp. 322–438.

11. The FBI's Changing Mission

1. The following categories of activities are designated as issue threats under NSTL as of December 30, 1991: (1) foreign intelligence activities directed at U.S. critical technologies as identified by the National Critical Technologies Panel; (2) foreign intelligence activities directed at the collection of U.S. industrial proprietary economic information and technology, the loss of which would undermine the U.S. strategic industrial position; (3) clandestine foreign intelligence activity in the United States; (4) foreign intelligence activities directed at the collection of information relating to defense establishments and related activities of national preparedness; (5) foreign intelligence activities involved in the proliferation of special weapons of mass destruction to delivery systems of those weapons of mass destruction; (6) foreign intelligence activities involving the targeting of U.S. intelligence and foreign affairs information and U.S. government officials; and (7) foreign intelligence activities involving perception management and active measures activities.

12. Covert Action: Neither Exceptional Tool Nor Magic Bullet

1. The most recent published manifestation is *The Need to Know: Report of the Twentieth Century Fund Task Force on Covert Action and American Democracy* (New York: Twentieth Century Fund Press, 1992).

2. For an example of this type of policy-making with respect to Central America in the 1980s, see Alexander Haig, *Caveat* (New York: Macmillan, 1984), pp. 128–129. This view of covert action was often prevalent in U.S. policy with respect to ruling Communist parties in the period following World War II.

3. There was not, so far as is known, a single document that might be described as "a covert action annex." There were, however, a variety of NSC directives that were translated by the covert action bureaucracies of the day, especially the Office of Policy Coordination (OPC), into what Harry Rositzke referred to favorably, and in their aggregate, as the "covert action annex to the Marshall Plan." Harry Rositzke, *The CIA's Secret Operations* (New York: Reader's Digest Press, 1977), p. 158. See also, Sallie Pisani, *The CIA and the Marshall Plan* (Lawrence, KS: University Press of Kansas, 1991) and Burton Hersh, *The Old Boys* (New York: Scribner's, 1992). As yet, there is no detailed, public account of the total U.S. covert action program in Western Europe during this period.

4. Defining covert action is a difficult enterprise. For example, where does covert action begin and counterintelligence (CI) leave off? Double agents can be developed to identify and neutralize a foreign intelligence service—traditional CI. But, at the same time, to be effective, double agents must pass on information to prove their bona fides. Unless this information is completely true, it will in some fashion mislead or deceive its recipient. When this happens, is this CI or CA (i.e., influencing the perception and hence the behavior of a foreign power in a secret or disguised manner)? A documented example of the use of double agents for both CI and CA purposes was the British Double Cross system in World War II, which, among other things, helped deceive the Nazis about the location of the D-Day landing.

   The difficulty in defining "covert action" precisely is evidenced in current law by the fact that the statute excludes from CA "traditional" counterintelligence, diplomatic, military, and law enforcement activities, but does not state precisely what those "traditional" activities might be. (P.L. 102-88, sec. 503[e][1–4]).

5. For a brief history of the evolution of the definition prior to the Intelligence Authorization Act of 1991, see Americo R. Cinquegrana, "Dancing in the Dark," *Houston Journal of International Law* 11, no. 1 (Fall 1988): 177–210.

6. A close reading of the Reagan administration's "Iran-Contra" operations tends to confirm this: the National Security Council found itself beholden to the CIA for operational information—and, in a number of cases, the logistics—it needed, while the CIA absorbed a flow of information from the NSC activities. Unfortunately, the NSC had little CI protection for its operations, as it might have had if it had been a properly conducted CA activity.

There is a view that CA is not inherently an intelligence activity and that it is only placed in the intelligence service for administrative or historical reasons. Some analysts and collectors take this view, believing intelligence is really only an "input" into policy and not an instrument of policy. They also reject the view that CI, too, is an instrument of policy. Some CI practitioners believe CI is part of intelligence, but CA is not. For elaboration of these various perspectives on the elements of intelligence, see Roy Godson, "Intelligence: An American Perspective," in *British and American Approaches to Intelligence*, edited by K. G. Robertson (New York: St. Martin's Press, 1987), pp. 3–36.

7. It should be noted that evaluating effectiveness or success in any foreign policy endeavor is not often easy. It is particularly difficult to determine when CA, on its own or in conjunction with other policy instruments, is effective. As yet, few indices for measuring (government-generated, or not) are available, let alone the data on which to apply the criteria. Mindful of these limitations, one can still seek to make tentative judgments.

8. For a brief overview of British efforts, see Christopher Andrew, *Her Majesty's Secret Service* (New York: Viking, 1986), pp. 208–212.

9. Ibid., pp. 212–221.

10. As yet, there is no single history concerning these efforts.

11. Thomas Powers, *The Man Who Kept the Secrets: Richard Helms and the CIA* (New York: Alfred A. Knopf, 1979), pp. 299–306.

12. There is no reliable history of this account. The *Washington Post*, *Washington Times*, and *New York Times* reported in late July 1988 that President Reagan had approved a covert plan to oust Noriega. The chairman of the Senate Intelligence Committee, David Boren, was quoted in the *New York Times* (July 28, 1988) as confirming the essence of the plan.

In April 1989, the *New York Times* reported that the Senate Intelligence Committee turned down the Bush administration's first plan to oust Noriega because it might have resulted in his death. By October of that year National Security Adviser Brent Scowcroft criticized the Senate Intelligence Committee and Congress for, in effect, handcuffing the administration's efforts to oust Noriega. *New York Times*, October 9, 1989.

13. Gregory F. Treverton, *Covert Action: The Limits of Intervention in the Postwar World* (New York: Basic Books, 1987), pp. 203–204.

14. Ibid., pp. 203, 204, and 206.

15. The CIA, however, was not a "rogue elephant." On the contrary, investigations designed in part to substantiate this charge indicate that the CIA generally acted within the guidelines established by the president and the NSC—even with regard to assassination plots. See, for example, "Alleged Assassination Plots Involving Foreign Leaders," Interim Report, U.S. Senate, Select Committee to Study Governmental Operations with Respect to Intelli-

gence Activities, 94th Cong., 1st sess., S.Rept. 94-465. See, en passim, Powers, *The Man Who Kept the Secrets*, and John Ranelagh, *The Agency: The Rise and Decline of the CIA* (New York: Simon & Schuster, 1987).

16. Arthur B. Darling, *The Central Intelligence Agency: An Instrument of Government, to 1950* (University Park, PA: Pennsylvania State University Press, 1990).

17. For the perceptions of an insider, see Stansfield Turner, *Secrecy and Democracy: The CIA in Transition* (Boston: Houghton Mifflin, 1985). For the perceptions of external observers see John Ranelagh, *The Agency*, chapters 15–19.

18. Gary J. Schmitt and Abram N. Shulsky, "The Theory and Practice of Separation of Powers: The Case of Covert Action," in *The Fettered Presidency*, edited by L. Gordon Crovitz and Jeremy A. Rabkin (Washington, DC: American Enterprise Institute, 1989), pp. 59–81. Gary Schmitt, "Oversight: What for and How Effective?" in *Intelligence Requirements for the 1980's: Intelligence and Policy*, edited by Roy Godson (Lexington, MA: Lexington Books, 1986), pp. 119–148. See also Robert Gates, "CIA and the Making of American Foreign Policy," *Foreign Affairs,* 77, no. 3 (Winter 1987/1988:225).

19. Cord Meyer, *Facing Reality: From World Federalism to the CIA* (Lanham, MD: University Press of America, 1980), pp. 91–94, 105–109.

20. Donald Purcell, "The Necessary Means for U.S. Covert Action in the 1980s," in *Intelligence Requirements for the 1980s: Covert Action*, edited by Roy Godson (Washington, DC: National Strategy Information Center, 1981), pp. 218–220.

21. *The Need to Know*, p. 5.

22. Mohammed Yousaf and Mark Adkin, *The Bear Trap* (London: Leo Cooper, 1992). See also Steve Coll, "Anatomy of a Victory: CIA's Covert War in Afghanistan," *Washington Post*, July 19, 1992; and "In CIA's Covert Afghan War Where to Draw Line Was Key," *Washington Post*, July 20, 1992.

23. B. Hugh Tovar, "Covert Action" in *Intelligence Requirements for the 1990s*, edited by Roy Godson (Lexington, MA: Lexington Books, 1989), pp. 220–221.

24. For a general discussion of this type of analysis, see Jack Davis's monograph, *The Challenge of Opportunity Analysis* (Center for the Study of Intelligence, Central Intelligence Agency, July 1992).

13.　Economic Espionage

1. *New York Times*, June 18, 1990; *Business Week*, October 14, 1991; *Wall Street Journal*, August 4, 1992; *Time*, February 22, 1993.

2. "Memorandum for all Assistant Secretaries and Bureau Directors from the Deputy Secretary of State," December 12, 1991.

3. "Christopher Makes Case for New Aid," *Washington Post*, March 23, 1993.

4. Turner, "Intelligence for a New World Order," *Foreign Affairs*, 70, no. 4 (Fall 1991): 151–152.

5. Ibid, p. 152.

6. Robert Reich, "Who Is Us?" *Harvard Business Review* (January–February 1990), p. 54 (emphasis added). See also Robert Reich, "Who Is Them?" *Harvard Business Review* (March–April 1991).

7. "The Idea of a CIA Linkup Spooks Some Area Executives," *Washington Post*, March 9, 1993.

8. *Time*, February 22, 1993.

9. Private communication with the author.

10. Speech by Robert M. Gates to the Economic Club of Detroit, April 13, 1992.

11. *New York Times*, April 5, 1993.

14.   Fighting Proliferation

1. This is not to say that the shift was not anticipated. See, for example, Barbara Starr, "DoD to Track TBM Proliferation," *Jane's Defense Weekly*, February 10, 1990, and "Third World SSM Threat Studied," *Jane's Defense Weekly*, November 16, 1991, regarding the creation of the U.S. Department of Defense Proliferation Countermeasures Working Group.

2. See, for example, testimony of Director of Central Intelligence James Woolsey, U.S. Senate, Committee on Governmental Affairs, *Hearing on Proliferation Threats of the 1990's*, (February 24, 1993) 103d Cong., 1st sess., S.Hrg. 103-208, pp. 8–18. See also, *Department of Defense Appropriations Act for FY 1993* (P.L. 102-396), sec. 1607; and Clinton administration initiative to expand proliferation concerns to items that result in "significant military capabilities" and that "would make a significant contribution to the military potential of countries that would prove detrimental to the national security and foreign policy of the United States." Proposed *Export Administration Act of 1994*, the White House, February 24, 1994.

3. Indeed, a weakness in most of the "counterproliferation" briefings now being given within the government is their emphasis on preempting and deterring smaller nations' use of strategic capabilities against the United States or its friends rather than on the grimmer but more likely challenge of having to absorb and respond to such strikes when preemption is not possible or deterrence fails.

4. See, for example, the agenda of the Arms Control and Disarmament Agency–sponsored conference on "Counter Proliferation" (May 24–25, 1993), which emphasized technology transfer, export controls, verification technologies, and information management.

5. Thus, current conventional arms control proposals rarely speak of banning the sale of planes or tanks but, instead, talk about increasing warning time by requiring nations to make such arms sales more public through UN registries and the like.

6. See *Defense Appropriations Act for FY 1993* (P.L. 102-396), sec. 1607 ("Iran-Iraq Arms Non-Proliferation Act of 1992"); and *The National Defense Authorization Act for FY 1993* (P.L. 103-160), sec. 1336 ("Report on Space Technology Proliferation").

7. For a discussion of the potential strategic significance of submarines in closed seas, accurate conventional missiles, and C³I technologies, see Henry Sokolski, "Nonapocalyptic Proliferation: A New Strategic Threat?" *Washington Quarterly*, 17, no. 2 (Spring 1994): 115–125.

8. See *Defense Appropriations for FY 1993*, sec. 1607. Regarding the growing interest in controlling "high leverage" weapon systems, see Charles Wolf, "U.S. Arms Exports Can Backfire," *Wall Street Journal*, June 21, 1994, p. A14.

9. An unclassified statement of this approach can be found in Defense Department testimony before the U.S. Senate, Committee on Governmental Affairs, Hearing on "Proliferation and Regional Security in the 1990's" (October 9, 1990) 101st Cong., 2d sess., S.Hrg. 101-1208, pp. 49–54. The approach has also been considered within the Department of Defense's Defense Intelligence Agency. See Dan Spohn, "Proliferation Production," unpublished staff working paper of the Office of the Defense Intelligence Officer for Research and Development, October 1992.

10. Abram Shulsky and Jennifer Sims, *What Is Intelligence?* (Washington, DC: Consortium for the Study of Intelligence, Working Group on Intelligence Reform, 1992), p. 32.

11. See Jack Davis, *The Challenge of Opportunity Analysis*, (Center for the Study of Intelligence, Central Intelligence Agency, July 1992).

12. See Kenneth deGraffenreid, "Intelligence and the Oval Office," in *Intelligence Requirements for the 1980s: Intelligence and Policy*, edited by Roy Godson (Lexington, MA: Lexington Books, 1986), p. 28.

13. See Jack Davis, *The Challenge of Opportunity Analysis*, p. 7.

14. This analysis is especially useful if effective public diplomacy efforts against proliferation developments are to be mounted.

15. See Andrew W. Marshall, *Long-Term Competition with the Soviets: A Framework for Strategic Analysis* (Santa Monica, CA: Rand Corporation, 1972); and Andrew W. Marshall, "Competitive Strategies: History and Background," Office of Net Assessment, Department of Defense, unpublished paper, March 3, 1988.

16. For a discussion of how economic pressures might lead to a less militarily threatening leadership in Iran, see Patrick Clawson, *Iran's Challenge to the*

West: How, When, Why (Washington, DC: The Washington Institute for Near East Policy, 1993); and Henry Sokolski, "Iran's Future Bomb," *Middle East Quarterly* 1, no. 2 (June 1994): 42–50.

15. The Future of Defense Intelligence

1. Throughout this chapter, the term *defense intelligence* is used as a convenience. In general, defense intelligence refers to intelligence originated by a Department of Defense (DoD) component, although intelligence for defense purposes can be provided by any member of the Intelligence Community. In fact, increasingly, intelligence, from whatever source, is intelligence for all in the government. Defense intelligence as an organization is a misnomer; there is no single, unified entity. Some components have separate statutory establishment. What all of the components of defense intelligence have in common is that they report—ultimately—to the secretary of defense. Defense intelligence consists of the Office of the Assistant Secretary of Defense for Command, Control, Communications and Intelligence (C^3I); the Defense Intelligence Agency (DIA); the intelligence elements of the military departments—namely, the Office of the Deputy Chief of Staff for Intelligence, Department of the Army and the U.S. Army Intelligence and Security Command, the director of naval intelligence and the Naval Intelligence Command, and the Office of the Assistant Chief of Staff, Intelligence, Headquarters U.S. Air Force and the Air Force Intelligence Command; intelligence elements from the military services assigned as forces to the unified combatant commands; and the Central Imagery Office, the National Reconnaissance Office, and the National Security Agency.

For the record, the opinions expressed in this paper are solely those of the author and do not represent the policy or viewpoints of the Department of Defense or the Intelligence Community.

2. Secretary of Defense Dick Cheney, *Defense Strategy for the 1990s: The Regional Defense Strategy*, January 1993, p. 7.

3. By war fighting, I mean any contingency involving hostilities, including low-intensity conflict.

4. Establishment of a deputy undersecretary of defense (policy review) and deputy assistant secretary of defense (intelligence); establishment of a deputy undersecretary of defense (command, control, communications and intelligence); establishment of an assistant secretary of defense (command, control, communications and intelligence) and transfer of intelligence and space policy directorate from deputy undersecretary of defense (policy) to assistant secretary of defense (command, control, communications and intelligence); transfer of counterintelligence and security countermeasures policy from the deputy undersecretary of defense (security policy) to assistant secretary of defense (command, control, communications and intelligence).

5. DIA was founded in 1961. The first draft of a joint intelligence doctrine, written shortly thereafter, remained in draft until the 1990s.

16. Reforming Intelligence: A Market Approach

1. The original version of this paper was written before I read William Harris's "Collection in the Intelligence Process," in *Intelligence Requirements for the 1980s: Clandestine Collection*, edited by Roy Godson (Washington, DC: National Strategy Information Center, 1983). The argument made in this essay is similar to that made by Harris.

2. Robert F. Nesbit, "Catching Up With Pomfret, Vermont—An Examination of Intelligence Dissemination Architectures" (MITRE Corporation, July 1993), unpublished manuscript.

3. See chapter 15 ("The Future of Defense Intelligence"), p. 226.

4. Harris also makes this proposal in "Collection in the Intelligence Process," op. cit. Following this paper's original publication as a Working Group monograph, the House Intelligence Committee requested that the Community Management Staff develop pilot programs that "should include a test of a market-type mechanism" for regulating intelligence production. See *Intelligence Authorization Act for Fiscal Year 1995: Report*, U.S. House of Representatives, Permanent Select Committee on Intelligence, 103d Cong., 2d sess. H.Rept. 103-541, pp. 30–31.

17. Intelligence and Law Enforcement

1. Roy Godson and William J. Olson, *International Organized Crime: Emerging Threat to U.S. Security* (Washington, DC: National Strategy Information Center, August 1993); and "Global Mafia," *Newsweek*, December 31, 1993, pp. 18–31.

18. Intelligence and the Revolution in Military Affairs

1. Recognition of the increasing importance of doctrinal and organizational innovation led to the term *revolution in military affairs* (RMA) gaining currency over the expression *military-technical revolution* (MTR). Some theorists refer to the MTR as the technology element of a military revolution, and RMA as the doctrinal and organizational exploitation of the MTR. A number of works have appeared in recent years dealing with the subject of RMAs, among them: John W. Bodnar, "The Military Technology Revolution: From Hardware to Information," *Naval War College Review* (Summer 1993); Paul Bracken, "The Military After Next," *Washington Quarterly* (Autumn 1993); James R. FitzSimonds and Jan M. van Tol, "Revolutions in Military Affairs," *Joint Force Quarterly* (Spring 1994); Andrew F. Krepinevich, "Keeping Pace With the Military-Technical Revolution," *Issues in Science and Technology*

(Summer 1994); and Andrew F. Krepinevich, "Cavalry to Computer: The Patterns of Military Revolutions," *National Interest* (Fall 1994).

2. The basic postulates of the RMA outlined here stem from theoretical work done in the Office of Net Assessment, Office of the Secretary of Defense, under Andrew Marshall and others. Some theorists do not include strategic bombing and strategic nuclear warfare in a list of RMAs because there has been no overt demonstration of their superiority in actual combat. However, the conduct of warfare has been changed profoundly by these innovations, and one could conclude that those who did not adapt successfully to these new regimens would have faced battlefield defeat.

3. Two additional elements often included in some constructs of the RMA are "advanced modeling and simulation" and "dominating maneuver." The basic technologies for advanced modeling and simulation are still in the early stages of development; the possible future implications of advanced modeling and simulation are addressed later. Dominating maneuver is postulated as a future analog to blitzkrieg or Inchon—a positioning of forces that leads to decisive battlefield results. Concepts for a revolutionary advance in maneuver warfare have yet to be fully developed.

4. Historic parallels have been drawn between the present era and the early years between World War I and World War II. The tank, aircraft, and radio had appeared on World War I battlefields, but it took two decades of doctrinal and organizational development with those systems to achieve the revolution of blitzkrieg. Some see the computer processing chip as equivalent to the internal combustion engine as the key "enabler" of the next revolutionary advance.

5. Gen. Gordon R. Sullivan, U.S. Army, and Col. James M. Dubik, U.S. Army, "War in the Information Age," *Military Review* (April 1994): 47.

6. "Owens: Get Smart Weapons," *Navy News & Undersea Technology*, October 3, 1994, p. 1.

7. Lt. Gen. Buster C. Glosson, USAF, "Impact of Precision Weapons on Air Combat Operations," *Airpower Journal* (Summer 1993): 9. Col. John Warden, USAF, one of the primary theorists in this area, defines a "center of gravity" as "that point where an enemy is most vulnerable and the point where an attack will have the best chance of being decisive" (John A. Warden III, *The Air Campaign: Planning for Combat* [Washington: National Defense University Press, 1988], p. 9). Warden postulates that any modern nation-state consists of five centers of gravity—leadership, key production, infrastructure, population, and fielded military forces—areas vital to the functioning and survival of the nation-state. His theory holds that all five of these aspects are vulnerable to attack and destruction by air power from the outset of hostilities. Other theorists maintain that any adversary—even those below the nation-state level—can be reduced to such strategic centers of gravity.

8. U.S. Air Force documents often refer to multiple centers of gravity. Navy doctrine states that "there can be only one center of gravity" of an enemy, but that this center of gravity can be attacked through "critical vulnerabilities," of which there can be many. *Naval Doctrine Publication 1: Naval Warfare*, (Naval Doctrine Command) 28 March 1994, p. 35.

9. Gen. Charles A. Horner, USAF, "Space Systems Pivotal to Modern Warfare," *Defense 94* (Issue 4): 20. *Naval Doctrine Publication 1* states that "good intelligence" produces intentions of potential enemies (p. 62).

10. William J. Perry, "Desert Storm and Deterrence," *Foreign Affairs* 70, no. 4 (Fall 1991): 66.

11. *Intelligence Successes and Failures in Operations Desert Shield/Desert Storm*, U.S. House of Representatives Committee on Armed Services, 103d Cong., 1st sess., August 1993, p. 1. Among the specific deficiencies noted were: (1) lack of timely and accurate battle damage assessment; (2) lack of communications capacity for intelligence dissemination; (3) poor collection asset allocation and intelligence dissemination due to service, agency, and command parochialism; (4) inability to convert raw information to actionable intelligence; (5) inability to establish a theater-wide intelligence architecture; (6) poor understanding of intelligence capabilities among combat commanders; (7) lack of standardization, connectivity, and interoperability for critical targeting data.

12. It is significant to note that the *Gulf War Air Power Survey* questioned whether the continuing limitations of attaining strategic leverage through air attack are even amenable to technical solutions. See Eliot A. Cohen, director, *Operations and Effects and Effectiveness*, vol 2. of *Gulf War Air Power Survey* (Washington, DC: Government Printing Office, 1993), pp. 361–370.

13. Maj. Gen. Kenneth R. Israel, USAF, "An Integrated Airborne Reconnaissance Strategy," *Unmanned Systems* (Summer 1994), p. 21.

14. See the *Unmanned Aerial Vehicles 1994 Master Plan* (Department of Defense: Unmanned Aerial Vehicles Joint Project Office, 1994).

15. The "extended reconnaissance" goal of the Defense Airborne Reconnaissance Office (DARO) aims at "the ability to supply responsive and sustained intelligence data from anywhere within enemy territory, day or night, regardless of weather as the needs of the war fighter dictate" (Israel, "An Integrated Airborne Reconnaissance Strategy," p. 17).

16. "Smart push" is a postulated future architecture that combines the best features of "intel pull" (the consumer receives only what he requests) and "intel push" (the consumer is fed everything that is available) support.

17. The number of actual hands-on analysts is not accurately known. Within the Intelligence Community itself, individual estimates of the percent of per-

sonnel actually devoted to basic intelligence analysis range from 1 percent to 60 percent.

18. The navy's Cooperative Engagement Concept (CEC), which links radar and surface-to-air missile assets from different platforms, is a first step along this path. Future experiments will link joint service antiair assets. For an overview of CEC, see Dean Barsaleau, "CEC: The Unprecedented Force Multiplier," *Surface Warfare* (September/October 1994).

19. Alvin Toffler and Heidi Toffler have popularized such notions as "knowledge warfare" and "cyberwar" in *War and Anti-War: Survival at the Dawn of the 21st Century* (Boston: Little, Brown, 1993).

20. Robert McQuie, "Battle Outcomes: Casualty Rates as a Measure of Defeat," *Army* (November 1987), is one noteworthy study that distinguished casualty rates from a decision maker's "recognition of defeat."

21. Unstated, but implicit in the U.S. military's efforts to exploit technology are the values of speeding up the pace of warfare, while reducing casualties to near zero.

22. In trying to induce an adversary to recognize defeat, the critical issue may not be what his critical centers of gravity really are, but what he *thinks* they are—perhaps an entirely different problem altogether.

23. A disturbing conclusion one might draw is that the United States will not be first to achieve the next RMA unless it can translate the RMA into a response to a vital national threat. On the other hand, some have postulated the existence of an "opportunity" RMA—profound peacetime innovation with technology that might have some future, but as yet undetermined, utility. Both carrier and amphibious warfare development in the United States in the 1920s and 1930s might fit this model. However, one can also argue that neither of these concepts came to fruition until significant combat reversals early in World War II forced the organizational changes necessary to exploit these new methods of warfare.

24. Stephen Rosen makes this point in his study of innovation in the military [("New Ways of War: Understanding Military Innovation," *International Security* 13, no. 1 (1988): 135.] Germany's impetus for profound innovation seems more attributable to an expectation of future war with Poland and France, with military forces constrained by the Versailles Treaty.

25. In his analysis of blitzkrieg, James Corum concluded that the Wehrmacht's "training factor alone would have proven decisive in 1940" against the Allies (James Corum, *The Roots of Blitzkrieg: Hans von Seeckt and German Military Reform* [Lawrence, KS: University Press of Kansas, 1992], p. 205). James Corum, Trevor Dupuy, Martin van Creveld, and others have documented the disproportionate battlefield effectiveness stemming from the relative training superiority of the Wehrmacht against all adversaries.

26. MEMS are micro-engineered devices—motors, actuators, gears, sensors, and such—on a scale ranging from a few millimeters down to that nearly invisible to the human eye. Postulated MEMS would be able to move, communicate, and perform simple functions, offering military applications ranging from intrusive sensing to the disabling of weapons and systems through microbiotics.

27. Russian theorists continue to offer the most in-depth work on the future nature of warfare and nontraditional weaponry. See, for example, Mary C. FitzGerald, "The Russian Image of Future War," *Comparative Strategy*, 13, no. 2 (1994). Nanotechnology involves molecular assembly of objects and components. See, for example, Charles Ostman, "Nanotechnology," *Midnight Engineering* (January–February 1994).

28. Microchip size and power may have already reached their practical limits using silicon technology. Ongoing work in synthesized DNA, for instance, may open the door to the trillion-bit storage devices and sophisticated artificial intelligence. See, for example, Pat Cooper, "Sci-Fi Vision May Become Reality for U.S. Air Force," *Defense News*, October 31–November 6, 1994, p. 1.

29. See, for example, Robert M. Epstein, "Patterns of Change and Continuity in Nineteenth-Century Warfare," *Journal of Military History* (July 1992).

30. Such was the character of the Axis powers in World War II. Neither Germany nor Japan—with a combined GDP less than half that of the United States—could be considered an individual peer. However, in combination, they were able to challenge the United States across the entire spectrum of warfare.

31. Significantly, human intelligence may also be the best source for intelligence relating to operations other than war.

32. A significant augmentation to this effort might be a joint military reserve Red Team with experts drawn from a broad range of civilian specialties.

33. See Patrick J. Garrity, *Why the Gulf War Still Matters: Foreign Perspectives on the War and the Future of International Security* (Los Alamos National Laboratory: Center for National Security Studies, July 1993).

34. The initial 1992 draft of the doctrine stated explicitly that conventional attack could elicit a nuclear response. See Charles Dick, "The Military Doctrine of the Russian Federation," *Jane's Intelligence Review*, Special Report No. 1, January 1994. One analyst has postulated that the improving capabilities of advanced conventional weapons may eventually cross a line of "disutility"—that point of "near certain suicide that comes with use." See Thomas J. Welch, "Technology Change and Security," *Washington Quarterly* (Spring 1990): 115.

LIST OF ABBREVIATIONS

ADDI	Associate Deputy Director for Intelligence, CIA
ADDO/MA	Associate Deputy Director for Operations, Military Affairs, CIA
ARPA	Advanced Research Projects Agency, Department of Defense
ASD	Assistant Secretary of Defense
CA	Covert Action
C^3I	Command, Control, Communications, and Intelligence
CI	Counterintelligence
CIA	Central Intelligence Agency
CIC	Counterintelligence Center
CINC	Commander in chief
CIPA	Classified Information Procedures Act
CRS	Congressional Research Service
DARO	Defense Airborne Reconnaissance Office
DCI	Director of Central Intelligence
DDI	Deputy Director for Intelligence, CIA
DDO	Deputy Director for Operations, CIA
DDP	Deputy Director for Plans, CIA
DEA	Drug Enforcement Agency
DECA	Developing Espionage and Counterintelligence Awareness
DGSE	Direction Générale de la Securité Exténeuve
DI	Directorate of Intelligence
DIA	Defense Intelligence Agency
DO	Directorate of Operations
DoD	Department of Defense
FBI	Federal Bureau of Investigation
FCI	Foreign Counterintelligence
FYDP	Future Years Defense Program
GDIP	General Defense Intelligence Program
GPS	Global Positioning System

GRU	Main Intelligence Directorate of [Russian] General Staff
HOTA	HUMINT Operational Tasking Authority
HPSCI	House Permanent Select Committee on Intelligence
HUMINT	Human Intelligence
IA	Intelligence Assessment
IAEA	International Atomic Energy Agency
IMINT	Imagery Intelligence
INR	Bureau of Intelligence and Research, Department of State
J-2	Joint Staff Intelligence Directorate
J-3	Joint Staff Operations Directorate
JIC	Joint Intelligence Center
KGB	Committee for State Security
MASINT	Measurement and Signature Intelligence
MEMS	Micro-electromechanical systems
MTCR	Missile Technology Control Regime
MTR	Military Technical Revolution
NASA	National Aeronautics and Space Administration
NED	National Endowment for Democracy
NFIP	National Foreign Intelligence Program
NIC	National Intelligence Council
NID	National Intelligence Daily
NIE	National Intelligence Estimate
NIO	National Intelligence Officer
NPT	Non-proliferation treaty
NRO	National Reconnaissance Office
NSA	National Security Agency
NSC	National Security Council
NSTL	National Security Threat List
OPC	Office of Policy Coordination
OSS	Office of Strategic Services
PFIAB	President's Foreign Intelligence Advisory Board
POM	[Defense] Program Objective Memoranda
RAB	Research and Analysis Branch, OSS
RMA	Revolution in Military Affairs
SE	Soviet East European Division, DO, CIA

SIGINT	Signals Intelligence
SPOT	*Satellite Pour l'Observation de la Terre*
SSCI	Senate Select Committee on Intelligence
TIARA	Tactical Intelligence and Related Activities
ULTRA	Intelligence derived from Allied decryption of German communications during World War II
X-2	Counterintelligence branch of OSS

ABOUT THE CONTRIBUTORS

John J. Coleman has worked in federal drug enforcement for three decades. At present, he is head of the Drug Enforcement Agency's New Jersey operations. Prior to his current position, Mr. Coleman served as assistant administrator for operations, DEA. As assistant administrator, he was principal adviser to the DEA Administrator and deputy administrator on all enforcement-related operations, including overseas enforcement programs.

John Despres is assistant secretary of commerce for export enforcement. Prior to becoming assistant secretary, Mr. Despres was a member of the professional staff of the Senate Select Committee on Intelligence. He has held senior positions in the Arms Control and Disarmament Agency, the departments of Energy, State, and Defense, and served as the national intelligence officer for nuclear proliferation in the late 1970s.

James R. FitzSimonds, a captain in the U.S. Navy, is military assistant to the director of net assessment, the Office of the Secretary of Defense. He has served in various operational intelligence posts, including intelligence officer for a battle group during Operation Desert Storm. His assignments ashore have included tours on the staff of the chief of naval operations and the CNO's Strategic Studies Group.

Randall M. Fort is Director, Special Projects, TRW avionics and surveillance group. Prior to joining TRW, Mr. Fort was deputy assistant secretary of state, functional analysis and research, bureau of intelligence and Research. He has also served as special assistant for national security affairs to the secretary of the treasury and as deputy executive eirector of the President's Foreign Intelligence Advisory Board.

Roy Godson is President of the National Strategy Information Center and an associate professor of Government at Georgetown University. In addition, he is coordinator of the Consortium for the Study of Intelligence, the editor of its series *Intelligence Requirements for the 1980s* and *Intelligence Requirements for the 1990s*, and author of *Dirty Tricks or*

Trump Cards: American Counterintelligence and Covert Action. He has also served as a consultant to the National Security Council and the President's Foreign Intelligence Advisory Board.

Samuel Halpern began his career in U.S. intelligence during World War II with the Office of Strategic Services. Following the war, he joined the Central Intelligence Agency and served in a number of senior positions within the operations directorate, including the post of executive assistant to three deputy directors of plans (later operations).

William Hood is the author of *Mole, Spy Wednesday*, and *Cry Spy*. Mr. Hood began his career in U.S. intelligence during World War II, serving in the Office of Strategic Service's counterintelligence division, X-2. After the war, he joined the Central Intelligence Agency and served in numerous senior posts within the agency's operations directorate. He retired from the CIA in 1975 while executive director of the counterintelligence staff.

Walter Jajko is deputy assistant to the secretary of defense for intelligence oversight. Previously, he was the director, special advisory staff, the office of the secretary of defense. A retired U.S. Air Force Reserve brigadier general, Mr. Jajko has served on the air staff in the Office of the Assistant Chief of Staff for Intelligence, in the Office of the Secretary of the Air Force, and in various strategic, tactical, and special operations units.

David Kay is assistant vice president, Science Applications International Corporation. Dr. Kay is a former head of the evaluation section, technical cooperation programs of the International Atomic Energy Agency and secretary general of the Uranium Institute. Following the Persian Gulf War, he was the chief UN inspector of Iraq's nuclear weapons program.

Richard Kerr, whose career with the Central Intelligence Agency spanned over thirty years, is a former deputy director of Central Intelligence. Prior to becoming deputy director, Mr. Kerr served as deputy director for intelligence. As DDI, he was head of the CIA's analytic branch. Currently Mr. Kerr is president of the Security Affairs Support Association and is also a national security affairs consultant.

Robert Kohler is executive vice president and general manager, TRW avionics and surveillance group and former president of ESL Incorporated. Prior to joining the private sector, Mr. Kohler was with the CIA for nineteen years, where he was involved in the development and operation of major technical collection systems. His last position with the Central Intelligence Agency was as director of the Office of Development and Engineering, Directorate of Science and Technology.

Douglas J. MacEachin was deputy director for intelligence, Central Intelligence Agency, from 1993 to 1995. Mr. MacEachin joined the agency in 1965 and has held a number of senior posts, including head of the agency's watch center and chief of the office of Soviet analysis. In the 1970s, he also served as a member of the U.S. (non-nuclear) arms negotiation delegation and director of the Strategic Warning Staff in the Pentagon.

Ernest May, former dean of Harvard College, is the Charles Warren Professor of American History at Harvard University. In addition to his many writings in the field of history and American diplomatic history, Dr. May is the editor of *Knowing One's Enemies*, a collection of essays on comparative intelligence assessments before World War I and World War II. Professor May also serves on the board of visitors of the Joint Military Intelligence College.

James Nolan retired from the Federal Bureau of Investigation in 1983 as deputy assistant director for intelligence. During his twenty-five year career in the bureau, Ambassador Nolan specialized in foreign counterintelligence operations and investigations. After leaving the FBI, he was named the first director of the Office of Foreign Missions, the Department of State.

Joseph S. Nye is assistant secretary of defense, international security affairs. Dr. Nye was previously chairman of the National Intelligence Council. Author of numerous volumes on U.S. national security and Dillon Professor of International Affairs, Dr. Nye has served as the director, Center for International Affairs, and as associate dean of arts and sciences at Harvard University.

Elizabeth R. Rindskopf was general counsel, Central Intelligence Agency, from 1990 to 1995. Prior to joining the agency, Ms. Rindskopf was Principal deputy legal advisor, the Department of State. She has also served as general counsel, National Security Agency. In addition to her work in the area of national security law, Ms. Rindskopf has served as a Legal Services attorney, and litigated federal civil rights and antitrust cases.

Henry S. Rowen is the Edward B. Rust Professor of Public Policy and Management, Graduate School of Business, Stanford University, and senior fellow, The Hoover Institution on War, Revolution and Peace. A former president of the Rand Corporation, Professor Rowen has also served as assistant secretary of defense, international security affairs, and as chairman of the National Intelligence Council.

Gary Schmitt is a senior fellow, the National Strategy Information Center in Washington, DC. He is the revising author of the second edition of *Silent Warfare*. Dr. Schmitt has served as executive director of the President's Foreign Intelligence Advisory Board and minority staff director of the Senate Select Committee on Intelligence. He has also been a fellow at the Brookings Institution and the *National Interest*.

Abram Shulsky, author of *Silent Warfare: Understanding the World of Intelligence*, is a consultant with the Rand Corporation. He has served in the Office of the Secretary of Defense and as director, Office of Strategic Arms Control Policy, Department of Defense. Prior to working in the Pentagon, Dr. Shulsky was the minority staff director of the Senate Select Committee on Intelligence and a consultant to the President's Foreign Intelligence Advisory Board.

Jennifer Sims is deputy assistant secretary of state, intelligence coordination, bureau of intelligence and research. Previously, Dr. Sims was a member of the professional staff of the Senate Select Committee on Intelligence. She has also served as U.S. coordinator of the multinational nuclear history program and a research fellow with the International Institute for Strategic Studies in London.

L. Britt Snider is currently staff director of the Commission on the Roles and Capabilities of the U.S. Intelligence Community. Prior to joining the commission staff, Mr. Snider was general counsel of the Senate Select Committee on Intelligence. He also served for ten years as deputy undersecretary of defense for counterintelligence and security.

Henry Sokolski is executive director of the Nonproliferation Policy Education Center in Washington, D.C. From 1988 to 1992, he was deputy to the assistant secretary of defense, international security affairs, for nonproliferation policy. Prior to working in the Pentagon, Mr. Sokolski served as Sen. Dan Quayle's (R-IN) military legislative assistant.

Patrick Watson is deputy assistant director, national se curity division, Federal Bureau of Investigation. He is responsible for the bureau's counterintelligence investigations. Mr. Watson has been with the FBI for three decades, serving in a number of senior posts in its foreign counterintelligence programs.

James Q. Wilson is James Collins Professor of Management, Graduate School of Business, University of California at Los Angeles. A former president of the American Political Science Association, Dr. Wilson has written numerous books on American government, public policy issues, and government organization, including *Bureaucracy: What Government Agencies Do and Why They Do It*. Dr. Wilson has also served as a member of the President's Foreign Intelligence Advisory Board.

Paul Wolfowitz is dean, School for Advanced International Studies, Johns Hopkins University. Dr. Wolfowitz has served as the under secretary of defense for policy, assistant secretary of state for East Asian and Pacific affairs, and as U.S. ambassador to Indonesia. In the mid-1970s, he was a member of the B-Team in the A-B Team experiment in competitive analysis concerning Soviet strategic capabilities and objectives and currently is a member of the Commission on the Roles and Capabilities of the U.S. Intelligence Community.